1 MONTH OF
FREE
READING

at

www.ForgottenBooks.com

By purchasing this book you are eligible for one month membership to ForgottenBooks.com, giving you unlimited access to our entire collection of over 1,000,000 titles via our web site and mobile apps.

To claim your free month visit:
www.forgottenbooks.com/free789754

ISBN 978-0-483-61746-9
PIBN 10789754

HOW TO BE HAPPY.

A COLLECTION OF BEAUTIFUL LESSONS INTENDED TO IN-
SPIRE NOBLE THOUGHTS AND ACTIONS, AND EN-
ABLE ONE TO BECOME USEFUL, LOVABLE,
——HAPPY AND WISE.——

BY

GRACE GOLD,

Author of "The Lost Memorandum," "Vows," "Every
Day Life," "Sowing and Reaping," "Bible
Christians," etc., etc.

AFFECTIONATELY DEDICATED

TO THE

YOUNG PEOPLE OF AMERICA.

——PUBLISHED BY——
F. & M. FRINK,
VALPARAISO, IND.

Preface

EVERY parent in the land desires their children to be happy.

No matter how bitter their own life has been, or how much anguish their own heart has known, they desire their offspring to escape these sorrows and would gladly see them placed where they could obtain peace, prosperity and happiness.

The author of this work does not claim she has discovered a new method whereby one can step from misery to happiness at a single bound, but she does claim there are certain laws which govern our lives for good or evil as we will, and in a sense we make our own destiny.

Happiness is what we are all seeking; but alas, how few find, or finding are able to retain it.

To be truly happy one must be loved; and to be loved, one must be lovable; and again, to be lovable one must in some way be useful, must possess something valuable in the eyes of others. It is the object of this book to give by its lessons, such information, as, if studied and practiced will enable one to become so useful and lovable that their society will be sought, others benefitted, prosperity will come and they will in spite of circumstances or surroundings live a truly beautiful life.

The author has spared no pains to obtain this valuable collection, many of which are the productions of the most celebrated writers.

Credit has been given each one so far as they were known, but no hesitancy has been made to use an article whose merit justifies its being placed in this work although the author was unknown, for we fully believe any one whom God has given the wonderful gift of touching human hearts as is indicated by these lessons are willing they shall be placed where they can be the means of encouraging, elevating and purifying humanity.

THE AUTHOR.

☀GREETING.☀

EAR YOUNG PEOPLE: I love you all, and desire you to be happy, not only in this world, but in the world to come.

The secret of being happy is to be good. Realizing this, and knowing my own life has been made bright and in many respects beautiful by the practice of such lessons, I take pleasure in coming to you with this humble volume laden with precious truths that will teach you how to be good and useful, thereby making you a blessing to yourselves and those around you.

This life is so short, and time so precious, I wish I could make you see and feel the importance of improving each moment for securing some benefit either for yourselves or those around you. So many have good resolutions they intend to carry out sometime in the future, but how few are doing their best to-day. Many neglect present duties and spend their time building for the future, castles without foundations. Dear ones I entreat you to attend to the duties of to-day which if faithfully performed will make a foundation so strong no misfortune can sweep it away.

Self sacrifice at first seems hard, but becomes at last a pleasure by continued practice, so then, "weary not in noble doing."

Hoping the lessons here given may be received in the same loving spirit they are given and cause you to make a deeper search for useful knowledge, I remain,

Your earnest friend,

GRACE GOLD.

WHATSOEVER things are true, whatsoever things are honest, whatsoever things are just, whatsoever things are pure, whatsoever things are lovely, whatsoever things are of good report; if there be any virtue, and if there be any praise, think on these things.

—BIBLE.

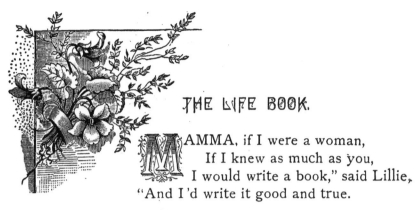

THE LIFE BOOK.

"MAMMA, if I were a woman,
　　If I knew as much as you,
　　I would write a book," said Lillie,
"And I'd write it good and true.

"I would make it just like talking,
　　As you talked to me last night,
So that every one who read it
　　Would love Jesus and do right."

"Every one, my love" said mamma,
　　"Must at least one book compose;
Each must write his own life-story,
　　From its drawing to the close.

"On a new unwritten volume,
　　Pure and spotless to the sight,
Loving ones confer a title,—
　　Baby hands begin to write.

"All through babyhood and childhood,
　　Youth, mid-life and trembling age,
Still those hands are writing, writing,
　　Never lifting from the page.

"Every word and every action,
　　Rude or gentle, wrong or right,
In its ugliness or beauty,
　　Live upon those pages white.

"Every deed of love and mercy
　　Shines upon those leaflets fair,
And if one has loved the Saviour
　　All his love is written there.

9

LIVE FOR SOMETHING.

THOUSANDS of men breathe, move and live; pass off the stage of life and are heard of no more. Why? They did not a particle of good in the world; and none were blest by them; none could point to them as the instruments of their redemption; not a line they wrote, not a word they spoke, could be recalled, and so they perish—their light went out in darkness, and they were not remembered more than the insect of yesterday. Will you thus live and die, O man immortal? Live for something. Do good, and leave behind you a monument of virtue that the storm of time can never destroy.

Write your name by kindness, love and mercy, on the hearts of the thousands you come in contact with year by year, and you will never be forgotten. No; your name will be as legible on the hearts you leave behind as the star on the brow of the evening. Good deeds will shine as bright as the stars of heaven.

HOW TO LIVE WELL.

AH, this is a subject of interest to everybody. This is the constant wish of every person of honest heart and pure desires. Success or failure in this means happiness or misery here, and heaven or hell at last. Says a writer: "To live well, economy is necessary." No matter if persons are rich, or have large incomes, they should be economical; for to waste is wicked. The master himself taught economy by precept and example; the apostles did the same. The first Christians led simple and economical lives; "neither said any of them aught of the things which he possessed was his own." They were "bought with a price." They and theirs all belonged to their Master, and were consecrated to his service. They lived well. Reader, if you would live well, go thou and do likewise.

HOW TO KEEP A SITUATION.

BE ready to throw in an odd half-hour, or an hour's time when it will be an accommodation, and don't seem to make a merit of it. Do it heartily. Though not a word be said your employer will make a note of it. Make yourself indispensible to him and he will lose many of the opposite kind before he will part with you. Those young men who watch the clock to see the very second their working hour is up—who leave, no matter what state the work may be in, at precisely the instant —who calculate the exact amount they can slight their work and yet not get reproved—will always be the first to receive the notice when times are dull, that their services are no longer required.

Sin is more to be feared than hell. If people were half as anxious to escape the former as they are the latter, their lives would be far purer than they are.

A WORKER'S PRAYER.

"For I have received of the Lord that which also I
delivered unto you."

LORD, *speak to me*, that I may speak
    In living echoes of Thy tone ;
As thou hast sought, so let me seek
    Thy erring children, lost and lone.

O *lead me*, Lord ; that I may lead
    The wandering and the wavering feet ;
O *feed me*, Lord, that I may feed
    Thy hungering ones with manna sweet.

O *strengthen me*, that while I stand
    Firm on the rock, and strong in Thee,
I may stretch out a loving hand
    To wrestlers in the troubled sea.

O *teach me*, Lord, that I may teach
    The precious things Thou dost impart ;
And wing my words, that they may reach
    The hidden depths of many a heart.

O give Thine own sweet *rest to me*
    That I may speak with soothing power
A word in season, as from Thee
    To weary ones in needful hour.

O *fill me* with thy fullness, Lord,
    Until my very heart o'erflow
In kindling thought and glowing word,
    Thy love to tell, Thy praise to show.

O *use me*, Lord, use even me,
    Just as Thou wilt, and when, and where ;
Until Thy blessed face I see,
    Thy rest, Thy joy, Thy glory share.
                  —FRANCES RIDLEY HAVERGAL.

THE WAY OF THE WORLD.

LAUGH, and the world laughs with you ;
    Weep and you weep alone ;
        For this brave old earth
        Must borrow its mirth,
It has troubles enough of its own.

Sing, and the hills will answer ;
Sigh, and 'tis lost on the air ;
    The echoes rebound
    To a joyful sound,
But shrink from voicing care.

Rejoice, and men will seek you ;
Grieve and they will turn and go ;
    They want full measure
    Of all your pleasure,
But they do not want your woe.

Be glad, and your friends are many ;
Be sad, and you will lose them all ;
    There are none to decline
    Your nectared wine,
But alone you must drink life's gall.

Feast, and your halls are crowded ;
Fast, and the world goes by ;
    Succeed and give,
    And it helps you to live,
But it cannot help you to die.

There is room in the halls of pleasure
For a long and a lordly train ;
    But one by one
    We must all file on
Through the narrow isles of pain.

—ANON.

CULTIVATE REFINEMENT.

DO not draw into your shell. So much is to be gained by contact with the outside world. The influence of the social current has the same effect upon human nature as that produced by the constant friction of the sea upon the pebbles on the beach. Rough corners are polished and sharp angles smoothed down into symmetrical proportions. But it is not enough to be simply in the swim. If you wish to be happy, cultivate that society which elevates and ennobles. Seek relaxation for mind and body among a set of people who hold broad views of living. Narrow-minded men and women, and the world is full of them, will only give you distorted ideas of life, ideas that will change the sunniest and most healthful disposition into one morose, churlish and ill-natured. Be careful then, whom you choose for your companions.

THERE is no life so humble that if it be true and genuinely human and obedient to God, it may not hope to shed some of His light. There is no life so meager, that the greatest, and wisest of us all can afford to despise it. We cannot know at what moment it may flash forth with the life of God.

In the voyage of life we should imitate the ancient mariners who, without losing sight of the earth, trusted to the heavenly signs for their guidance.

If you would sleep well, take a clear conscience to bed with you.

THE PURE IN HEART.

THE pure in heart, the pure in thought,
Shall learn the law the Master taught,
Shall turn from ill and earthly strife,
And seek the summits high in life.

The pure in heart, the pure in deed,
Shall sow each hour some fruitful seed,
Which falling here and falling there,
Shall plant for harvest rich and rare.

The pure in heart, the pure in word,
Make music, the sweetest ever heard,
And wake the tones of gracious good,
The tones of peace and brotherhood!

The pure in heart, the pure in prayer,
Shall feel God's presence everywhere;
Shall seek His work on every side,
And know that life is glorified.

"FEELING HURT."

SOME women are always "feeling hurt" at some-
thing,—nobody knows what, very likely, or cares,
after awhile. They make the world miserable,
and themselves doubly so. They are the torment of
their families, the terror of their friends, the disgust of
their employers.

Now sensitiveness is not a sign of sense. To put it
on the very lowest ground of selfish policy, the woman
who "feels hurt" and shows it, makes a ruinous mis-

take. People are apt to hate you in proportion as they hurt you. Your real lovers are those who feel that they have helped or pleased you. If one believes that, why not get out of it a little worldly and womanly wisdom? To go comfortably through this world one needs a certain amount of liking and affection—even, I was going to say, of admiration. Who likes a friend who is always taking offence at something said or unsaid? Who can admire long, or love, the one that notes suspiciously your every look and word for signs of neglect or waning regard? Who never gives her own love grandly and heartily, but is always scrutinizing what she gets in return to see if she hasn't been cheated in the measure? The "most meanest thing a woman can do" (if one may misquote Cable) is to "feel hurt."

I say a woman, because I think this particularly a woman's vice. Some men have it—womanish men. For the very reason that our life is a love-life, our mistakes and our sins are the faults of the loving. And this is such a very hypocrite of a fault, pretending oftentimes to be dear love itself, that I want you girls to begin at once and root it out, declare war against it, in the name of all that is blessed and peaceful and lovely and lovable.

Of course you have outgrown the childish trick of "getting mad"—taking offence openly at every word that is spoken. Now go a step further and resolve that you will not see offence if it is possible to screen your eyes with any mantle of charity. If your best friend walks out of church arm in arm with another and newer one, tossing you a careless nod across the aisle, don't go home and cry about it. Have you forgotten how near-sighted she is? The poor girl never saw you! Somebody doesn't answer your letters by return mail; forgets to make you a present at Christmas; doesn't remember your birthday. The poorest thing you can do is to "feel hurt" about it.

Nine times out of ten, it was unmeant and accidental. The one real slight is best avenged by taking not the least notice of it.

The fact is people do not often go out of their way to slight and annoy others in every-day intercourse. In the main, people are well-intentioned, kindly disposed; but people are also busy and careless. Take no heed to every word that is spoken. Do not allow yourself to set up an inquisition over other people's words and actions. Mild doses of common-sense taken daily as a tonic will go far to prevent attacks of low-mindedness; for slight pin-pricks of neglect and unkindness, the faith-cure is sovereign—trust in the real affection of friends, whatever their faults of manner. For real internal injuries and heart troubles, there is nothing like forgiveness and "the poultice of silence."

Keep a good stock of these simple remedies on hand, dear girls. You will have troubles and slights and injustice; it is the common lot. But as you value success in life, as you love your friends, as you love yourself —don't feel hurt! You will lose respect; you will even, perhaps, lose confidence in yourself, as surely as you do.

How long we live, not years but actions tell.

HOW TO BE HAPPY.

ARE you almost disgusted
   With life, little man?
   I will tell you a wonderful trick
That will bring you contentment,
   If any thing can—
Do something for somebody, quick;
Do something for somebody, quick!

Are you awfully tired
   With play, little girl?
Weary, discouraged, and sick?
I'll tell you the loveliest
   Game in the world—
Do something for somebody, quick;
Do something for somebody, quick!

Though it rains like the rain
   Of the flood, little man,
And the clouds are forbidding and thick,
You can make the sun shine
   In your soul, little man—
Do something for somebody, quick;
Do something for somebody, quick!

Though the skies are like brass
   Over head, little girl,
And the walk like a well heated brick;
And are earthly affairs
   In a terrible whirl!
Do something for somebody, quick!
Do something for somebody, quick!

STAND FOR THE TRUTH.

ET me advise you to wear no armor for your backs when you have determined to follow the track of truth. Receive upon your breast-plate of righteousness the sword cuts of your adversaries; the stern metal shall turn the edge of your foeman's weapon. Let the right be your Lord paramount, and for the rest be free and your own masters still. Follow truth for her own sake; follow her in evil report; let not many waters quench your love to her. Bow to no customs if they be evil. Yield to no established rules if they involve a lie. Do not evil though good should come of it.

"Consequences!" This is the devil's argument. Leave consequences to God, but do right. If friends fail thee, do the right. Be genuine, real, sincere, upright, and godlike. The world's maxim is, trim your sails and yield to circumstances. But if you would do any good in your generation, you must be made of sterner stuff, and help make your times rather than be made by them.

You must not yield to customs, but, like an anvil, endure all the blows until the hammers break themselves. When misrepresented, use no crooked means to clear yourself. Clouds do not last long. If in the course of duty you are tried by the distrust of friends, gird up your loins and say in your heart, I was not driven to virtue by encouragement of friends, nor will I be repelled from it by their coldness. Finally, be just, and fear not; corruption wins not more than honesty; truth lives and reigns when falsehood dies and rots.

—CHAS. SPURGEON.

THE BOYS WHO WILL WIN.

HERE'S to the boys who are always ready
   To do their best at their play or work;
Never afraid, as some are of labor—
   Never trying a task to shirk.

Never saying, "I cannot do it,"
   And putting it off "till by-and-by,"
But facing each task with a sturdy courage,
   A willing heart, and brave "I'll try."

Such are boys we all depend on,
   Such are the boys who will some day win.
They shut the doors of their hearts and guard them
   Against vain thoughts that would fain come in.

Though only the boys, as age is reckoned,
   They are really men at heart, say I,
And it makes me glad and proud to see them,
   And the world will be proud of them by-and-by.

ABOUT GOOD MANNERS.

MANY women, particularly the more youthful ones, commit through carelessness or thoughtlessness many breaches of good manners which need but a reminder to be speedily remedied. To begin with, the sweet tooth of the average American girl tempts her to eat candy in the street and at the theaters, though she may be quite aware that to do so is not

good form.   The same girl who would scorn to eat pea-
nuts and condems those delicacies as "vulgar," munch-
es away on caramels or buttercups in public vehicles,
public thoroughfares and public places of amusement.

Many young women, the best hearted in the world,
will wound their parent's hearts by openly correcting or
contradicting them, forgetting that their own superior
knowledge does not show up to advantage when parad-
ed at the expense of good manners.   This habit on the
part of the younger members of society is one that
should be nipped in the bud at once.   Suppose father
or mother do mispronounce a word, make a mis-state-
ment, or fall into an error of grammar, does it make
things any better by emphasizing their faults so openly?
The first law of good manners is consideration and re-
spect for those older than ourselves, therefore that,
outside of any other promptings, should restrain the
flippant correction of parents before strangers at least.

To discuss your clothes, your servants or your do-
mestic affairs is to stamp yourself ill-bred.   General
conversation is the only sort tolerated in the best cir-
cles.   Do not talk and laugh at the theater or other
places of amusement, annoying those about you who
came to enjoy the performance and not your conversa-
tion.   Do not stare at people and then discuss them so
that there is no possibility of their mistaking the topic
of your conversation; in fact, let consideration for oth-
ers be your watchword and refinement your code, and
your manners will improve steadily under such person-
al discipline.

MOTHERS AS SWEETHEARTS.

THERE is nothing that so pleases the fond mother as the gentle ways of a sweetheart in her son. If he greets her with a smile, throws his arms about her and pats her cheek and caresses her in the fond ways of an affectionate nature, she may chide him as a simple boy and laughingly question the sincerity of his demonstrations, but they bring a glow of pleasure to her heart that sweeps away the shadows of care and makes her the happiest among God's creatures. Sons may make friends here and there as they go through life as the creatures of destiny, but one who never deserts them, never loses faith or abandons hope is the mother whose yearning for love he so often repels or neglects.

COMMIT THY WAY TO GOD.

COMMIT thy way to God.
　　The weight which makes thee faint;
Worlds are to Him no load,
　　To Him breathe thy complaint.
He who for winds and clouds
　　Maketh a pathway free,
Through wastes, or hostile crowds,
　　Can make a way for thee.

Hope, thee, though woes be doubled;
　　Hope, and be undismayed;

Let not thy heart be troubled,
  Nor let it be afraid.
This prison where thou art,
  Thy God will break it soon,
And flood with light thy heart,
  In his own blessed noon

Up! up! the day is breaking,
  Say to the cares, good night!
Thy troubles from thee shake,
  Like dreams in day's fresh light.
Thou wearest not the crown,
  Nor the best course can tell;
God sitteth on the throne,
  And guideth all things well.

DOING ANOTHER'S DUTY.

THE true lady shows her training in every word and gesture; but the pretended is too often caught napping. A little girl, shopping with her mother one day, was sitting contentedly on a counter-stool, watching the people as they came in and out.

Presently she saw a lady, elegantly dressed, who stopped at their counter, and handed a water-proof and umbrella to the young girl in charge.

"Take care of these things till I call for them," she said in an autocratic tone, and sailed away.

The bright eyes of the child followed her. The little face wore a look of distress.

"Why, mamma," she whispered, "she didn't even say 'please'."

Sooner than she expected the lady returned.

"I will take my things," she said.

There was some delay in finding them.

"I hope you haven't lost or misplaced them," she said to the young girl in a severe tone.

Neither misfortune had occurred. The articles were found, and taking them without a word, the lady walked out. This was more than the child could bear. Leaning over so that her sweet face came close to that of the clerk, she said graciously, "Thank you!"

SELF EXAMINATION.

AM I full of self or full of spirit? Am I living and working for Christ or self? Do I preach for reputation, salary, position, or Christ? Am I constrained by the love of Christ? Does my activity spring from physical vivacity, nervous force, ambitious ends, or is it inspired by supreme love for Christ? Am I zealous of my rights, prerogatives, dignities, or am I zealous only for Christ and the salvation of souls? Do I preach in deadness to self, no thought of reputation, only eyeing God's glory and the eternal welfare of men? Do I set God, the judgment, hell and heaven always before me? Am I long suffering? Are my sharpest rebukes seasoned with tenderness? My most solemn warning delivered with tears? Am I humble, self-forgetful, prayerful and holy? Do the people grow in holiness and divine troops under my ministry? Not simply do I get my assessments in full, not so many baptized and added to the roll. All these things may be done and death prevail. But are people advancing in faith, in prayer, in holiness, in love? Is this advance evident and marked? Is my ministry fruitful in this regard? A nearness to God, a fitness for heaven, a growing separation for, and antagonism to the world, a freedom from sin, the Spirit abounding, the flesh crucified?

A WORKINGMAN'S TRIBUTE TO PAPERS.

WORKING man in this city who was complaining of hard times recently was asked how he could afford to take a newspaper. "Well," said he, "I hope I shall never be too poor to take a paper. I thought I was too poor for ten years after I was married. My wife suggested that I take a paper regularly, and I did so, and it was the most economical stroke of my life. It kept me at home, afforded me pleasure and instruction and was a comfort to the whole family. I had to stop the use of tobacco for a whole year once in order to pay for the paper, and the result was that I have not cared for tobacco since, and in that one item I have saved enough to pay for several papers. So long as I have money enough to buy bread with I will have money enough to pay for a news-paper. There is no man too poor to read a paper. It is the cheapest investment he can make, both for himself and his family. It is the last expense I will lop off. I will drink my tea and coffee without sugar before I miss my paper, I can better afford to do so."

25

WHAT BECAME OF A LIE.

FIRST, somebody told it,
  Then the room wouldn't hold it,
  So the busy tongues rolled it
    Till they got it outside;
Then the crowd came across it,
And never once lost it
But tossed it and tossed it
  Till it grew long and wide.

From a very small lie, Sir,
It grew deep and high, Sir,
Till it reached to the sky, Sir,
  And frightened the moon;
For she hid her sweet face, Sir,
In a veil of cloud-lace, Sir,
At the dreadful disgrace, Sir,
  That had happened at noon.

This lie brought forth others,
Dark sisters and brothers,
And fathers and mothers—
  A terrible crew;
And while headlong they hurried,
The people they flurried,
And troubled and worried,
  As lies always do.

And so, evil boded,
This monstrous Lie goaded,
Till at last it exploded
  In smoke and in shame.
When from mud and from mire
The pieces flew higher
And hit the sad liar,
  And killed his good name!

—Mrs. M. A. Kidder.

26

"IF WE KNEW."

IF we knew, when walking thoughtless
　　In the noisy crowded way,
　　That some pearl of wondrous whiteness
　　Close beside our path-way lay,
We would pause where now we hasten,
　　We would often look around,
Lest our careless feet should trample
　　Some rare jewel to the ground.

If we knew what forms were fainting
　　For the shade that we should fling;
If we knew what lips were parching
　　For the water we could bring,
We would haste with eager foot-steps,
　　We would work with willing hands,
Bearing cups of cooling water,
　　Planting rows of shading palms.

If we knew when friends around us
　　Closely pressed to say good-bye,
Which among the lips that kissed us
　　First would 'neath the daisies lie,
We would clasp our arms around them,
　　Looking on them through our tears;
Tender words of love eternal
　　We would whisper in their ears.

If we knew what lives were darkened
　　By some thoughtless word of ours,
Which had ever lain among them
　　Like the frost among the flowers;

Oh, with what sincere repentings,
   With what anguish of regret,
While our eyes were overflowing,
   We would cry, Forgive! Forget!

If we knew—Alas! and do we
   Ever care or seek to know
Whether bitter herbs or roses
   In our neighbors' gardens grow ?
God forgive us ! Lest hereafter
   Our hearts break to hear Him say,
"Careless child, I never knew you,
   From my presence flee away."

READ.

READ continually, only reserving such time for re-
laxation and the duties of life as your situation may
require.   Don't sit with your hands folded and
mouth open, doing nothing; these are minutes which
you are wasting—minutes make hours, hours make days
and weeks, and all combined are swiftly flying towards
eternity.   Then read!—read everything and anything,
except low and trashy subjects; there is no branch of
art or science, or of literature, from which, properly
perused, you may not get some valuable information.

The difference between the reader and the sluggard,
who sits in the easy-chair asleep in the evening, is as
great as the contrast between a fool and a sensible per-
son; the former goes about the world, sees, hears, thinks
and digests the results of his observation during his
travels; he will presently give these reflections to the

world in a new and interesting shape, and thus make other readers. But the sluggard is a useless character, and not worth the ink to describe him.

Read an almanac, if you cannot get a paper; and he must be poor indeed, as the bard singeth, who cannot afford a subscription to some journal in this age of the world. At all events, leave no means untried to cultivate and improve the spare hours which you will have during the winter months. If you are waiting somewhere on business, take out your paper and peruse its columns; you will soon find the advantage of the practice.

Time shall overwhelm all things, and render mines useless, gems of no value. The thief may in an hour destroy the labor of a lifetime in accumulating a fortune, but no power, short of a Divine one, can wrest the riches of a well stored mind from its possessor. Again we say—read!

CONSIDER your blessings more than your troubles; look on the bright side of life rather than on the dark side; see your neighbor's virtues rather than his failings; speak cheerfully, not despondingly; give thanks instead of grumbling.

Truth is the property of God; the pursuit is what belongs to man.

Divine love is a sacred flower which in its earthly bud is happiness, and in its full bloom is heaven.

29

THE UNSOWN SEED.

I SAW a garden, in springtime,
   Prepared with the greatest care,
And I thought when comes the summer,
   Rare flowers will be blooming there.
But summer found in the garden
   Full many a noxious weed,
With never a flower among them,
   For none had sown the seed.

I saw a life that gave promise
   Of a harvest rich and rare,
Had the fertile soil been tended,
   And the seed been planted there.
Neglected and unplanted—
   O'ergrown with sin's foul weeds—
O, the flowers we might gather
   Did we only sow the seed!

Had we sown the seeds of virtue,
   Of holy love and truth,
Of charity and kindness,
   In the springtime of our youth;
In the autumn we'd have gathered
   A harvest rich and rare—
A harvest of fragrant flowers
   Been blooming for us there.

We'd have never cause to murmur
  At the hardness of our lot ;
Our lives full of contentment—
  In palace or in cot.
Did we improve the golden springtime,
  Root out each noxious weed—
What a bountiful harvest waits us,
  Did we only sow the seed !

VACATION SONG.

 HAVE closed my books and hidden my slate,
And thrown my satchel across the gate,
My school is out for a season of rest,
And now for the schoolroom I love the best !

My schoolroom lies on the meadow wide,
Where under the clover the sunbeams hide ;
Where the long vines cling to the mossy bars,
And the daisies twinkle like fallen stars ;

Where clusters of butter cups gild the scene,
Like showers of gold-dust thrown over the green,
And the wind's flying footsteps are traced, as they pass,
By the dance of the sorrel and the dip of the grass.

My lessons are written in clouds and trees,
And no one whispers, except the breeze,
Who sometimes blows from a secret place,
A stray, sweet blossom against my face.

My school bell rings in the rippling stream
Which hides itself, like a school-boy's dream,
Under a shadow and out of sight,
But laughing still for its own delight.

31

My schoolmates there are the birds and bees,
And the saucy squirrel, less wise than these,
For he only learns in all the weeks,
How many chestnuts will fill his cheeks.

My teacher is patient, and never yet
A lesson of hers did once forget ;
For wonderful love do her lips impart,
And all her lessons are learned by heart.

O come ! O come ! or we shall be late,
And autumn will fasten the golden gate.
Of all the schoolrooms, in east or west,
The school of nature I love the best.

WHAT'S DONE

FOR GOD CAN NEVER DIE.

O, ye who spend your strength for naught,
And loathe what you've so dearly bought,
Toilers of earth and time and sense
Oh, what shall be your recompense
Of all that's done beneath the sky ?
But this is immortality.
What's done for earth, fails by and by,
What's done for God, can never die.

Ho, ye who join the eager strife,
For gold, or fame, or pride of life,
Who pamper lusts of flesh or eye,
And for the world, with worldlings vie,
Death will undo your toil so vain
And leave you no abiding gain,
What's done for time, ends by and by,
What's done for God, can never die.

Mountains may crumble back to dust,
.Scepters and crown deceive our trust
And fail, desire may perish—lust ;
By moth, or rust, or thief, or fire,
Our treasures fail, our hope expire ;
What's done for sense, fails by and by,
What's done for God, can never die.

Then do for God what-e'er you can,
O mortal, and immortal man ;
A wasted life ah me to grieve,
Eternity cannot retrieve.
A fruitful life for man and God
Eternity will well reward.
Probation ceases by and by,
What's done for God can never die.

SWEET WORDS.

"MY dearest of Mothers." I heard the words repeated in soft tones by my next door neighbor at an island farm-house where we were sojourning. "My dearest of mothers." My friend was a widow, and her son, an affectionate talented fellow, was engineering in Idaho. In one of his late letters he had said at the close, "and now, my dearest of mothers, good-bye." Did he guess, I wonder, how the little petting phrase would please the heart that loved him so? Did he think she would say it over softly to herself as she sat alone in her room?

The home days were over. The babies with their sweet ways, their joy-giving and their trouble-making, had grown to noisy boys, then to self-asserting men; they were out in the world making their way; brains busy, thoughts absorbed, hearts full; yet here was one who remembered the mother, still in middle life, loving and needing love the same as when her boys were her very own in the very dear child's home. He wrote her long letters, describing his adventurous, changeable life; the strange companions by whom he was surrounded; the wondrous scenery of the wild western world. It was all intensely enjoyed; but better than all were the loving phrases that showed the son's affectionate heart. I wonder if the boys know how dear they are to their mothers, and how little attentions, little gifts, tender words, flying visits, cheer and warm the hearts that have born the test of years and sorrow.

Life is a little chilly to mothers whose homes are things of the past. Even if they remain in the home, the rooms seem very bare and silent after the children are gone. It is as if summer had flown, with its nest and bird-songs, and autum winds are blowing. Then the love of the sons and daughters is like the sunshine or warm fires to the heart that sadly miss them. Let us hope there are many sons who write, "My dearest of Mothers.

OFTEN the most useful Christians are those who serve their Master in little things: he never despises the day of small things, or else he would not hide his oaks in tiny acorns, or the wealth of a wheat field in bags of little seeds.

34

HE CHOSE THIS PATH FOR THEE.

HE chose this path for thee,
No feeble chance, nor hard relentless fate ;
But love, His love, hath placed thy footsteps here.
He knew the way was rough and desolate:
Knew how thy heart would often sink with fear,
Yet tenderly He whispered, "Child, I see
This path is best for thee."

He chose this path for thee,
Though well He knew sharp thorns would pierce thy feet,
Knew how the bramble would obstruct thy way,
Knew all the hidden dangers thou would'st meet,
Knew how thy faith would falter day by day;
And still the whisper echoed, "Yes I see
This path is best for thee."

He chose this path for thee;
And well He knew that thou must tread alone
Its gloomy vales, and ford each flowing stream;
Knew how thy bleeding heart would sobbing moan,
"Dear Lord, to wake and find it all a dream!"
Love scanned it all, yet still could say, "I see
This path is best for thee."

He chose this path for thee;
E'en while He knew the fearful midnight gloom
Thy timid, shrinking soul must travel through:
How towering rocks would oft before thee loom
And phantoms grim would meet thy frightened view;
Still comes the whisper, "My beloved, I see
This path is best for thee."

He chose this path for thee.
What need'st thou more?   This sweeter truth to know,
   That all along these strange, bewildered ways,
O'er rocky steeps where dark rivers flow,
   His loving arm will bear thee ,"all the day."
A few steps more, and thou thyself shalt see
   This path is best for thee.

WAIT.

IF not even one little step is plain to us, "ye nexte thynge" is to wait.   Sometimes that is God's will for us.   At least, it is never His will that we shall take a step into the darkness.   He never hurries us.   We had better always wait than rush on when we are not quite sure of the way.   Often in our impatience we do rush things, which after a little while were not God's "nexte thynge" for us at all.   That was Peter's mistake when he cut off a man's ear in the garden, and it led to sore trouble and humiliation a little later.   There are many quick, impulsive people who are continually doing "next things" wrong, and who find their next thing trying· to undo the last.   We must always wait for God, and never take a step which He has not made light for us.

—J. R. MILLER.

The only way to abolish poverty is to dig yourself, or get some one to dig for you whose work is worth more than his wages.

LOOK HIGHER UP.

"IS this the door?" I asked my-self, hunting up an address in a bewildering street. "I ought to know it."

"No," I said, "I doubt if this is the door."

I chanced though to look higher up, and there was the name I sought after, a name honored, beloved, valued. Looking lower, I failed to notice that help. I saw it now, standing out in clear, distinct letters.

A simple incident, but it set me busily to thinking.

There are many of us trying some door of blessing. Bewildered, we look and may be disappointed. We are in sorrow. It may be the disappointment of afflic-tion, of sickness, of business losses. We look along the range of human resources and human helps, ever seeking some door of peace. Look higher up. Look unto the name of Him called "Wonderful." Measur-less are His resources, giving a personal presence to support us, an individual reconciliation to our losses, strength now. Look unto Jesus!

We are perplexed about duty. But it may not be

the thing that perplexes so much as the way; not the end, but our course to do it. We want wisdom. We need advice. We seek it at human lips; we err if we stop there. Look higher up! Look unto the name of Him called "Counselor." Ask the Savior. Look unto Jesus!

We are tempted. We are weak before the hour of decision and helpless after it. We cry, "No man careth for my soul." Self then shall be the friend showing sympathy, self the friend that promises the strength of its co-operation. "Is not this the door?" some one asks. "That door is a snare," we say. No; victory has another portal. Look up higher! Look unto Him called the "Mighty God." He is able to save from sin and save unto holiness. Look higher up, unto Jesus!

When the end comes, when our feet may falter in death; when our sight may be dim, how precious the name of the Unchangeable. One, the same yesterday, to-day, and forever, his glorious name shining out in letters of fire! In the hour of dying may we look on high, and looking we shall see, as we pass into the Father's house, no more to go out forever.

THE chief beauty in every mother's face, lies in its expression which mirrors the sincerity, the gentleness, the intelligence within. "Her face," says Lovett, "was the benediction of the world, coming from her true and tender soul." That beauty every woman can gain by a pure and loving life.

FOR LOVE'S SAKE.

OMETIMES I am tempted to murmur
   That life is flitting away,
With only a round of trifles
   Filling each busy day;
Dusting nooks and corners,
  Making the house look fair,
And patiently taking on me
  The burden of woman's care.

Comforting childish sorrows,
   And charming the childish heart
With the simple song and story
  Told with a mother's art;
Setting the dear home-table,
  And clearing the meal away,
And going on little errands
  In the twilight of the day.

One day is just like another!
  Sewing and piecing well
Little jackets and trousers
  So neatly that none can tell
Where the seams and joinings—
  Ah!—the seamy side of life
Is kept out of sight by the magic
  Of many a mother and wife.

And oft when I'm ready to murmur
  That life is flitting away,
With the selfsame round of duties
  Filling each busy day,

39

It comes to my spirit sweetly,
  With the grace of a thought divine:
"You are living, toiling for love's sake,
And loving should ne'er repine.

"You are guiding the little footsteps
  In the way they ought to walk;
You are dropping a word for Jesus
  In the midst of your household talk;
Living your life for love's sake
  Till the homely cares grow sweet,
And sacred the self-denial
  That is laid at the Master's feet."

HE who overlooks a small occasion will have lost his eyesight when a great one comes. Never wait for a chance to do good, never seek for some great thing, but improve each small opportunity as it comes to you, and some day you will be surprised to find that the truly great occasion of your life would have been overlooked had you not been keeping track of the small things.

At thirty we are all trying to cut our names in big letters upon the walls of this tenement life; twenty years later we have carved it, or shut up our jacknife.

—O. W. HOLMES.

There is nothing more difficult than to make a friend of a foe; nothing more easy than to make a foe of a friend.

ONLY THE PRESENT.

BEFORE me in billowy mist,
　　Floats visions of greatness and fame ;
　　Deeds of chivalry, kindness, and love,
That one day shall make me a name.
I see great acts of charity
That some day I shall perform,
The orphans I'll cheer, the widows relieve,
And hearts I shall gladden and warm.

I see myself petted, and loved,
Respected and courted by all,
Because I reached out to the needy
And heeded humanity's call.
Of course it was only my duty,
But that doesn't alter the case,
That people will flatter and smile,
And speak words of praise to my face.

I smile as I look at the phantom,
For self is exalted you know ;
In the future these deeds I shall do,
No time for them now, Oh no !
I have work for myself to do,
I have cares of my own just now,
But by and by when riches shall come,
Then all the world before me shall bow.

For I'll bind the hearts that are broken,
I'll lift up the helpless and weak,

Encourage the weary and feeble
And no reward will I seek.
I will smile on those who look sad,
I will speak in tones low and sweet,
Yes, all this in the future I'll do
When all around me is complete.

But higher and thicker the mist arose
Till all was darkness and gloom ;
Then all at once the light streamed in
And a being I knew not whom,
Came gliding forward and gently said :
" My child, why dream of future years,
Unless thou dost the present improve
It will bring thee nothing but sorrow and tears."

"Boast not thyself of the future,
We need thy work just now, to-day,
Look forth on the fields already white,
Then up and be doing !   Do not delay !
If in other days thy work had been needed,
In other days thy life had been given.
This is the time for thee to labor
For Him whose side for thee was riven."

The vision fled, and I awoke
To find, alas, it was terribly true
That I was idling my life away
When all around was so much to do.
With a prayer to Heaven for pardon
O'er the wasted days long and pleasant
I'll arise and work, redeeming the time,
For, we've only the present !   Only the present !

ONCE there was a king who employed his people to weave for him, The silk and paterns were all given by the king. He told them when difficulty arose they should send for him, and never fear troubling him.

Among the men and women busy at looms was a little child whom the king did not think too young to work. Often alone at her work cheerfully and patiently she labored. One day, when the men and women were distressed at the sight of their failures, the silks were tangled and the weaving unlike the patern, they gathered around the child and said: "Tell us how it is that you are so happy in your work. We are always in difficulties."

"Then why do you not send to the king?" said the little weaver; "He told us that we might do so."

"So we do, night and morning."

"Ah," said the child. "But I send directly when I find I have a tangle."

So let us all take our wants and troubles to the Lord in prayer. He invites us to do so, and promises to help us.

To be able to converse well is a valuable gift. Of one so gifted Joanna Baillie says:

"He is so full of pleasant anecdote,
So rich, so gay, so poignant in his wit,
Time vanishes before him as he speaks."

WHY SOME DON'T WORK.

BECAUSE they can't have their own way in every-
thing.

Because they don't receive abundant applause of
men for each effort put forth.

Because some one has misjudged them or perhaps
unintentionally slighted them.

Because they have not their eyes open to the good
they might do if they tried.

Because they are chronic invalids and live in doubt-
ing castles, and all their time is occupied complaining
about themselves and fighting against their doubts.

Because they are not set on fire by the elements of
divine love, as God intended, and are in some degree
in a cold and back-slidden state.

Because the viper of indifference has got hold of
them as they have been warming by the world's fire,
and swollen them up with pride of heart.

NO HONEST LABOR SHOULD BRING SHAME.

CONSCIENTIOUS effort raises the most humble
labor to the highest plane. The shirk is out of
place in any sphere, and no matter whether his
work is what the world styles humble or genteel, it is
belittled by his indolence and want of attention. But
the individual who makes each effort a complete one,

44

who looks after the minutest detail with the same fidelity that a matter of the utmost importance would command, renders the most commonplace duty respectable and worthy.

A certain merchant who had commenced life in humble circumstances, and, by labor and honesty, had achieved a striking success, was disputing with a fellow-tradesman.

"You used to drive a delivery wagon for my father, and do the sweeping and chores about his store," said the other tauntingly.

"I did," was the reply; "and more than that, I did it well."

No honest labor should bring shame to the person who engages in it, save to him who seeks to shirk the responsibilities of his calling. Work that is well done always commands respect, and proves that the workman is a person of character.

The man who sees only the dollar and cents at the end of his labor is the one who usually leaves his work crude and unfinished.

The pecuniary reward of toil is a great and desirable incentive to industry, but there is something in addition to this to be desired.

"To be a successful speaker or writer," says a famous thinker, "a man must be of intense spirit, and must put part of himself into his discourse."

The same is also true of workmen in any other sphere of activity. To be a successful carpenter, blacksmith, teacher, or professional man, one must put his individuality into his work. He must regard each detail as important, and must labor with the thought before him that a well-completed task is of itself part of the reward he shall receive for his labor. The success of the individual who works in this spirit, no matter what may be his duties, is assured from the beginning.

BE CONTENT.

BE content with such things as ye have. Some people have better things, others have worse. You, perhaps, can not have the better, and you have no desire for the worse; then be content with what you have. You may have had better things in the past, you may have worse things in the future. Be thankful for the present and be content. If your lot is a hard one you may improve it, but not by murmuring, fretting or repining. Just here to-day learn the lesson of contentment and wait on God for brighter days, for richer fruits, for purer joys.

No blessing comes to the murmuring, complaining, discontented heart. When once this evil demon of discontent has entered into the soul nothing is right. Even the "angel's food" was not good enough for the murmuring Israelites, and "the corn of heaven" could not satisfy those whose souls were filled with the discontent of earth. But when once the heart has found its rest in God, and all its murmurings are hushed in sweet submission to His will, there is peace in believing, joy in the Holy Ghost, and a hallowed confidence in the kind providence of Him who hath done all things well.

COURAGE.

THE world is bright to all who dare ;
   The world is sweet to all who do ;
   There comes an answer to the prayer
    Of all who to themselves are true.

The hill that in the distance glooms,
   On near approach, to smile is found ;
Its verdure and its sweet perfumes
   Are balm to every bleeding wound.

The mine is barred to indolence,
   The dewy pearl hides in the sea,
The "golden fleece" is found far hence,
   "Beyond the Alps lies Italy."

No good e'er comes to idle dreams ;
   To wish is but to wish in vain ;
The polished shaft of marble gleams
   Not for the stranger unto pain.

All things of honest worth are brought
   By toil and patience, faith and love ;
Each step in life's great ladder wrought
   By which the soul may mount above.

Oh, could I speak one word of cheer
   To those who languish in the strife !
Oh, could I wipe away the tear
   And let them see their crown of life !

Press on with courage true and bold ;
   Press on with pulses beating high ;
The morning breaks her bars of gold !
   The sun in splendor mounts the sky !

REAL FRIENDS.

THE best thing that can happen to a nervous girl is to be liked." Leave out the "nervous girl" and substitute "anyone," and the aphorism will hold good. Real friends are the choicest of possess- ions, not only for the superficial pleasures they confer, but because of the reflex influence which true affection exerts on its object as on its giver. Scores of self-de- nying, charitable acts owe their origin to this source. A friend who has confidence in your ability inspires you to your best endeavors. The admiration of a friend in- creases the self-respect and hence attractiveness of the plainest person. Cordial friendship awakens friendship in return and brightens the darkest periods of life. It is an easy thing to give friendship, and the poorest and the humblest has it in his power to bestow this happi- ness, which is more lasting in its effects and more help- ful than any other gift. Count over your list of friends and determine to increase it.

A RECEIPT FOR HAPPINESS.

IT is simple: When you rise in the morning, form a resolution to make the day a happy one to a fellow- creature. It is easily done. A left off garment to the man who needs it; a kind word to the sorrowful; an encouraging expression to the striving—trifles in themselves light as air—will do it at least for the twenty-four hours. And if you are young depend upon it, it will tell when you are old; and if you are old rest assured it will send you gently and happily down the stream of time to eternity. Look at the result. You send one person, only one, happily through the day; and it is three hundred and sixty-five during the year; and suppose you live forty years only after you commence this course, you have made fourteen thousand and six hundred human beings happy, at all events for a time. Now worthy reader is it not simple, and is it not worth accomplishing?

NEVER TOO OLD TO LEARN.

SIR Henry Spellman neglected the sciences in his youth, but commenced the study of them when he was about fifty and sixty years of age. After this time he became a most learned antiquary and lawyer.

Dr. Johnson applied himself to the Dutch language but a few days before he died.

Franklin did not commence his philosophical researches till he reached his fiftieth year.

Socrates, at an extreme old age, learned to play on musical instruments.

Cato, at eighty years of age, began to study the Greek language.

Constant occupation prevents temptation.
Conscience is never dilatory in her warnings.
Confine your tongue lest it confine you.

THE SCULPTOR BOY.

CHISEL in hand stood a sculptor boy,
  With his marble block before him,
And his face lit up with a smile of joy
  As an angel dream passed o'er him.
He carved that dream on the yielding stone
  With many a sharp incision ;
In Heaven's own light the sculptor shone—
  He had caught that angel vision.

Sculptors of life are we as we stand
  With our lives uncarved before us,
Waiting the hour, when, at God's command,
  Our life-dream passes o'er us.
Let us carve it, then, on the yielding stone
  With many a sharp incision ;
Its heavenly beauty shall be our own—
  Our lives that angel vision.

                              —W. C. DOANE.

LONG LIFE.

COUNT not thy life by calendars ; for
  Years shall pass thee by unheeded, whilst an hour—
  Some litttle fleeting hour, too quickly past—
May stamp itself so deeply on thy brain,
Thy latest years shall live upon its joy.
His life is longest, not whose boneless gums,
Sunk eyes, wan cheeks, and snow-white hairs bespeak
Life's limits ; no ! but he whose memory
Is thickest set with those delicious scenes
'Tis sweet to ponder o'er when even falls:

THE HAPPIEST BOY.

WHO is the happiest boy you know? Who has the best time? Is it the one who last winter had the biggest toboggan, or who now has the most marbles, or wears the best clothes? Let's see.

Once there was a king who had a little boy whom he loved. He gave him beautiful rooms to live in, and pictures and toys and books. He gave him a pony to ride, and a row boat on a lake, and servants. He provided teachers who were to give him knowledge that would make him good and great.

But for all this the young prince was not happy. He wore a frown wherever he went, and was always wishing for something he did not have.

At length, one day a magician came to court. He saw the boy, and said to the king: "I can make your son happy, but you must pay me my own price for telling the secret."

"Well," said the king, "what you ask I will give."

So the magician took the boy into a private room. He wrote something with a white substance on a piece of paper. Next he gave the boy a candle, and told him to light it and hold it under the paper, and then see what he could read. Then he went away and asked no price at all. The boy did as he had been told, and the white letters turned into a beautiful blue. They formed these words:

"Do a kindness to some one every day!"

The prince made use of the secret, and became the happiest boy in the kingdom.

DOING HIS WILL.

IF the voice of the Master bid me,
 "Go, buckle the armor on,
Go, stand where the fight is the thickest,
 And strike till the victory's won,"—
I count that the joy of serving
 Will prompt me to go unswerving.

Yet, when the din and clamor
 I can hear, yet comes no call,
And I fold my hands while the valiant
 Smite their foes, till they shrink and fall,—
I fret that such fate should bind me,
 And the Master in idleness find me.

But the voice that nerved for the battle
 I hear as the din grows still,
And it whispers me this sweet plaudit,
 "Fret not, you too, did my will."
Sweet message, my soul elating,
 "You served me by only waiting."

COMMON politeness is very simple, very easy, very cheap. It costs nothing in effort; it is no tax on either the physical or mental powers; it is always gratefully received by polite people, and it gratifies giver as well as receiver. It makes all within the range of its influence happier and better, and it smooths many of the rough paths of life.

PATIENCE.

WHEN we look back at close of day,
　　Whether it close in sun or rain,
We yet can say, "It is a way
　　We shall not have to walk again."

For should we live a hundred years—
　　A life of praise, a life of blame,
A life of joy, a life of tears—
　　We would not see two days the same.

Out of the vast, eternal store
　　New duties and new joys arise ;
Strange clouds of grief shall gloom us o'er,
　　Fresh bursts of hope shall clear the skies.

Each day a gift!　And life is made
　　Only of days, with gifts between.
To-day a burden?　Quick 'tis weighed,
　　And you shall have a day unseen.

Sweet Patience!　Other angel bands
　　On urgent errands sweep the skies,
To-day but let me hold thy hands,
　　And gaze into thy steadfast eyes!

The Lord Jesus is a stone of stumbling to every self-righteous sinner; but to the believer he is the Stone of help.

PATIENCE WITH THE LIVING.

SWEET friend, when thou and I are gone
  Beyond earth's weary labor,
When small shall be our need of grace
  From comrade or from neighbor ;
Passed all the strife, the toil, the care,
  And done with all the sighing,
What tender truth shall we have gained,
  Alas! by simply dying ?

Then lips too chary of their praise
  Will tell our merits over,
And eyes too swift our faults to see
  Shall no defects discover.
Then hands that would not lift a stone
  Where stones were thick to cumber
Our steep hill-path, will scatter flowers
  Above our pillowed slumber.

Sweet friend, perchance both thou and I,
  Ere love is past forgiving,
Should take the earnest lesson home—
  Be patient with the living.
To-day's repressed rebuke may save
  Our blinding tears to-morrow;
Then patience—e'en when keenest edge
  May whet a nameless sorrow.

'Tis easy to be gentle when
  Death's silence shames our clamor,
And easy to discern the best
  Through memory's mystic glamour ;
But wise it were for thee and me,
  Ere love is past forgiving,
To take the tender lesson home—
  Be patient with the living.

54

A LOVING HEART.

THE woman with a loving heart is sure to look up-
on the bright side of life, and by her example in-
duce others to do so. She sees a good reason
for all the unwelcome events which others call bad luck.
She believes in silver linings, and likes to point them
out to others. A week of rain or fog, an avalanche
of unexpected guests, a dishonest servant, an unbecom-
ing bonnet, or any other of the thousand minor inflec-
tions of everyday life, have no power to disturb the
deep calm of her soul. The love light is still in her
eyes, whether the days be dark or bright. It is she
who conquers the grim old uncle and the dyspeptic
aunt. The crossest baby reaches out its arms to her,
and is comforted; old people and strangers always ask
the way of her in the crowded street. She has a good
word to say for the man or woman who is under the
world's ban of reproach. Gossip pains her, and she
never voluntarily listens to it. Her gentle heart helps
her to see the reason for every poor sinner's mis-step,
and condones every fault. She might not serve with
acceptance on the judge's bench, but she is a very
agreeable person to know. If you seek to find the
happy and fortunate woman in your circle, they will
generally be those who were born with loving hearts,
or, if not so endowed by nature, they have cultivated,
by help of grace, this choice possession, and so have a
double claim to its rewards.

FAMILIARITIES OF YOUNG GIRLS.

THERE is very little left to call the people you love if you lavish words of affection on every stranger whom you meet. If you call a young woman whom you have known just half an hour "Dear," and one whom you have known three days "Darling," there will be no tender endearing term for you to address to those who have your whole heart. Girls who are not of necessity gushing are often apt to speak in the most familiar manner. Good speech is certainly pure silver, but there are so many times when silence would outweigh it and be perfect gold. To tell of one's family affairs, to tell of one's joys and worries to some one who has a sympathetic manner and seems to invite it, is at once a weakness and a misfortune. To write a letter in which you use endearing terms, in which you discuss personal matters, is more than merely indiscreet—it is dangerous. Don't you think if you are a bit familiar in speech or with a pen to a man that he is going to meet this more than half way? Don't you think if you call him by his first name he is very apt to call you by yours, and perhaps before people whom you do not care to have think lightly of you? If you permit him to speak of things not usually discussed, do not imagine for one moment he is going to regard the conversation as confidential. He will always tell it to somebody and then you can imagine how much further down in the esteem of two people you have gone.

Don't permit any man to be familiar with you to the extent of calling you "Old Girl," or citing you as "One of the boys." You don't belong among the boys, and you shouldn't be counted there. Don't let any man, unless you are betrothed to him, kiss you. Lips are of little worth to John which have been pressed by Tom, Dick and Harry.

WHAT TO TEACH THE BOYS.

TO be obedient.

To have patience.

To read books worth reading.

To be temperate in all things.

To keep themselves neat and clean.

To shun evil company and rough ways.

To take off their hats when they enter the house.

To get their lessons and obey the rules of the school.

Always to be employed in some useful occupation.

Never to chew, smoke, drink or use profane language.

To keep early hours and always be punctual and industrious.

To be polite at all times and always have a kind word for everybody.

To avoid contracting loose habits and to strive to be manly always.

To be kind and courteous to each other in the school-room and on the street.

MIND!

MIND your TONGUE! Don't let it speak hasty, cruel, unkind, or wicked words.

Mind your EYES! Don't permit them to look on wicked books, pictures or objects!

Mind your EARS! Don't suffer them to listen to wicked speeches, songs or words.

Mind your LIPS! Don't let tobacco foul them. Don't let strong drink pass them. Don't let the food of the glutton enter between them.

Mind your HANDS! Don't let them steal or fight, or write any evil words.

Mind your FEET! Don't let them walk in the steps of the wicked.

Mind your HEART! Don't let the love of sin dwell in it. Don't give it to Satan, but ask Jesus to make it his throne.

BE SOMETHING FIRST-RATE.

A MODERN philosopher has been saying that every man who can be a first-rate something—as every man can be who is a man at all—has no right to be a first-rate something, for a first-rate something, is no better than a first-rate nothing. A young man who wants to do any thing can soon find out what he can do best. It does not matter much what he does, so long as he can do it a little better than any one else. It is in business or occupation as it is in pastimes or amusement. The champion is at the head of his class. John L. Sullivan is not a charming all-around man; but as he can beat any one else in prize fighting, he is a hero. He may be brutal and beastly; but fair worshipers of heroes have sought to know him.

It is the same with the leaders of armies. The object of war is to kill the enemy. The most successful warrior is the one who kills most, or gets credit for it, as a matter of course. Private soldiers do the killing; but the generals get the promotion and thanks of their government. Eminence in any profession must be won by honest endeavor and earnest and patient application. Money can not make a great man of a little one. Money may put a little man in a big place; but that only makes him look smaller. The pity of it all is that so many men are content to be nothing when they might be something.

It makes no difference if a man only blacks boots for a living. Let him do his work always a little better than any one else and he will have the call. Very many men do not do the best they can under all circumstances. They have too little ambition to do so for themselves, and too little interest in anything else to make a success in life.

One of the most effectual ways of pleasing and of making one's self loved is to be cheerful. Joy softens more hearts than tears.

THE CHILD'S PRAYER.

INTO her chamber went
 A little girl one day,
And by her chair she knelt,
 And thus began to pray:—
"Jesus, my eyes I close,
Thy form I cannot see;
If thou art near me, Lord,
 I pray thee speak to me."
A still small voice she heard within her soul—
"What is it child? I hear thee; tell the whole."

"I pray thee, Lord," she said,
 "That Thou wilt condescend
To tarry in my heart,
 And ever be my friend.
The path of life is dark,
 I would not go astray;
Oh! let me have Thy hand
 To lead me in the way."
"Fear not; I will not leave thee, child, alone."
She thought she heard a soft hand press her own.

"They tell me, Lord, that all
 The living pass away,
And even children may.
 Oh! let my parents live
Till I a woman grow;
 For if they die what can
A little orphan do?"
"Fear not, my child: whatever ill may come
I'll not forsake thee till I bring thee home."

Her little prayer was said
And from her chamber now
She passed forth with the light
Of heaven upon her brow.
"Mother, I've seen the Lord,
His hand in mine I felt,
And oh! I heard Him say,
As by my chair I knelt:—
"Fear not, my child; whatever ill may come
I'll not forsake thee till I bring thee home."

ALL REQUIRED.

IF your station is an humble one, fill it to the best of your ability, and that is all that will be required of you. God only wants now and then a Paul, a Luther, a Calvin, or a Moody; but he always wants, and the world always wants, a multitude of men and women ready to bury their lives in the tunnels and mines of society, away from the gaze of those who seek a less noble and a less enduring work. To a vast number of such self-denying, humble workers, like those "of whom the world was not worthy," the state, the church and society are most deeply indebted to-day; and though their names are unknown and their deeds are unsung, yet in the world to come they may have a fuller joy and a more blessed inheritance than many who are occupying a more conspicuous place, and seem to be doing a larger work in the world.

The more communion we enjoy with God, the more we reverence His majesty and adore His perfections.

PARTING.

AS years slip by, more thoughtful do we grow
    When unto those we love farewell is said :
    To youth Time moves with steps of lagging tread,
And hence they deem to all his flight is slow.
But when maturer, higher growth we know,
    And light on our imperfect sight is shed,
    We came to feel a month, a year, swift fled,
May mean a weight of overwhelming woe.

With clasp of hand or loving kiss we part,
And words of fondness, linking heart to heart,
    Speaking of what shall be when we again
Answer with smiles the look of trustful eyes ;
But if this be no more beneath the skies,
    Unutterable the heritage of pain.

ADVICE TO LITTLE ONES.

BE very kind, dear children to your grandmother.
    I know sometimes little folks think grandma is fus-
    sy; and that she thinks such a *little* noise is too
much. But, dear children, you can think how hard it
is for grandma to bear noise, pleasure and trouble all
mixed, when your mamma and all your uncles and
aunts were children like you. She used to be just as
patient as your mamma is with you. If it had not been
for dear good grandma, you would not have had such
a dear loving mamma. It was she who taught mamma
to be so nice and good, and mamma is trying to teach
you now.

ONE VERSE A DAY.

EALIZING the truth of the statement that very few persons are in the habit of memorizing Scripture, a number of Christians have agreed upon a systematic arrangement by which there shall be a uniform study of the word of God. Only one verse each day. It seems so little, but in the course of a year it will treasure up in the heart twelve chapters of thirty verses each.

In the time of temptation we need the Word hid in the heart. When "the fiery darts of the wicked" once were hurled against the man Christ Jesus, He neither used nor needed other defense than "It is written," and, mortified and discomfitted, "the devil leaveth him, and behold, the angels came and ministered unto Him." The Lord will magnify the law, and make it honorable in the deliverance of His people when beset by sore temptation. "Thy word have I hid in my heart," says David "that I might not sin against Thee." Yet the "word" which was so precious to David was all comprised in a few books of the Old Testament, now considered by many dry and obsolete.

In time of distress what can bring comfort and consolation but the tender, gracious words of our heavenly Father, cherished in the heart as its most precious treasure?

Not by bread alone, but "by every word that proceedeth out of the mouth of God shall man live." Is not the lack of this daily food the cause of that absence of spiritual life which we so constantly deplore? In our busy, hurried lives if there is no time to feed upon the word, the soul is starved. Hide it in the heart, and amid all life's pressing cares and anxieties we can meditate upon it day and night.

So in time of doubt—in this questioning age, when we live in an atmosphere of unbelief, which benumbs the senses and deprives the soul of the power of resistance, our only weapon is "the sword of the Spirit, which is the word of God." If we would have our faith increased, if we would enjoy the peace and repose which comes from perfect trust in God, we must know God. "They that know thy name," says the Psalmist, "will put their trust in Thee." How can we know God save by daily studying the revelations which He has made of Himself?

SIX GOOD RULES.

ACQUIRE THOROUGHLY. This puts the knowledge in.
REVIEW FREQUENTLY. This keeps the knowledge.
PLAN YOUR WORK. This begins well.
NEVER THINK OF SELF. Selfishness spoils all.
NEVER LOOK BACK. Waste no time over failures.
EARN, SAVE, GIVE ALL YOU CAN FOR JESUS. Happiness.

IT is easy to say, 'Know thyself,' but who is to introduce you? Most people go through life without making the advantageous acquaintance in question; and if a friend should take the liberty of introducing you to yourself you would hate him forever."

THE BATTLE OF LIFE.

GO forth to the battle of life, my boy,
Go while it is called to-day ;
For the years go out and the years come in,
Regardless of those who may lose or win,
Of those who may work or play.

And the troops march steadily on, my boy,
To the army gone before ;
You may hear the sound of their falling feet
Go down to the river where two worlds meet :
They go to return no more.

There's a place for you in the ranks, my boy,
And duty, too, assigned ;
Step in to the front with a cheerful face ;
Be quick or another may take your place
And you may be left behind.

There's work to be done by the way, my boy,
That you can never tread again—
Work for the loftiest, lowliest men—
Work for the plow, plane, spindle, and pen—
Work for the hands and the brain.

The serpent will follow your steps, my boy,
To lay your feet a snare ;
And pleasure sits in her fairy bowers,
With garlands of poppies and lotus of flowers
Inwreathing her golden hair.

Temptations will wait by the way, my boy,—
Temptations without and within ;
And spirits of evil, with robes as fair
As those which the angels in Heaven might wear,
Will lure you to deadly sin.

Then put on the armor of God, my boy—
In the beautiful days of youth ;
Put on the helmet and breast-plate and shield,
And the sword that the feeblest arm may wield
In the cause of right and truth.

Then go to the battle of life, my boy,
With the peace of the gospel shod,
And before high heaven do the best you can
For the great reward and the good of man,
For the kingdom and the crown of God.

GOOD ADVICE.

MY advice is," said Isaac Walton, "that you en-
deavor to be honestly rich, or contentedly poor:
but be sure that your riches are justly got, or
you spoil all. For it is well said, 'He that loses his
conscience has nothing left that is worth keeping.'
Therefore be sure you look to that. And in the next
place look to your health: and if you have it, praise
God, and value it next to a good conscience; for
health is a blessing that money cannot buy; therefore
value it, and be thankful for it. As for money, neglect

it not; but note there is no necessity for being rich.

"I have a rich neighbor who is always so busy he has no leisure to laugh: the whole business of his life is to get money, and more money. That he may still get more and more money, he is still drudging on, and says that Solomon says, 'The diligent hand maketh rich;' and it is true indeed. But he considers not that it is not in the power of riches to make a man happy; for it was wisely said by a man of great observation, 'There be as many miseries beyond riches as on this side of them.' And yet God deliver us from pinching poverty; and grant, that having enough, we may be content and thankful. Let us not repine, or so much as think the gifts of God unequally dealt, if we see another abound with riches; when, as God knows, the cares that are the keys that keep those riches, hang often so heavily at the rich man's girdle, they clog him with weary days and restless nights, even when others sleep quietly.

"I have heard a grave divine say, that God has two dwellings; one in heaven, and the other in the meek and thankful heart; which Almighty God grant to me."

SUPPOSING all the points of Atheism were formed into a kind of a creed, I would fain ask whether it would not require an infinitely greater measure of faith than any set of articles which they so violently oppose.

BE KIND TO MOTHER.

MY boys, be kind to mother,
    For she's been kind to you ;
    She's sought to lead you safely
      Your life's brief pathway through.
She's cared for you and loved you,
    And tried to save you pain,
And gave a kindly counsel—
    I hope not all in vain.

She wants to see you happy,
    She wants you to be true ;
Her hope and pride are centered,
    Believe it, boy, in you.
How much of joy and comfort
    Is in your power to give
This faithful loving mother,
    If rightfully you live.

Be manly, true and honest
    In everything that's done,
And show her that her counsel
    Is treated by her son ;
Be kind when old age sprinkles
    Its snowflakes in her hair,
And make her last days happy
    With loving words of care.
              —W. J. SLOAN.

Faith like the diamond, is valuable in proportion to the degree of light it can catch and reflect.

WITH THY MIGHT.

IF there is a disgusting specimen of physical mechanism, in some faint measure animated by what is commonly understood to be a soul, in this fallen world, it is a downright lazy person. To drone this drawling, yawning, supremely tired characteristic into a professedly christian life is an attempt to harmonize most unnatural associations. While these constitutionally languid people, with two strong hands that only hang down until their strength seems almost paralyzed to weakness, are to be in some sense pitied, they are to be in a very positive sense seriously blamed. A natural tendency to indolence, if indulged, marvelously increases by such fostering. Especially is laziness an abhorrent abomination when personifying a gospel minister. If there is a soporific curse on this earth which tends to paralyze the moral and spiritual force of a church, it is a minister who has a relish for nothing but resting, eating and sleeping. When the church finds they have a walking, or rather moping specimen of inherited tiredness, the best way they can do is to call a meeting and pray God to either put some sort of life or ambition into him, or in some gracious way rid the church of him. It is feared that there is occasionally one who is too superlatively lazy to work, and thinks it would be a nice thing to take up the ministry and live at ease.

69

Such are only suited to "wearing out the patience of the saints." It is very evident that God never calls such a conglomeration of indolence to the office and work of the ministry. God calls to labor, to earnest activities. The lazy minister should either shake off this sloth and get to work for God, or give place to some one who will work.

A WOMAN'S WIT.

DR Adler tells a good story about a verbal sparring match between the Emperor Hadrian and a rabbi. Said the Emperor: "Why, your God is represented as a thief, for he surprised Adam in his sleep and robbed him of one of his ribs." The rabbi's daughter craved permission to reply and when her request was granted she said: "Let me implore thine imperial protection. A great outrage has been inflicted upon us." "What has happened?" said the Emperor. She answered, "In the darkness of the night an audacious thief broke into our house. He took a silver flagon from our chest of plate and left a gold one in its place." "Would that such a robber would visit my place every day!" said Hadrian. "And was not the Creator such a thief as this?" retorted the girl; "For he stole from Adam a rib, and in lieu thereof gave unto him a living, loving wife."

A little knowledge wisely used is better than all knowledge disused.

AFTER.

WE know that when the clouds look darkest
      And spreads their shade around—
   If we could look beyond their portals,
      The sunshine would be found ;
And when the storm beats o'er us fiercely,
   Crushing our flowers to earth—
That when the tempest's reign is over
   They will have fairer birth.

So, when life's cares almost o'erwhelm us,
   And we sink down dismayed,
When hope's fair promises all fail us,
   And—even trust betrayed—
Fairer for having been o'ershadowed,
   Our blessings will shine forth
After the storm is over. Its coming
   Has proved true friendship's worth.

IT is a very short way of argument, to call one a com-
   promiser, or if in a very great hurry, and with a
   larger stock of zeal than experience, to call those who
differ with us in judgment "wolves in sheep's clothing,"
and other not very musical terms. But then this is
only one of the incidentals of this transitory life; and
as much as within us lies, we will look on the bright
side. Sometimes farther acquaintance will demonstrate
integrity where it was not looked for. In the midst of
all, the best is, that our own and the faults of others
may, through faith in Christ, be no more remembered
against us. There is wrong enough to correct. Let
us see to that at home first and help others afterwards.

71

THE SHEPHERD'S APPEAL.

HAVE you seen my lamb that has gone astray,
    Afar from the shepherd's fold,
Away in the deserts "wild and bare,"
    Or on the mountain cold?
Have you ever sought to bring it back
    By a word, or a look, or a prayer,
Or followed it on where it wandered alone,
    And tried to reclaim it there?

Ye gather each week in the place of prayer,
    And ye speak of your love for me,
And pray that your daily life may bear
    Some fruit that the world may see.
Ye mean it well; but, when once away,
    Do you live that life of prayer?
Is the soul of the lamb that's gone astray
    Your chief and greatest care?

Ye speak of the good that ye mean to do
    Among your fellow men;
Yet ye tarry oft 'mid the joys of earth
    They are watching your footsteps then.
And while ye have stopped for pleasure or ease
    The lamb that has gone astray
Has wandered farther 'mid darkness and sin
    Along the forbidden way.

Ye meet in your counting-house rooms for gain,
    And count the cost each day;
Do ye ever count what the cost may be
    Of the lamb that has gone astray?

The cost of that soul will far out-weigh
 Your stocks and your piles of gold.
Can you leave your gain and wealth untold
 To gather it into the fold ?

It is perishing now in the bleak and cold
 While ye might have saved its life.
Are ye thinking too much of your ease and your gains
 To enter the Christian strife ?
When the reck'ning is called and the balance made,
 Will the wealth of a single day ·
Atone for the loss of a dying soul—
 For the lamb that has gone astray ?

       —F. MARSH.

WOMAN'S INFLUENCE.

WOMAN holds the balance of power over man;
and she can throw that balance to the side she
will—either for his good or for his ruin. Her
influence can make man pure, brave and strong, or
make him stoop to things so weak and unbecoming;
things not criminal, perhaps, yet so beneath a proper
dignity that the blushes of shame will mantle his cheek
when away from that presence. Whiskey makes a man
beastly, money will make him avaricious, woman can
make life good or evil—as she chooses.

       —MARION MURPHY.

Never purchase friends by gifts, for if you cease to
give they will cease to love.

FROM LITTLE TO GREAT.

MANY years ago, an invalid lady whose home was in the country, visited a large city near which she lived, on a sultry August day. She had business in some of the smaller streets and alleys, and was appalled at the number of pale, puny and sick babies in their mother's arms who were literally dying for a breath of fresh air. What should she do?

"I cannot save all," she said, "but I may save one. There is room for a mother and her child at home."

She took the one mother and her child to her country home, kept them for a fortnight, and then took them home and brought others. Her neighbors followed her example. The next summer the number of children entertained amounted to hundreds; the next thousands.

Another woman who lived in the city and had no money to give was vexed that she could not help in the most gracious charity.

"I can at least tell others of it," she said. She wrote an account of it for a New York newspaper.

A third woman possessed of great wealth, sent a thousand dollars to the editor with the request that he should open a fund for this noble purpose. The Fresh Air charity was the result. The various organizations throughout the United States for the removal of the poor children from the poisonous air of the cities to the country have grown out of this first attempt of a single weak woman to save one dying baby.

During the last two years the charity has taken root in England and on the continent. No one but God knows how many lives have been saved by it.

If the woman who thought of it on that torrid day as she passed, sick and weary, through the slums, had decided, "I cannot save all, why should I trouble myself with one?" how many lives that might have been saved would have been lost!

LIFE'S BURDENS.

LIFE has a burden for every man's shoulders,
    None may escape from its burdens and care,
Miss it in youth and 'twill come when you're old,
    And fit you as close as the garments you wear.
Sorrow comes into our lives uninvited,
    Robbing our hearts of their treasures of song.
Lovers grow cold and friendships are slighted,
    Yet somehow or other we worry along.
Somehow or other the path grows brighter—
    Just when we mourn there are none to befriend,
Hope in the heart makes the burden seem lighter,
    And somehow or other we get to the end.

The worthy man who does good in this life will receive in the age to come, "a reward for that which he hath done" as well as be blessed now in the act of doing right.

DON'T TAKE IT TO HEART.

THERE'S many a trouble
  Would break like a bubble,
And into the waters of Lethe depart,
    Did not we re-hearse it,
    And tenderly nurse it,
And give it a permanent place in our heart.·

    There's many a sorrow
    Would vanish to-morrow,
Were we not unwilling to furnish the wings,
    So sadly intruding
    And quickly brooding,
It hatches out all sorts of horrible things.

    How welcome the seeming
    Of looks that are beaming,
Whether one's wealthy or whether one's poor,
    Eyes bright as a berry,
    Cheeks red as a cherry,
The groan and the curse and the heart-ache can cure.

    Resolve to be merry,
    All worry to ferry
Across the famed waters that bid us forget ;
    And no longer tearful,
    But happy and cheerful,
We feel life has much that's worth living for yet.

THY WILL BE DONE.

I HAVE only one prayer to pray
To the dear Lord up in heaven
Who watches over and cares for me
And everything needful hath given.

But I was long, so long in learning,
Though the letters were bright as the sun,.
But I've got them at last, thank God!
It is this : Thy will be done.

Thy will be done! 'Tis music now
To my heart, where once 'twas pain.
For I've found He doeth all things well,
What once was loss, I find is gain.

So many, many, times I have prayed
For things I thought must be so.
And murmured 'gainst God for granting not,
But now I thank Him for saying "No."

So much better He doeth for me,
Than I could ever think or ask,
I've learned whatever He bids me do,
To call a pleasant and cheerful task.

Whatever the way, whether dark or light
Come sickness, sorrow or pain.
My Father I know with all-seeing eye,
Will bring about my eternal gain.

77

When loved ones are taken from my embrace,
And trouble shall come without measure,
I still will trust.   He'll guide my steps,
Whither he hath taken my treasure.

There are sweets enough in Jesus
For the bitterest cup of woe
That ever was pressed to earthly lips,
If the drinker could see it so.

But we see now with human eyes,
As we wander sad and lone ;
Take courage heart !   We soon shall know
As even also we are known.

Thy will be done !   God grant our eyes
May look towards His Son.
Not lips alone, but heart still cry,
Thy will be done !   Thy will be done !

IF it were possible to enter heaven and find no Father there, heaven would be the grave of hope.   But what will make the heavenly house a home is that it will have, not friends and brethren only, but a Father, whose presence will fill it, and make itself felt in the pulse of every heart.

A man that studieth revenge keepeth his own wounds green, which otherwise would heal and do well.

THE CRUSE THAT FAILETH NOT.

IS thy cruse of comfort wasting ? Rise and share
    it with another,
And through all the years of famine, it shall
    serve thee and thy brother.

Love divine will fill thy storehouse, or thy hand-
    full still renew;
Scanty fare for one will often make a royal feast
    for two.

For thy heart grows rich in giving : all its wealth
    is living grain ;
Seeds which mildew in the garner, scattered, fill
    with gold the plain.

Is the burden hard and heavy ? Do thy steps drag
    wearily ?
Help to bear thy brother's burden ; God will bear
    both it and thee.

Numb and weary on the mountains, wouldst thou
    sleep amidst the snow ?
Chafe that frozen form beside thee, and together
    both shall glow.

Art thou stricken in life's battle ? None but God
    its void can fill ;
Nothing but a ceaseless Fountain can its cease-
    less longing still.

Is the heart a living power ? Self-entwined, its
    strength sinks low ;
It can only live in loving, and by serving love will
    grow.

79

DON'T GET SOUR.

A MAN will always find enough in this world of worry and want, to try his patience and test his good nature; but, whatever comes, he had better keep sweet. Sweetness is the condition of preservation. Whatever is naturally sweet must be kept sweet or become worthless. Fruit is good for nothing after it sours. A man looses his attractions when he sours on the world, and his best friends included. We know of able ministers whose usefulness is practically at an end because they are thought to be "sour." They speak, look, and act their acidity. Some one in times past slighted them; and the sweetness of their hearts began to acquire the quality of tartness. The coagulating process kept right on, its work is now completed.

Coleridge speaks of a "sour, gloomy, miserable man." You can find that man to-day in every rank of life, but the pity is that any christian minister is so. Who wants to follow the leadings, or receive the teaching of a crabbed, peevish, discontented pastor? His look is forlorn, his speech crusty and harsh, and his temper morose. It is all he can do to get into a mood to pray. He dare not show his acrimonious spirit when addressing the eternal throne, and so for a moment he calls back his banished sweetness and talks pleasantly with God. The people hear him and fancy that he will be sociably agreeable again, but no sooner does he rise from his knees than the old acerbity is manifested in every lineament of his countenance. Poor man! He is not what he once was. He turned sour before he stopped to think, and he cannot work himself back to his former state. It is easy to turn molasses into vinegar, but not easy to transform vinegar into molasses. If you are sweet to-day keep sweet. Guard yourself against morose feelings. Laugh when you want to frown, and sing when you feel like scolding. Curb your temper. If you must drink worm-wood, don't ask others to share your cup. Walk not in darkness. Get into the sunshine. Take on brightness. Consider what is good and beautiful and true, and ask God to help you to assimilate these qualities into your own unhappy nature.

TRUE POLITENESS.

TRUE politeness is always free from ostentation. To do a kind act and then publish it to the world is not polite, and to do an act in hope of reward is not polite. The effusiveness of a waiter who expects a fee, the porter tipping his hat to the hotel guest, or the boy who directs you on your way and then holds out his hand for a cent—these acts spring from mercenary motives, and although agreeable are certainly not polite.

A New York man who went on a trip with his wife to Boston tells that in the elevator of his hotel he met a pleasant-faced and quiet-spoken gentleman, who, on seeing strangers desirous of seeing the city, escorted the couple about for nearly half a day. Among the places visited were the City Hall and the mayor's office.

"Which is the mayor?" asked the New Yorker of his guide, there being half a dozen persons in the office as they entered.

"I am the mayor," was the astonishing reply.

That was true politeness, and if it pervades Boston, the city has a right to call itself the "Hub."

NEVER BE IDLE.

IDLENESS means ruin just as stagnation means decay. You can catch better things than early worms by rising early in the morning sometimes, that will paint your cheek, quicken your pulse, brighten your eye, and give you such an appetite as will make breakfast a treat, tea a delight, and—no room for supper. Besides, it's only one early bird that catches the worm. Every early boy can catch the benefit I speak of. And what the boy learns to love, the man will turn to account, while his hay will be better and more abundant than an idler's, his corn, his carrots and his cucumbers will be finer, better and more abundant, too; and just when the idle man is thinking he ought to have a fortune, the early one will be wrapping his up and running off to the bank with it. The boy who says it is music to hear the milk man and chimney-sweep from between the sheets will most likely take his bed to escape his creditors by and by.

FAITH.

I SAT and mused ;
    I felt so weary with the strife,
  I asked myself the question, "Is the prize
    I strive so hard to win,
Worth all the toil, rebuff and pain,
  The jostle and the din ?"
I listened ;
And a voice, from where I knew not, came
And to my heart it whispered :
    "The prize heed not ; that aim would selfish be ;
Work thou with all thy might and mind,
    And leave the rest to me."

" But who art thou ?" I asked.
    " I thought the prize to be a stimulant to urge me on ;
    To elbow through the crowd ; to lead ;
To trample under foot all that oppressed,
    And thus make greater speed."
The voice replied :
    "If thou wouldst learn my name, heed my behest—
Think naught of self, nor what will be thy gain ;
Relinquish not one whit of toil, whatever be thy pain."

Musing, my eyelids drooped ;
I slept, and dreamed :
    Floating in azure blue,
A castle was within, painted with sun-tint rays—
    It seemed so real I thought my dream were true.
Spurred by ambition's lusts,
So eager to possess, I forged my way

Through swamp, up craggy height, o'er desert
    sands;
It seemed within my grasp! I reached ;—
    And lo! I woke with empty, clenched hands.

Walking, I looked me round ; demolished was the
    castle
    That builded in my dream ; I only saw
    Instead of it the wreck;
I had naught left me but to learn the name
Of him who spake ; I followed as he bade me,
    And found his name was Faith.

HOW TO DO GOOD.

HE who waits to do a great deal of good at once, will never do anything. Life is made up of little things. It is but once in an age that occasion is offered for doing good. True greatness consists in being great in little things. How are railroads built? By one shovel at a time. Thus drops make the ocean. Hence we should be willing to do a little good at one time and never wait to do a great deal of good at once. If we would do much good in the world, we must be willing to do it in the little things, little acts one after another; speaking a word here, giving a tract there, and setting a good example all the time; we must do the first thing we can, and the next and then the next, and keep on doing good. This is the way to accomplish anything. Thus only shall we do all the good in our power.

COMFORT ONE ANOTHER.

COMFORT one another
    For the way is growing dreary,
    The feet are often weary, ·
And the heart is very sad.
    There's a heavy burden-bearing,
    When it seems that none are caring,
And we half forget that we were ever glad.

Comfort one another
    With the hand-clasp close and tender,
    With the sweetness love can render,
And the looks of friendly eyes.
    Do not wait with grace unspoken,
    While life's daily bread is broken ;
Gentle speech is oft like manna from the skies.

Comfort one another :
    There are words of music ringing
    Down the ages, sweet as singing
Of the happy choirs above.
    Ransomed saint and mighty angel,
    Lift the grand, deep-voiced evangel,
Where for-ever they are praising the eternal love.

Comfort one another
    By the hope of Him who sought us,
    In our peril—Him who bought us,
Paying with His precious blood ;
    By the faith that will not alter,
    Trusting strength that will not falter,
Leaning on the One divinely good.

Comfort one another :
>   Let the grave gloom lie beyond you,
>   While the Spirit's words remind you
> Of the home beyond the tomb ;
>   Where no more is pain or parting,
>   Fever's flush to tear-drop starting,
> But the presence of the Lord, and for all His
>   people, room.

WIND IS NOT WORK.

WIND is not work any more in the religious line than in the commercial. We say of a man in the commercial world who is given to blowing about his business and his accomplishments, what he is going to do, etc., that he is a blow-hard, and men have little confidence in such a person. A successful business man who has many traveling men in his employ said: "Give me a man who says little and works much." In the religious field to-day, we need to look out for those who are full of wind in regard to God's work and who are given to boasting and really blowing about what they are going to do; but watch them, they never do anything else. They are religious blow-hards. You and I cannot judge of each other's work and we ought not to try to, but when we see one given to empty words and plans, we ought to pray earnestly that God would show him the danger and then look out for ourselves that we do not fall into a similar habit. It is extremely easy to talk and stop and let it end there.

"Few words and much work", should be our motto.

THE BRAIN.

OUR brains are seventy-year clocks. The Angel of Life winds them up once for all, and closes the case and gives the key into the hands of the Angel of Resurrection. Tick tac! tick tác! go the wheels of thought; our will cannot stop them; they cannot stop themselves; sleep cannot still them; madness only makes them go faster; death alone can break into the case, and seize the ever-swinging pendulum, which we call the heart, silence at last the clinking of the terrible escapement we have carried so long beneath our wrinkled foreheads.

OLIVER W. HOLMES.

YOUR HISTORY.

IT is said of Peter the Great, Emperor of Russia, that once, when out in a sailing boat, he became so angry at some offense given by one of the men, that he seized him and was about to throw him overboard. The man had but time to say, "You may drown me but your history will tell of it." Struck by the force of this fact, the Emperor relaxed his hold and desisted from his terrible purpose.

Boys and girls, do you know that the acts and words of every day will make up something of your history? Once in a while some act will be performed that will mark a special point in your life. It may be an act of blessing, it may be some dreadful dark deed; in either case it will loom up out of the past, and will determine in great part the character you shall form and the reputation you shall bear for life. As the colors and figures woven into a fabric determine its character, so the acts, the words, the thoughts, that are woven into your every day life will determine with unfailing accuracy what your life shall be.

HOW DO YOU DO?

HOW do you do? "I do with my might
Just as I'm told, when I'm told to do right.
I strive for promotion by doing my best,
My mother and teacher can tell you the rest.
I speak when I'm spoken to, come when they call,
And strive to be kind and respectful to all.
It is nothing to boast of, what-ever I do,
I wish it were more and were better, don't you?"

How do you feel? "Sorry and mean,
When I do a wrong act, whether hidden or seen.
But I feel like a bobolink, joyous and bright,
When I take the straight path and try to do right.
It sometimes seems hard, but it turns out the best,
And then I feel glad and can laugh with the rest.
I can caper and jump, and turn somersaults too;
It may not look nice, but I like it, don't you?"

What do you know? "Very little, it's true,
Compared with my elders, but that's nothing new.
If I study in earnest I hope to know more

88

When I get to be twenty and on to four-score.
Wisdom may come with gray hairs, if not now,
When wrinkles of care settle deep on my brow,
And boys will look up and honor me then,
When I'm a judge and stand among men."

What do you do? "I study and work;
I don't want to be a mean sneak or a shirk.
I have my home duties, and do them with care,
In that and every thing try to be square;
Tobacco and liquor I shun as a foe,
And stand by my colors wher-ever I go.
What more can I do, except love and obey
My Maker and parents and heed what they say."

BECAUSE SHE WAS BLIND.

 SUFFICIENT excuse for pettishness, and selfishness, and grumbling, one might suppose. But what a reason for giving!

At a missionary meeting in Paris, a poor blind woman put twenty seven francs into the plate. "You cannot afford so much," said the man who was holding the plate. "Yes, sir, I can," she answered. On being pressed to tell how she could give so much she said: "I am blind; and I said to my fellow straw-workers, 'how much money do you spend in the year for oil for your lamps, when it is too dark to work nights?' They added it up in their minds, and found it was twenty-seven francs. So," said the poor woman, "I found that I save twenty-seven francs in the year because I am blind, and do not need a lamp; and I give it to send light to the dark heathen lands."

89

SONGS IN THE NIGHT.

IT is said of a little bird that it will never learn to sing the song its master would have it sing, while there is light in the cage. It learns a snatch of every song it hears, but it will not learn a full separate melody of its own. But the master covers the cage and makes it dark all about the bird, and then it listens and learns the song that is taught it, until it becomes its own. Ever after that it sings that song in the light.

It is much so with us. We will not sing the song God would have us sing till He puts us into the darkness of true conviction. Then the blessed Saviour can teach us a new song, and ever we will sing it in the light He gives. The sweetest songs are sung by those who have just come out of darkness and God "who giveth song in the night" will give us joy and peace in believing, that our songs, begun in the darkness of sorrow, like the angel anthems over the plains of Bethlehem, shall roll on in perpetual fullness of the perfect day that is to come.

"Sing we the song to angels given
　High o'er the plains of Bethlehem ;
Glory to God in highest heaven,
　And peace on earth, good will to men.

Loud as the thunder's mighty roar
　Roll back the anthem to the sky ;
And, breaking on the eternal shore,
　May its glad echoes never die."

AIM HIGH.

AIM high, my boy, and strive to climb
   The heights where heroes stand,
Whose purposes were all sublime,
   And aspirations grand.

Each hero's life, a lesson is,
   And if you read it well,
It gives you help and strength, and this
   Is what it has to tell :

Be true ; be earnest for the right
   In every time and place ;
Toward high endeavor's beacon light
   Set steadfastly your face.

Be brave of heart ; if sore defeat
   O'er-take you in the way,
Then with fresh zeal and courage meet
   The foe another day.

The great men of the world are those
   Who swerved not left nor right
When base, ignoble men opposed,
   But kept the goal in sight !

Though baffled, beaten for a time,
   From each defeat we gain
A strength that makes the strife sublime,
   And takes away its pain.

Be brave, be steadfast, and be true ;
   And ever, as you climb,
Keep God's clear beacon light in view,
   And win, in His good time.

RESPONSIBILITIES.

IT is a high, solemn, almost awful thought for every individual man, that his earthly influence, which has commencement, will never, through all ages, were he the very meanest of us, have an end! What is done has always blended itself with the boundless, ever-living, ever-working universe, 'and will also work there for good or evil, openly or secretly, throughout all time. But the life of every man is as the wellspring of a stream, whose small beginnings are indeed plain to all, but whose ulterior course and destination, as it winds through the expanse of the infinite years, only the Omniscient can discern. Will it mingle with neighboring rivulets as a tributary, or receive them as their sovereign? Is it to be a nameless brook, and will its tiny waters, among millions of brooks and rills, increase the current of some world's river? Or is it to be itself a Rhine or Danube, whose going forth are to the uttermost lands, its floods an everlasting boundary line on the globe itself, the bulwark and highway of whole kingdoms and continents? We know not; only in either case we know its path is to the great ocean; its waters, where they are but a handful, are here, and cannot be annihilated or permanently held back.

—CARLYLE.

O Lord, Thou knowest how busy I must be this day. If I forget Thee, do not Thou forget me.

—SIR JACOB ASHLEY.

92

KEEP BUSY.

IF you expect God to choose you for a great work, be busy; he seldom selects idlers. When he wished a deliverer for Israel, he went into the wilderness for Moses, who was watching sheep; when he wanted a man to save his people from the Midianites, he sent for Gideon, who was threshing wheat; when he wanted a man after his own heart to be king of Israel, he sent for David who was keeping sheep. Idlers do not suit; the Lord wishes those who are not only willing to work, but who are hard at it. Idlers are too often lazy, and that may be the cause of their idleness. Such seldom have ambition to take care of themselves, let alone caring for the Lord's work. But idlers suit Satan exactly. He likes such as have no ambition, for they make the best slaves. The devil wants slaves for his work, but God wants something better. He wishes men and women who have ambition, who take an interest in their work; he wishes persons who are anxious to rise, for he means to promote them some day. From servants he adopts them into his family, and makes them as children.

***

Those who place their hope in another world have in a great measure conquered the dread of death and unreasonable love of life.

A BOY.

THERE'S something in a noble boy,
   A brave, free-hearted, careless one,
   With his unchecked, unbidden joy,
    His dread of books and love of fun ;
And in his clear and ready smile,
Unshaded by a thought of guile ;
   And unrepressed by sadness—
Which brings me to my childhood back,
As if I trod its very track,
   And felt its very gladness.

And yet it is not in his play,
   When every trace of thought is lost,
And not when you would call him gay,
   That his bright presence thrills me most.
His shout may ring upon the hill,
   His voice be echoed in the hall.
His merry laugh like music thrill,
   And I in sadness hear it all—
For like the wrinkles on my brow,
I scarcely notice such things now.

But when, amid the earnest game,
   He stops, as if he music heard,
And, heedless of his shouted name
   As of the carol of a bird,
Stands gazing on the empty air,
As if some dream were passing there,
   'Tis then that on his face I look—
His beautiful but thoughtful face—
   And, like a long forgotten book,
Its sweet, familiar meaning trace.

94

Remembering a thousand things
Which passed me on those golden wings,
  Which time has fettered now ;
Things that came o'er me with a thrill,
And left me silent, sad and still,
  And threw upon my brow
A holier and a gentler cast,
That was too innocent to last

'Tis strange how thoughts upon a child
  Will like a presence sometimes press ;
And when his pulse is beating wild,
  And life itself is in excess—
When foot and hand, and ear and eye,
  Are all with ardor straining high—
    How in his heart will spring
  A feeling whose mysterious thrall
  Is stronger, sweeter far than all !
    And on its silent wing,
  How with the clouds, he'll float away,
  As wandering and as lost as they.

CHRISTIAN COURTESY.

AT a sanitarium, recently, a young collegian was no-
ticeable for his kind and courteous treatment of
invalids there. Every day he gave time and at-
tention to one and another of the patients, particularly
to the one most helpless. His manner always seemed
to say, "It is real pleasure to me to be of use to you."
So gentle, so courteous, did he show these attentions,
that he became a marked figure in groups gathered in

halls or parlors, attracting to himself the regard and good will of all who saw him. It was not a surprise to be told that he was preparing for the ministry, and it needs no prophet's vision to fore-see for him power and usefulness through his rare gift of christian courtesy.

Why was this young man so particularly noticeable? Was it not because courtesy like his is conspicuously infrequent? Are our young men in college, or out of college, generally characterized by courtesy? Are respect and kindness, good will and consideration, shown to others by the majority? And, not to single out young men, but men in middle life, or advanced in years, marked by courtesy in manner? Are not the men who take pains to treat others politely the exceptions? Certain conventional forms of politeness are observed in society life; but these do not govern the actions of men in the places of business, on the streets, in traveling, and elsewhere. A truly courteous man will be so in his office, or in the cars, as well as in the parlor. He will treat strangers kindly, will respond to their questions, and listen to their statements as pleasantly as to those whom he calls his friends.

"The train of years goes slowly out of sight,
Time freighted each and into darkness bound,
And leaves but a feeble, fading light
To copy negatives from memory's ground ;
But even these so indistinct at first,
We straightway spoil with our shallow tears,
As though 'twere folly that we chose the worst,
And leave us nothing but our silly fears."

WORTH REMEMBERING.

THE wisest fellows, as we think, are those who agree with us.

Contentment does not demand conditions, it makes them.

Whistling does not make the locomotive go, it is the silent steam.

Now is always the very best time if we will only make it so.

To be really yourself you must be different from those around you.

The ups and downs of life are better than being down all the time.

Man may growl, grumble and fight, but it has no effect upon natural right.

WANTS OF DAILY LIFE.

LEARN to entwine with prayer the small cares, trifling sorrows, and the little wants of daily life. Whatever effects you—be it a changed look, an altered tone, an unkind word, a wrong, a wound, a demand you cannot meet, a sorrow you cannot disclose— turn it into prayer and send it up to God. Disclosures you may not make to man, you may make to the Lord. Men may be too little for your great matters. God is not too great for your small ones. Only give yourself to prayer, whatever be the occasion that calls for it.

STEPPING ON A SHADOW.

ONE dark night a man who was about to leave a steamboat saw what he supposed to be a gang-plank, but it was only a shadow. He stepped out upon it, and, of course, fell into the water below.

He thought he was taking the right way, but his thinking so did not make any difference in the result so long as he really did not take it.

Just so in matters of far greater importance. You must be *right*, not merely suppose you are right, if you are to avoid the evil consequences of wrong-doing. This man might have put it to the proof whether it was the gang-plank or not, before trusting himself upon it. Do not be like him but test your beliefs and see if they are well grounded. Many a young man has been ruin-ed by a course of conduct which at first he felt sure would do him no harm. Many a man has followed his own notions of what is right, instead of taking God's word as a guide, and wakened in eternity to find that he has stepped on a shadow and fallen.

THE BEST PLACES OPEN.

THE average excellence of the age is high; but one of its imperative needs is great leaders, and these in every department of human endeavor. Turn over the historical pages where you will, and one truth remains the same, that a supreme man has always made a supreme event.

To be practical, we ask an observation to business concerns. They have grown so large and spread so widely, as to need men of consummate ability for their direction.

Dr. Mains tells of several prominent New York firms which are hunting for an individual "at the top," and though he may command his own price, they have not yet found him. A first-rate insurance company recently revealed the salary of the head manager.

"Is that not an enormous price?" we asked a financial authority.

"No, sir," responded he, "it is purely a good business price, considering the man."

Money is no object, providing the leader of the future "fills the bill." The highest skill, with perfect trustworthiness added, is just now in great demand.

There are problems, social and political, which non-thinking people are apt to think insolvable. The truer statement is: We need commanding men to think them out; men whose moral and mental understanding will insure respect, whose judgments will catch the listening ear. And we believe these leaders are coming. They may be developed out of our very need. If any market is governed by supply and demand, this one is. Even as we write we are convinced that climbing slowly but surely to the top are the watchmen who shall first discern the dawn. And as the revolution gave us Washington, the civil war Lincoln, so shall difficulties and labor troubles produce in like manner the men who can solve them. This much is safe, that every young man has a brilliant future for his character and usefulness providing he has character and usefulness for his future.

The elevated rights of a more advanced civilization are before our eyes. Who, like Napoleon crossing the Alps, will rush forward to their summit and bid his fellows follow?. Certainly no temporizer; no coward, paltering with the truth; nor yet the "smart" man who lacks moral fiber. Expedience cannot always rule. Right must and only perpetually endure. The poets sing this; the philosophers who think, and orators who persuade, say—for them (and for us, if we are among them) there is "room at the top." All honors men pay to their greatest benefactors are just where they have ever been,—within the reach of a young man's brave and pure endeavor.

GOD WANTS OUR LOVE.

GOD is not expecting very much of us in the way of conduct. His joy is not in the things we do, but in seeing his own image reflected in us. It is the love of the child every true parent wants, and not its service. All that the service can do is to testify to the love in the heart. What God wants first of all, is love, not work.

I hate to see a thing done by halves; if it be right, do it boldly; if it be wrong, leave it alone.

—GILPIN.

THE CROSS AND THE CROWN.

THE cross for only a day,
　　The crown forever and aye ;
The one for a night that will soon be gone,
And one for eternity's glorious morn.

　　The cross, then, I 'll cheerfully bear,
　　Nor sorrow for loss or care ;
For a moment only the path and the strife,
But through endless ages the crown of life.

　　The cross till the conflict's done,
　　The crown when the victory's won :
My cross never more remembered above
While wearing the crown of this matchless love.

　　His cross I 'll never forget,
　　His marks on his brow are set ;
On his precious hands, on his feet and side,
To tell what He bore for the church, his bride.

　　My cross I 'll think of no more,
　　But strive for the crown set before ;
That ever through ages my song may be
Of his cross that purchased my crown for me.

　　The work of redemption done,
　　His cross and his crown are done ;
The crimson and gold will forever blend
In the crown of Jesus, the sinner's friend.

NO DANGER OF PERSECUTION.

THERE is a kind of fish that resembles sea-grass. It hides itself in the midst of marine vegetation. Below is the head, looking like the bulb of the plant, and above is the body and the tail, looking like the blade of sea grass. The ocean currents sway the fish and the grass alike, and so the little fish escapes being devoured by its enemies. They swim along, and one can hardly perceive where fish leaves off and grass begins, so perfect is the disguise.

Now, there are a great many christians whose lives are so blended with the world that they cannot easily be distinguished. They are swayed by worldly maxims and habits; they share with the world in its sinful pleasure. The difference between such christians and worldlings is not apparent. If this is the kind of christian life you are living, you need not be afraid of persecution; the world will not think it worth while to molest such a christian as that. You will not know what it is to drink of the cup that Christ drank of, and to be baptized with the baptism that He was baptized with. But let a man confess Christ as his Master; let him engage in some aggressive christian work, and he will meet the same opposition which was experienced by the One who said, ''I came not to send peace, but a sword.''

—EDWARD JUDSON.

102

A WOMAN'S FACE.

THE lines of a woman's face are the tracings of her life history. Temper, emotions, principles, are plainly written there. A woman who exists like an oyster can keep her face unlined. The woman who lives, must expect to show the march of years. Too many women play with their emotions; they cater to nervous excitement. Then reality fails to furnish the necessary portion; fiction, sensational reports of disasters—commercial, social, accidental—becomes the basis of supply. To thrill becomes as necessary as to breathe, and every emotion leaves its tell-tale mark and becomes the enemy that deprives life of power.

ALL FOR THE BEST.

SECURE is that soul in the midst of affliction
  Who sees in each sorrow the hand of his God,
  And knowing all things for his good work together,
    Unquestioning bows 'neath each stroke of the rod :
Oh, blest is that heart that, when tossed by tempest,
  Can cling to this hope as a bird to its nest,
And say, with a faith by each trial made stronger,
  "The dear Father knows—it is all for the best."

Each blossom of hope in our lives may be blighted,
  Swept by adversity's pitiless blast ;
Clouds of misfortune o'ershadow our pathway,
  Friends of a life-time prove false at the last ;

The heart may be sad and the way may be lonely,
  And rough be the path by the weary feet pressed,
Yet faith pleadeth ever, oh, fail not to trust Him :
  "The dear Father knows—it is all for the best."

The seed that, with weeping, we sow for the Master,
  Unquickened, may lie where it fell by the way ;
Prayers that were wrung from our hearts deepest anguish,
  Unanswered remain, though we cease not to pray ;
The Father may hide for a moment His presence,
  And the soul by its doubts and its fears be distressed,
But faith whispers low, "Though He slay thee, yet trust
    Him."
  "The dear Father knows—it is all for the best."

These light afflictions, which but for a moment
  The Father hath sent us His promise to seal,
Are naught to the weight of glory eternal,
  And far more exceeding, which God shall reveal.
Some day we shall know *why* the crosses were given,
  For the angels will summon us home to our rest,
Where, with faith lost in sight, and with vision grown
    clearer,
  We shall see as God sees, and shall know it was best.

GOD will have us sure of a thing by knowing the heart whence it comes; that is the only worthy assurance. To know He will have us go in at the great door of obedient faith; and if anybody thinks he has found a back stair he will find it will land him at a doorless wall.

—George McDonald.

HIS OWN.

DO you think that the Lord forgets you,
　　Because you must fight and pray,
　And reap the sorrow-harvest
　　You've sown from day to day ?
Do you think that He lets you suffer
　And never heeds your moan ?
Ah no ! for the dear Lord Jesus
　Will *never* forget His own.

Do you think because your heart aches
　With a bitter, cruel pain,
And your life's sweet, happy sunshine
　Is shadowed by storm and rain,
And the music is hushed and silenced
　Till you hear but the undertone,
That the dear Lord Jesus forgets you ?
　He never forgets His own.

Do you think that because your loved ones.
　Are lying cold and still
Where you cannot hear their voices
　Or work their careless will,
And the struggle you've made together
　Must now be fought alone,
That the dear Lord Jesus forgets you ?
　He never forgets His own.

Do you think that because the sorrow
　All human hearts must know,
Has come to you or the darling
　You loved and cherished so,

And the things you want have vanished,
  The things you would call your own,
That the dear Lord Jesus forgets you ?
  He never forgets His own.

And we're all His own dear children,
  And He holds us all as dear
As you do the wayward baby
  Who creeps to your heart so near;
And if we only listen
  We can hear His tender tone :
"Oh, rest in peace, my children ;
  I never forget my own."

—Ethel M. Colson.

CONQUERING DEFEAT.

IN every life there are mistakes and sins. The holiest do not live perfect. The strongest are liable to fall into sudden and unexpected temptation. The wisest will commit grave errors and follies at some time. We should know well in such cases how to deal with our sins. They must not simply be self-condoned and left lying on the path behind us while we hurry on, nor must they bring despair to our hearts as we sorrow over them; they must be sincerely and heartily repented of, and forgiveness for them sought at the feet of Him we have offended and grieved. Then we must rise from disaster and defeat, stronger, purer, nobler, through Christ victorious over our own sins and a conqueror over our own defeat.

SWEET-MINDED.

S O great is the influence of a sweet-minded woman on those around her that it is almost boundless. It is to her, that friends come in seasons of sorrow and sickness, for help and comfort; one soothing touch of her kindly hand works wonders in the feverish child; a few words let fall from her lips in the ears of a sorrow-stricken sister, do much to raise the load of grief that is bowing its victim down to the dust in anguish. The husband comes home worn out with the pressure of business, and feeling irritable with the world in general; but when he enters the cozy sitting-room, and sees the blaze of the bright fire, and meets his wife's smiling face, he succumbs in a moment to the soothing influence which acts as the balm of Giliad to his wounded spirits that are wearied with the stern realities of life. The rough school-boy flies into a rage from taunts of his companions, to find solace in his mother's smile; the little one, full of grief with her large trouble, finds a haven of rest in its mother's breast; and so one might go on with instance after instance of the influence that a sweet-minded woman has in the social life with which she is connected. Beauty is an insignificant power when compared to hers.

~~~~~~~~~

If good people would make goodness agreeable, and smile instead of frowning in their virtue, how many they would gain to the good cause.

FACE TO FACE WITH TROUBLE.

YOU are face to face with trouble,
  And the skies are murk and gray :
You hardly know which way to turn,
  You are almost dazed you say.
And at night you wake to wonder
  What the next day's news will bring ;
Your pillow is brushed by a phantom care
  With a grim and ghastly wing.

You are face to face with trouble ;
  A child has gone astray ;
A ship is wrecked on the bitter sea ;
  There's a note you cannot pay ;
Your brave right hand is feeble ;
  Your sight is growing blind ;
Perhaps a friend is cold and stern,
  Who was ever warm and kind.

You are face to face with trouble ;
  No wonder you cannot sleep ;
But stay, and think of the promise,
  The Lord will safely keep,
And lead you out of the thicket,
  And into the pasture land ;
You have only to walk straight onward,
  Holding the dear Lord's hand.

You are face to face with trouble ;
  And did you forget to look,
As the good old father taught you,
  For help in the dear old book ?

You have heard the tempter whisper,
  And you've had no heart to pray,
And God has dropped from your scheme of life
  O ! for many a weary day !

Then face to face with trouble ;
  It is thus He calls you back
From the land of dearth and famine
  To the land that has no lack.
You would not hear in the sunshine ;
  You hear in the midnight gloom ;
Behold, His tapers kindle
  Like the stars in the quiet room.

O ! face to face with trouble,
  Friend, I have often stood ;
To learn that pain hath sweetness,
  To know that God is good.
Arise, and meet the daylight!
  Be strong and do your best !
With an honest heart, and a child-like faith
  That God will do the rest.

—MARGARET E. SANGSTER.

Holy Greenham often prayed that he might keep his young zeal with his old discretion.

IN HIS STEPS.

SLOWLY with bowed head I walked,
    And life seemed dark to me ;
I knew the clouds overhead
    No sun my eyes could see.

But as I walked, beside my path
    I saw a flow'ret rare,
And stopped to pick the earth-born star
    Amid the wild winds there.

While as I stopped my fingers pressed
    Another by its side,
And step by step I seemed to find
    My path-way glorified.

In quick surprise I looked ahead,
    And knew my Lord was there ;
Every where His feet had pressed
    A flower was springing fair.

And while my hands with blossoms filled
    I clasped in love the while
He turned with eyes of tenderness,
    And waited with a smile.

" Ah, timid one, could you not trust
    My love for you ?" He said ;
And then were scattered all my clouds,
    And sun-light came instead.

And often times since He's come,
    To deck my path with flowers,
And brought me with his hand of love
    A joy 'mid falling showers.

                            —E. H. SHANNON.

PATIENCE IN WAITING.

I STAND erect and look ahead,
  A shining goal I see,
Just how, or what, I do not know,
  But know that it's enough for me.

And thus I struggle sore and long
  That shining goal to reach,
But mind seems dumb, and tongue seems numb,
  I cannot teach or preach.

And then I would my hands employ,
  My way to work along,
But find alas! my hands are tied,
  Then plaintive is my song.

Then I with willing feet would run,
  But find, they too are fast,
I cannot even creep along—
  And time is flying past.

But then I heard a gentle voice,
  From heav'n 'twas surely sent,
So full of love and sympathy
  It stilled my discontent.

It said not much—but "Only wait
  Till I have wrought in thee
A work sufficient for thy need,
  Then on thy course canst flee.

III

Then thou shalt win the longed-for race
    And serve thy Master well,
And angels of the God in heaven
    Shall of thy waiting tell.

And thou shalt conqueror be at last,
    When pain and work are o'er ;
And then in heav'n with all that serve
    Shall reign forevermore."

—CORA M. FOWLER.

MACAULAY'S TRIBUTE TO HIS MOTHER.

CHILDREN, look in those eyes, listen to that dear voice, notice the feeling of a single touch that is bestowed upon you by that hand! Make much of it while yet you have the most precious of all gifts, a loving mother. Read the unfathomable love of those eyes; the kind anxiety of that tone and look, however slight your pain. In after life you may have friends; but never will you have again the inexpressible love and gentleness lavished upon you which none but a mother bestows. Often do I sigh in the struggle with the hard, uncaring world for the sweet, deep security I felt when, of an evening, nestling in her bosom, I listened to some quiet tale suitable to my age, read in her untiring voice. Never can I forget her sweet glances cast upon me when I appeared asleep; never her kiss of peace at night. Years have passed away since we laid her beside my father in the church yard; yet still her voice whispers from the grave, and her eye watches over me, as I visit spots long since hallowed to the memory of my mother.

MY STRENGTH.

I SAT in the deep'ning twilight,
　With faith that was weak and dim,
The dear Lord stood beside me ;
　But I had no thought of Him ;
My spirit was weary of sinning,
　But blind faith could not see
The love of a pitying Saviour,
　E'en then so near to me.

And looking on all the failures,
　The wrong and sin of the day,
The many times I have left my Lord
　For the broad and sinful way.
"How can I be His disciple,
　His child ?" I wearily cried,
And unto my sorrows and weakness
　My Savior gently replied:

"Child, is it thy strength that shall conquer
This daily temptation and sin ?—
Thy righteousness that shall help thee
　Life's victories bravely to win ?
Trust not in thyself; when thou'rt weary
　And longing from sin to be free,
Look upward for help through the trial,
　My grace is sufficient for thee !"

Then I turned away in the twilight,
　With faith growing strong and clear ;

I had not known through the weary day
  That the Lord had been so near.
And now when my spirit is weary
  And my way I cannot see,
I think of the loving, helpful words
  That the dear Lord said to me.

I whisper them over and over,
  Fresh courage they lend to the day,
And morning, and noontime, and evening
  Make bright with hope's sunshine my way,
Till with faith that no longer is troubled,
  His dear face I no longer can see,
While I know tho' my strength is but weakness,
  His grace is sufficient for me.

               —M. L. BRAY.

A CATECHISM.

DID you ever see a counterfeit ten dollar bill? Yes. Why was it counterfeited? Because it was worth counterfeiting. Was the ten dollar bill to blame? No.

Did you ever see a scrap of brown paper counterfeited? No. Why? Because it was not worth counterfeiting.

Did you ever see a counterfeit Christian? Yes, lots of them. Why was he counterfeited? Because he was worth counterfeiting. Was he to blame? No.

Did you ever see a counterfeit infidel? No; never. Why? You answer. I am through.

HOME FIRST.

HOME FIRST.

LET home stand first before all things. No matter how high your ambition may transcend its duties, no matter how far your talents or your influence may reach beyond its doors, before everything else build up a kind home! Be not its slave; be its minister.

Let it not be enough that it is swept and garnished, that its silver is brilliant, that its food delicious, but feed the life in it, feed the truth in it, feed thought and aspiration, feed all charity and gentleness in it.

Then from its walls shall come forth the true woman and true man, who shall together rule and bless the land.

Is it an overwrought picture? We think not.

What honor can be greater than to found such a home? What dignity higher than to reign its undisputed and honored mistress? What is the ability to speak from a public platform to a large audience, or the wisdom that may command a seat on the judge's bench, compared to that which can insure and preside over a true home that husband and children "rise and call her blessed?"

To be the guiding star, the ruling spirit, in such a position, is higher honor than to rule an empire.

~~~~~~~~~

It is one of the easiest, as one of the meanest things to be funny at other folk's expense.

WORK will never cease with me till coffin lids are screwed down. It may be here, or it may be somewhere else, but under God's providence I am going to work out my life. Let me see the man who will stop me. As long as there's sympathy for the discouraged, patience for the impatient, love for the unloved, a tongue for those who cannot speak, so long as there are men who need God and cannot see Him, so long I'll do God's work among the poor and needy in this world. I never sought a high place; I was sent here by Providence, and Providence has kept me here. I shall stay here or go, by God's providence; live or die when God calls me. Living or dying, I am the Lord's. My question is simply this: ''Lord, what wilt Thou have me to do?'' That I mean to do, though there were ten thousand devils in the way. Hell and the devil can't stop me.

—HENRY WARD BEECHER.

BUILDING.

SOULS are built as temples are—
Sunken deep, unseen, unknown,
Lies the sure foundation stone.
Then the courses framed to bear,
Lift the cloisters pillared fair.
Last of all the airy spire,
Soaring heavenward, higher and higher,
Nearest sun and nearest star.

Souls are built as temples are—
Inch by inch in gradual rise
Mount the layered masonries.
Warring questions have their day,
Kings arise and pass away,
Labors vanish one by one,
Still the temple is not done,
Still completion seems afar.

Souls are built as temples are—
Here a carving rich and quaint,
There the image of a saint ;
Here a deep-hued pane to tell
Sacred truth or miracle ;
Every little helps the much,
Every careful, careless, touch
Adds a charm or leaves a scar.

Souls are built as temples are—
Based on truth's eternal law,
Sure and steadfast, without flaw,
Through the sunshine, through the snows,
Up and on the building goes ;
Every fair thing finds its place,
Every hard thing lends a grace
Every hand may make or mar.

—Susan Coolidge.

Prayer is so mighty an instrument that no one ever
thoroughly mastered all its keys.   They sweep along
the infinite scale of man's wants and of God's goodness.

—Hugh Miller.

A HOLY LIFE.

A HOLY life is made up of a number of small things —little words, not eloquent speeches or sermons; little deeds, not miracles or battles nor one great heroic act of mighty martyrdom, make up the true Christian life. The constant sunbeams, not the lightning; the waters of Siloam "that go softly" in the meek mission of refreshment, not "waters of the river, great and many," rushing down in noisy torrents, are the true symbols of a holy life.

The avoidance of little evils, little sins, little inconsistencies, little weaknesses, little follies, indiscretions, and imprudences, little foibles, little indulgences of the flesh—the avoidance of such little things as those go far to make up at least the negative beauty of a holy life.

—BONAR.

THE SIN OF OMISSION.

IT isn't the thing you do, dear,
　　It's the thing you leave undone
　Which gives you a bit of heartache
　　At the setting of the sun ;
The tender words forgotten,
　　The letter you did not write,
The flower you might have sent, dear,
　　Are your haunting ghosts to-night.

The stone you might have lifted
　Out of the brother's way,
The bit of hearth-stone counsel
　You were hurried too much to say ;
The loving touch of the hand, dear,
　The gentle and winsome tone
That you had no time or thought for,
　With troubles enough of your own.

These little acts of kindness,
　So easily out of mind,
These chances to be angels
　Which even mortals find—
They come in night and silence,
　Each child's reproachful wraith,
When hopes are faint and flagging,
　And a blight has dropped on faith.

For life is all too short, dear,
　And sorrow is all too great,
To suffer our slow compassion
　That tarries until too late ;
And it's not the thing you do, dear,
　It's the thing you leave undone
Which gives you the bitter heartaches
　At the setting of the sun.
　　　　　　　—MARGARET E. SANGSTER.

TRUST IN GOD AND DO THE RIGHT.

COURAGE, brother, do not stumble,
　　Though thy path be dark as night ;
　There's a star to guide the humble ;—
　　"Trust in God and do the right."

Let the road be rough and dreary,
　And its end far out of sight,
Foot it bravely ! strong or weary,
　"Trust in God and do the right."

Perish policy and cunning !
　Perish all that fears the light !
Whether losing, whether winning,
　"Trust in God and do the right."

Trust no party, sect, or faction ;
　Trust no leaders in the fight ;
But in every word and action
　Trust in God and do the right."

Trust no lovely forms of passion,
　Friends may look like angels bright ;
Trust no custom, school, or fashion,
　"Trust in God and do the right."

Simple rule, and safest guide,
　Inward peace and inward might,
Star upon our path abiding,
　"Trust in God and do the right."

Some will hate thee, some will love thee,
　Some will flatter, some will slight ;
Cease from man and look above thee,
　"Trust in God and do the right."

TO ACHIEVE TRUE SUCCESS.

WHAT will assure success? It needs a combination of sound elements to achieve true success. —call it nerve and brains, or over-drawn assurance, whatever you will. The spirit of push, unbounded perseverance, of untiring patience, is a recognized feature of the true American, and there is no reason to mourn its existence, it is a necessary factor in modern life. In the midst of the rush and hurry of these days a man will be left far in the rear who does not make himself aggressive.

Mere brain power is not enough, there must be some means whereby the ability can be manifested. The man of mere intellect may be a fine scholar and a thoughtful reader, but he can never mingle successfully in the business actualities of the world at large. It needs a determination to make the world feel the brain power of the man, this is the means. It need not be shown in a way to annoy or disgust; quietly or persistently the intellect may be made to influence others. The genius of the head may be exerted by the grasp of the hand and the genial familiarity which follows thereby. It requires pluck and courage. To wait in the lowermost place to get an invitation to come higher is a pretty poor policy nowadays. If you don't let it be known that you are around some other fellow will climb over you and achieve wealth and renown. Keep looking onward and going onward. Don't stand still. To stand still in business is but to go backward.

—A. H. REVELL.

LOVE'S POWER.

TWO ladies were overheard talking. Said one, "Do you know Mrs. ——?" "O, yes," was the reply. "She is a good woman." "Yes she is so full of love herself that she seems to fill everybody else with the same spirit; she draws everybody to her." Then the voices were lost in the crowd, and we heard no more with the outward ear, but a voice kept singing in our heart—

> "Love is the grace that shall live and sing
>   When faith and hope shall cease,
> And sound from every joyful string
>   Through all the realms of bliss."

But now abideth faith, hope, love; and the greatest of these is love." Ah, yes, "Love suffereth long, and is kind; love envieth not; love vaunteth not itself, is not puffed up, doth not behave itself unseemly, seeketh not its own, is not provoked, taketh not account of evil: rejoiceth not in unrighteousness, but rejoiceth with the truth: beareth all things, believeth all things, hopeth all things, endureth all things. Love never faileth!" What a model minister's wife must she be who is full of grace like that! What a model person anywhere, in any station! Can I, even I, aspire to such a model? "Beloved, let us love one another, for love is of God; God is love; and he that dwelleth in love dwelleth in God, and God in him;" "Because the love of God is shed abroad in our hearts by the Holy Ghost which is given unto us."

THE SONGS OF HOME.

THE world is full of wondrous song,
    We pause to hearken, and we hear,
    Forever sounding, far and near,
Those sweet vibrations, soft or strong.
    Yet sweeter sounds, and far more dear
Than to the outward sense can come,
    Is memory's music, soft and clear,
    That rings upon the inward ear,
        The loved, old songs of home.

We catch the music of the May,
    The tender voice of bird or breeze,
    That trembles tuneful through the trees,
And faint and sweet from far away
    The mingled murmur of the seas.
    Yet sweeter, dearer far than these,
Though sirens sang across the foam,
    Are echoed through life's silences,
        The loved, old songs of home.

The old, old tunes, the sweet old words
    That lips grown silent loved to sing,
    How close around the heart they cling,
Smiting its truest, tenderest chords.
    Let all the world with music ring,
Where 'er we rest, where 'er we roam ;
    Not one can touch so sweet a string,
    Or to the heart such rapture bring
        As those loved songs of home.

—EMMA S. CARTER.

STEP BY STEP.

HEAVEN is not reached by a single bound
   But we build the ladder by which we rise
From the lowly earth to the vaulted skies
   And we mount to its summit round by round.

I count these things to be grandly true,
   That a noble deed is a step toward God—
Lifting the soul from the common sod
   To a purer air, and a broader view.

We rise by the things that are under our feet,
   By what we have mastered in greed and gain,
By the pride deposed, and the passion slain,
   And the vanquished ill, we hourly meet.

We hope, we resolve, we aspire, we trust
   When the morning calls to its life and light,
But our hearts grow weary and 'ere the night,
   Our lives are trailing in sordid dust.

Wings for the angels, but feet for the men,
   We must borrow the wings to find the way—
We may hope, and resolve, and aspire and pray,
   But our feet must rise, or we fall again.

Only in dream is the ladder thrown
   From the weary earth, to the sapphire wall;
But the dreams depart and the visions fall
   And the sleeper wakes on his pillow of stone.

Heaven is not reached by a single bound,
   But we build the ladder by which we rise
From the lowly earth to the vaulted skies,
   And we mount to its summit round by round.
                —J. G. HOLLAND.

TO YOUNG MEN.

"SOWING WILD OATS," OR WHAT SHALL THE HARVEST BE?

WHEN a man sows in the natural world he expects to reap. There is not a farmer who goes out to sow, but expects a harvest. Another thing—they all expect to reap more than they sow. And they expect to reap the same as they sow. If they sow wheat, they expect to reap wheat. If they sow oats, they won't expect to gather watermelons. If they plant an apple-tree, they don't look for peaches on it. If they plant a grape-vine, they expect to find grapes, not pumpkins. They will look for just the very seed they sow. Let me say right here, that ignorance of what they sowed will make no difference in the reaping. It would not do for a man to say, "I didn't know but what it was wheat I was sowing, when I sowed tares." That makes no difference. If I go out and sow tares thinking that it is wheat, I've got to gather tares all the same. That is a universal law. If a man learns the carpenter's trade, he don't expect to be a watch-maker, he expects to be a carpenter. The man who goes to college and studies hard, expects to reap for those long years of toil and labor. It is the same in the spiritual world. Whatsoever a man or a nation sows, he and they must reap. The reaping time will come. Men may think God is winking at sin now-a-days, and isn't going to punish it, because he does not execute his judgments speedily; but be not deceived, God is not mocked, and whatsoever a man soweth that shall he also reap. I tremble for those young men who laugh in a scoffing way and say, "I am sowing my wild oats." You have got to reap them. There are some before me now reaping them, who only a few years ago were scoffing in the same way. The rich man who fared luxuriously, while the poor man sat at his gate, and the dogs came and licked his sores, the reaping time has come for him now. He would gladly change place with that beggar now.

Yes, there will be a change by and by. Men may go on scoffing and making light of the Bible, but they will find it to be true by and by. I think there is one passage that you will admit is true. You very often see it in the daily papers, that "murder will out" when some terrible crime that has been covered up for years has come to light. And there is one passage I would like to get every one to remember: "Be sure your sin will find you out." There are a great many things in this world we are not sure of, but this we can always be sure of, that our sins will find us out. I don't care how deep you dig the grave in which you try to bury them. Look at the sons of Jacob. They thought they had covered up their sins, and their father never would find out what they had done with Joseph. And the old man mourned him for twenty long years. But at last, after all these long years had gone, away down in Egypt, there Joseph stood before them. How they began to tremble. Oh, it has found them out. Their sin had overtaken them. Young men, you may have committed some sin many years ago, and you think nothing is known about it. Don't you flatter yourself. God knows all about it, and be sure your sin will find you out. Your own conscience may turn witness against you by and by. If you sow tares you will reap disappointment, you will reap despair, you will reap death and hell. If you sow to the Spirit you shall reap joy and happiness and eternal life. The reaping time is come. What is the harvest going to be? If you confess your sin, God will have mercy; He delights in mercy.

—D. L. Moody.

She Knew The Author.

IT is said that a gentleman in conversation with a lady upon the subject of certain of the utterances of the poet Browning insisted that his interpretation of the poet was correct because he was a friend of Browning, and enjoyed his personal acquaintance. Afterward he chaffed the lady for her faith in the Scriptures, which he said was childish and unmeaning. "But you forget," was the reply, "That I am acquainted with the author." It is this acquaintance with God that makes his word so true, so precious, so comforting to the devout believer. If we know God, we shall surely recognize his word.

The man who depends on the spur of the moment often discovers that particular moment hasn't any spur.

FORGIVENESS.

NOTHING is harder than to forgive a malicious wrong, a harm done us, in a matter where we know we are right.

Sir Eardley Wilmot was an English baronet, widely known as a leader in social life, a man of great personal dignity, and force of character. Having been a distinguished Chief Justice of the Court of Common Pleas, he was often consulted by friends as to perplexing social questions.

On one occasion a statesman came to him, in great excitement over an injury just inflicted on him by a political leader. He told the story with warmth, and used strong ephithets in describing the malice which had inflicted the wrong.

"Is not my indignation righteous?" he asked impetuously. "Will it not be manly to resent such an injury?"

"Yes," was the calm reply. "It will be manly to resent it, but it will be God-like to forgive it."

The answer was so unexpected and so convincing that the statesman had not another word to say. He afterward confessed to a friend that Sir Eardley's words caused his anger to suddenly depart, leaving him a different and a much better man.

~~~~~~~~~~

Spiritual life is strong just in the proportion in which it can propagate itself, and inoculate others with its essential power.

MOTHER'S WAY.

OFT within our little cottage,
    As the shadows gently fall,
While the sunlight touches softly
    One sweet face upon the wall,
Do we gather close together,
    And in hushed and tender tone,
Ask each other's full forgiveness
    For the wrong that each has done.
Should you wonder why this custom
    At the ending of the day,
Eye and voice would quickly answer,
    "It was once our mother's way."

If our home be bright and cheery,
    If it holds a welcome true,
Opening wide its door of greeting
    To the many not the few;
If we share our Father's bounty
    With the needy, day by day,
'Tis because our hearts remember,
    "This was mother's way."

Sometimes when our hearts grow weary,
    Or our task seems very long,
When our burdens look too heavy,
    And we deem the right all wrong,
Then we gain a new, fresh courage,
    As we rise and brightly say,
"Let us do our duty bravely,
    This was our dear mother's way."

129

Thus we keep the memory precious,
　　While we never cease to pray,
That at last, when lengthening shadows
　　Mark the evening of life's day,
They may find us waiting calmly,
　　"To go home our mother's way."

WHATEVER YOU DO, DO CHEERFULLY.

WHATEVER you do, do cheerfully,
　　As if your heart was in it,
　　'Twill smooth the way to the goal you seek,
　　And give you strength to win it.
For little of silver and gold you'll get,
If you make up your mind to frown and fret ;
Little of joy for a lonely hour,
If you never have planted a single flower,
What though the task a hard one be,
　　Still with a smile begin it ;
And whatever you do, do cheerfully,
　　As if your heart was in it.

The help you give with a cheery word
　　Is a double help to your neighbor,
For it puts a song in the weary heart
　　That knoweth no rest from labor.
For little you'll know of real delight
If you work for yourself from morn till night,
And never have a penny to spend,
Or a loving thought for a needy friend ;
The thread of life will longer wear,
　　If with a song you spin it ;
So whatever you do, do cheerfully,
　　As if your heart was in it.

ABILITY AND OPPORTUNITY.

THESE are the conditions of success. Give a man power and a field in which to use it, and he must accomplish something. He may not do and become all he desires, and dreams of, but his life cannot be a failure. I never hear men complaining of the want of ability. The most successful think that they could do great things if they only had the chance. Somehow or other something or somebody has always been in the way. Providence has hedged them in so that they could not carry out their plans. They knew just how to get rich, but they lacked opportunity.

Sit down by one who thus complains and ask him to tell you the story of his life. Before he gets half through, he will give you the occasion to ask him, "Why didn't you do so at that time? Why didn't you stick to that piece of land and improve it, or to that business and develop it? Is not the present owner of that property rich? Is not the man who took up the business you abandoned successful?" He will probably reply: "Yes, that was an opportunity; but I did not think so then. I saw it when it was too late." In telling his story he will probably say, of his own accord, half a dozen times, "If I had known how things were going to turn, I might have done as well as Mr. A. That farm of his was offered to me. I knew that it was a good one, and cheap, but I knew that it would require a great deal of hard work to get it cleared and fenced, to plant trees, vines, etc., and to secure water for irrigation. I did not like to undertake it. I am sorry that I didn't. It was one of my opportunities.''

The truth is, God gives to all of us ability and opportunity enough to enable us to be moderately successful. If we fail, in ninety-five cases out of a hundred it is our own fault. We neglect to improve our talents with which our Creator endowed us, or we fail to enter the door he opened for us. A man cannot expect his whole life shall be made up of opportunities, that they will meet him at regular intervals as he goes on, like milestones by the roadside. Usually he has one or two, and if he neglects them, he is like a man who takes the wrong road where several meet. The further he goes the worse he fares.

A man's opportunity usually has some relation to his ability. It is an opening for a man of his talents and means. It is an opening for him to use what he has, faithfully and to the utmost. It requires toil, self-denial and faith. If he says, ''I want a better opportunity than that, I am worthy of a higher position than it offers;'' or if he says, ''I won't work as hard and economize as closely as that opportunity demands,'' he may, in after years, see the folly of pride and indolence.

There are young men all over the land who want to get rich, and yet they scorn such opportunities as A. T. Steward and Commodore Vanderbilt improved. They want to begin, not as these men did, at the bottom of the ladder, but half way up. They want somebody to give them a lift, or carry them up in a balloon, so that they can avoid the early and arduous struggles of the majority of those who have been successful. No wonder that such men fail, and then complain of Providence. Grumbling is usually a miserable expedient that people resort to, to drown the reproaches of conscience. They know that they have been foolish, but they try to persuade themselves they have been unfortunate.

IT CANNOT BE DONE.

"GATHER up my influence and bury it with me," were the dying words of a young man to the weeping friends at his bedside. What a wish is this? What a deep anguish of heart there must have been as the young man reflected upon his past life—a life which had not been what it should have been. With what deep regrets must his very soul have been filled as he thought of those young men he had influenced for evil; influences which he felt ought to be eradicated, and which led him faintly, but pleadingly, to breath out such a dying request, "Gather up my influence and bury it with me."

Young men, the influence of your lives for good or evil cannot be gathered up by your friends after death, no matter how earnestly you may plead. Then, remember, your influence is now going out from you; you alone are now responsible; you have now the power to govern and shape it. Then live noble, true, heroic, God-like lives.

ONLY ONE MOTHER.

YOU have only one mother my boy,
Whose heart you can gladden with joy,
Or cause it to ache,
Till ready to break,
So cherish that mother, my boy.

You have only one mother, who will
Stick to you through good and through ill,
And love you, although
The world is your foe—
So care for that love ever still.

You have only one mother to pray
That in the good path you may stay;
Who for you won't spare
Self-sacrifice rare—
So worship that mother alway.

You have only one mother to make
A home ever sweet for your sake,
Who toils day and night
For you with delight—
To help her all pains ever take.

You have only one mother, just one—
Remember that always, my son ;
None can or will do
What she has for you,
What have you for her ever done ?

THEY WERE ALL POOR BOYS.

JOHN Adams, second President, was the son of a farmer of very moderate means. The only start he had was a good education.

Andrew Jackson was born in a log hut in North Carolina, and was raised in the pine-woods for which the State is famous.

James K. Polk spent the earlier years of his life helping to dig a living out of a new farm in North Carolina. He was afterwards a clerk in a country store.

Millard Fillmore was the son of a New York farmer, and his home a very humble one. He learned the business of clothier.

James Buchanan was born in a small town in the Alleghany Mountains. His father cut the logs and built a house in what was then a wilderness.

Abraham Lincoln was the son of a very poor farmer in Kentucky, and lived in a log cabin until he was twenty-one years old.

Andrew Johnson was apprenticed to a tailor at the age of ten years by his widowed mother. He never was able to attend school, and picked up all the education he ever had.

General Grant lived the life of a common boy in a common house on the bank of the Ohio River, until he was seventeen years of age.

James A. Garfield was born in a log cabin. He worked on the farm until he was strong enough to use carpenter tools, when he learned the trade. He afterwards worked on the canal.

OVERWORK AND UNDERWORK.

EVERY one has heard of the danger of overwork, yet few understand just where the danger lies. A man can hardly overwork himself if he takes care of himself in other respects—secures a normal amount of sleep, breathes pure air, takes exercise, and eats food moderately.

The main trouble is that the man who is overworking is violating fundamental conditions of health. He burns his candle at both ends.

With due care, a man with good heredity is capable of safely doing an almost incredible amount of solid work. Mr. Gladstone at eighty-three, with no show of weariness, carried the weight of the British Empire. The celebrated John Wesley did more work than almost any other man of the last century; but he observed the laws of health, and still active, reached his eighty-eighth year.

Much of the so-called overwork is the overwork of worry, care, anxiety and haste. These make the severest draft on the vitality of the system.

We seldom hear of Quakers dying of overwork, and yet they are a very industrious people. The pupil who has prematurely broken down in his studies might have gone on under even heavier loads if there had been nothing to fret him in his home surroundings, and competition, examinations and scholarship markings had no place in our school system. The fact is, work, and plenty of it, is healthy in a high degree.

And this leads us to say that a lack of work, of the brain or hand, is highly injurious. Underworking may be as harmful as overworking to the brain if not to the body. Nations living in conditions in which livelihood come almost without effort are in every way feeble. Close confinement in prison tends to idiocy.

Further, when the mental faculties are not called into action the moral also lie dormant, and the lower propensities become all-controlling. In all ages the corruptions of the higher classes are due to this fact. Few worse things can befall one than to have nothing to do.

VISIT YOUR PARENTS.

IF you live in the same place, let your steps be—if possible daily—a familiar one in the old home; if you are miles away—yea, many miles away—make it your business to go to your parents. In this matter do not regard time or expense; the one is well spent, and the other will be, even a hundred-fold, repaid. When some day the word reaches you, flashed over the telegraph, that your mother is gone, you will not think them much, those hours of travel which at last bore you to the loved one's side.

The brightest bow we only trace upon the darkest skies.

—Frances Ridley Havergal.

137

ACQUIESCENCE IN THE DIVINE WILL.

WHAT know I of what is best,
　　Oh! my Father! kind and wise!
Thy great love is manifest,
　　Let whatever scenes arise;
Health or sickness, choose for me;
As thou pleasest, let it be.

What know I of what is best?
　　Who could always bear the light?
In thy changeless love I rest,
　　Knowing well thy ways are right.
Light or darkness, choose for me;
As thou pleasest, let it be.

What know I of what is best?
　　Human knowledge is but small;
Trusting thee my soul is blest,
　　Kept by thee, I cannot fall;
Pain or pleasure, choose for me;
As thou pleasest, let it be.

What know I of what is best?
　　'Tis enough that thou art nigh;
Since my hand by thine is pressed,
　　Who can be more safe than I?
Strength or weakness, choose for me;
As thou pleasest, let it be.

What know I of what is best?
  Earth and heaven alike are mine ;
Grace can stand the sternest test,
  Living, dying, I am thine ;
Life or death, Lord, choose for me ;
As thou pleasest let it be.

A WORTHY AMBITION.

YOUNG man! if God has given you brains, heart and voice, speak out. There are great reforms to be carried on. The whole nation needs awakening. Speak out, sir, and your speech will be welcome, wherever and on whatever particular branch of reform you choose to make yourself heard. Lift up your voice for that which is "honest, lovely, and of good report." Not in mere word harangue, not in windy palaver, not in grandiloquent spouting, not in weary, drawling verbosity—not in jabbering garrulity which is heard only when the speaker must be delivered of a speech. But in the words of true, sanctified earnestness, opening your mouth because you have something useful to say, saying it with the genuine, unstudied eloquence which comes right from the heart, and in all cases closing your mouth the moment you have done.

Do you wish to sow that which will produce fruit? Then "cast thy bread (truth) upon the waters (before the people) for thou shalt find it after many days." Ecclesiastes 11: 1.

139

THE EARNEST MINISTER.

COULD I but preach as I saw the woe
Which, like a sea, spreads over all below,
As if I heard earth's weeping millions cry,
"Give us the light before we faint and die,"
With eloquence of words and tears, I then
Would rouse the church to pity dying men.

Oh, could I preach as if my heart was fired,
By gazing on the cross where Christ expired—
As if it felt the mighty love that he,
By dying pangs, proved his own love to be—
How soon would guilty, stubborn souls embrace
The joyful tidings of redeeming grace !

Oh, could I preach as Christ would have me do
With heaven and hell immediately in view—
With heart inflamed with pure, seraphic love,
Like those that wait and minister above—
What victories, then, would from my labor spring
To honor Christ, my blessed Lord and King !

Oh, could I preach as if I saw the day—
Dark day of doom, of sorrow and dismay,
When weeping mercy shall in tears retire,
And burning justice wrap the world in fire—
How would the thoughtless and the giddy hear,
And apathy give way to anxious fear.

Oh, could I preach as I will wish at last,
When days and months and rolling years are past,
And just before me in deep mystery, lies
The world unseen as yet by human eyes,
How would I agonize to love to bring
Mankind in sweet submission to their King.

WANT OF DECISION.

A GREAT deal of labor is lost in the world for the want of a little courage. Every day sends to their graves a number of obscure men, who have only remained in obscurity because their timidity has prevented them from making a first effort, and who, if they had only been induced to begin, would in all probability have gone great lengths in the career of fame. The fact is, that in doing anything in the world worth doing, we must not stand shivering on the bank, thinking of the cold and danger, but jump in and scramble through as well as we can. It will not do to be perpetually calculating risks and adjusting nice chances; it all did very well before the flood, when a man could consult his friends upon an intended publication for a hundred and fifty years, and live to see its success for six or seven centuries afterwards; but at present a man waits and doubts, and consults his brother, and uncles, and his particular friends, until one day he finds that he is sixty-five years of age, and that he has lost so much time in consulting first cousins and particular friends, that he has no more time to follow their advice. There is so little time for over-squeamishness at present, that the opportunity slips away. The very period of life at which a man chooses to venture, if ever, is so confined that it is no bad rule to preach up the necessity, in such instances, of a little violence done to the feelings and efforts made in defiance of strict and sober calculations.

—Sidney Smith.

THE MOTHER.

THERE is no human love like a mother's love. There is no human tenderness like a mother's tenderness. And there is no such time for a mother displaying her love and tenderness toward her child as in the child's earliest years of life. That time neglected, no future can make good the loss to either mother or child. That time well improved, all the years that follow it can profit by its improvement. Even God Himself measures His Fatherly love by a motherly standard. "As one whom his mother comforteth, so I will comfort you," He says. What more than this could be asked? Many a strong man who was first comforted by his mother's loving, tender words and ways, while he was a helpless child, has never lost his grateful, trusting dependence on that mother's ministry of affection and sympathy.

When gruff old Dr. Johnson was fifty years old, he wrote to his aged mother as if he were still her wayward but loving boy: "You have been the best mother, and I believe the best woman in the world. I thank you for the indulgence to me, and beg forgiveness for all that I have done ill, and all that I have omitted to do well."

John Quincy Adams did not part with his mother until he was nearly or quite fifty years of age, yet his cry, even then, was: "O God, could she have been spared yet a little longer. Without her the world feels like a solitude."

When President Nott, of Union College, was more than ninety years old, and had been a college president for half a century, as sense and strength failed him in his dying hours, the memory of his mother's tenderness was fresh and potent; and he could be hushed to needed sleep by a gentle patting on the shoulder, and the singing to him of the old-time lullabys, as if his mother was still sitting by his bed-side in loving ministry, as she had been well nigh a century before. The true son never grows old to a true mother.

WORTH OF CHARACTER.

HE two most precious things this side the grave are our reputation and our life. But it is to be lamented that the most contemptible whisper may deprive us of the one, and the weakest weapon of the other. A wise man, therefore, will be more anxious to deserve a fair name than to possess it, and this will teach him so to live, as not to be afraid to die.

—Geo. H. Colton

HE earnest men are so few in the world that their very earnestness becomes at once the badge of their nobility, and as men in a crowd instinctively make room for one who seems eager to force his way through it, so mankind everywhere open their ranks to one who rushes zealously toward some object lying beyond them.

--Timothy Dwight, D. D.

NOTHING TO PAY.

NOTHING to pay! Ah, nothing to pay!
Never a word of excuse to say!
Year after year thou hast filled the score,
Owing thy Lord still more and more.
    Hear the voice of Jesus say,
"Verily thou hast nothing to pay!
Ruined, lost, art thou, and yet
I forgive thee all thy debt."

Nothing to pay! The debt is so great;
What will you do with the awful weight?
How shall the way of escape be made?
Nothing to pay! yet it must be paid!
    Hear the voice of Jesus say,
"Verily thou hast nothing to pay!
All has been put to my account,
I have paid the full amount."

Nothing to pay; yes, nothing to pay!
Jesus has cleared all the debt away,
Blotted it out with His bleeding hand!
Free and forgiven, and loved you stand,
    Hear the voice of Jesus say,
"Verily thou hast nothing to pay!
Paid is the debt, and the debtor free!
Now I ask thee? lovest thou ME?"
—FRANCES R. HAVERGAL.

<hr>

All useless misery is certainly folly, and he that feels
evils before they come, may be deservedly censured,
yet surely to dread the future is more reasonable than
to lament the past.

SMILES.

OW little they cost, and how much good they do. What a cold and cheerless world this would be without them. And yet we do not have half enough of them.

I believe many a poor drunkard or fallen woman might be won back to the right path, if they could have kind words, and looks, instead of frowns, cold shoulders, and hard words. What humanity needs is more sympathy and love, to feel that some one cares for them. A good way is to give a friendly nod and a bright smile to every one, even those we are not acquainted with.

I remember once spending the day with a lady friend, and during the time had occasion to pass the "kitchen help;" as I did so, I gave her a nod and smile, but should never have thought of it again had not my friend told me shortly after that she had a compliment for me, and then went on to say that the girl had just said:

"Sure Missis, and ye have a very beautiful lady in the parlor to-day."

She asked what made her say that, and she replied:

"Because she looked right at me and laughed."

"You ought to see how happy she is over it," said my friend.

Poor creature, I knew she was not accustumed to smiles. It did not matter to her that day, that her mistress had company and she had extra work to do, so long as the "beautiful lady" had smiled on her.

We may not see the reward of our smiles so soon, but we must sow, if we ever expect to reap.

I know a lady who is the most successful Sunday-school teacher I ever saw. During the ten years she has been in our school, she has had charge of every department, and with such marked success as to cause envy in some instances.

Do you ask her secret? She simply smiles on each one and makes them feel they are *wanted right there.*

Dear young people, you may with-hold your confidence, be cautious of your words, not lavish of your love; but if you wish to be happy and make others so, freely give your smiles.

ADVICE.

BOYS, if in this world you would succeed,
　　You must be brave and true :
　　Don't stand aloof and slight your work,
　　Because 'tis hard to do.
If troubles come and sorrows rise
　　Then show yourself a man ;
Let courage nerve you for your work,
　　And do the best you can."

JUST ONE DAY.

IT ought not to be hard to live well just one day. Anyone should be able to carry his burden, or fight his battle, or endure his sorrow, or stand faithful at his post, or do his work, however hard, for just one day. Anyone should be able to remember God and keep his heart open toward heaven; and remember his fellow in need and suffering, keep his hand stretched out in helpfulness, for just one day. Yet that is all there is to do. We never have more than one day to live. We have no to-morrows. God never gives us years, nor weeks; he gives us only days. If we will fill the little days with faithfulness, the great years will pile up monuments and blessings.

OLD FRIENDS.

THERE are no friends like old friends,
  And none so good and true
 We greet them when we meet them,
  As roses greet the dew ;
No other friends are dearer,
  Though born of kindred mold :
And while we prize the new ones,
  We treasure more the old.

There are no friends like old friends,
  To help us with the load
That all must bear who journey
  O'er life's uneven road :

147

And when the unconquered sorrows
   The weary hours invest—
The kindly words of old friends
   Are always found the best.

There are no friends like old friends,
   Where e'er we dwell or roam—
In lands beyond the ocean,
   Or near the bounds of home :
And when they smile to gladden,
   Or sometimes frown to guide,
We fondly wish those old friends
   Were always by our side.

There are no friends like old friends,
   To calm our frequent fears,
When shadows fall and deepen
   Through life's declining years :
And when our faltering footsteps
   Approach the Great Divide,
We'll long to meet the old friends
   Who wait the other side.

           —DAVID B. SICKLES.

EACH one of us is bound to make the little circle in which he lives better and happier; each of us is bound to see that out of that small circle the widest good may flow; each of us may have fixed in his mind the thought that out of a single household may flow influences that shall stimulate the whole commonwealth and the whole civilized world.

           —DEAN STANLEY.

148

OUR MISSION.

"OUR mission, our mission," repeated little Nellie S. one Sunday afternoon, "Teacher said all, everybody."

"What is it Nellie?" asked the mother who had heard the child's soliloquy.

"Why mamma you see our lesson to-day was about Christ's mission, how he came to seek and save the lost, and teacher said we all had a mission, even little boys and girls."

"What is a mission, Nellie?" asked the mother, wishing to know if her daughter really understood what she was talking about.

"I don't know as I can tell you just exactly, teacher told us all about it, but I don't remember all she said."

"Never mind to tell me all she said, just tell me what you think it is."

Nellie hesitated a moment, then said: "I suppose it is—*is just what God wants us to do.*"

"Very good, my dear, now what do you think He wants you to do?"

"That is what I was thinking about all the way home, and I haven't found out yet; but I am going to keep thinking and thinking till I find out, then I am just going to *go right at and do it.*" Nellie was right. How grand if we all like her would keep thinking and thinking, and asking God what He would have us do, and like her, go straight and do it.

Some people from a lack of willingness to do what is required of them, attempt to deny they have a mission. But upon serious reflection I think all will agree they have a work to do, a work God requires at their hand, nor will He hold him guiltless who attempts to shift the responsibility upon another.

It is true a few have been mistaken in regard to their mission.

Paul, at one time really thought his mission was to persecute the saints, make havoc in the churches, enter into houses hailing men and women, and committing them to prison. But it was not long before Jesus met him and deprived him of his sight; and it was at that time when the world was shut out, that God got Paul's attention sufficiently to give him his true mission. Acts 26: 16-17-18. As soon as the change had taken place and Paul received his sight, "straightway he preached Christ," increasing in moral strength and boldness each day until he became the most zealous of all apostles. So God wants us as soon as we enter upon His work to continually look to Him for a supply of strength and grace and boldly proclaim His truth.

Joshua, when commanded to lead the children of Israel, after the death of Moses, was commanded to "be strong and of a good courage;" and again the Lord said: "Be thou strong and very courageous." Ezekiel, when he was commanded to go and preach to a rebellious nation, was commanded to speak the words of the Lord "whether they would hear, or whether they would forbear."

And so we might go on through a long catalogue of

the names of God's servants whom He has commanded to go forth in His name, doing His bidding regardless of the opposition or opinion of men.

Right here is where many fail in these days. The opinions, oppositions, and ridicule of men, the criticism as to their mode of doing, hinder many really good people from attempting that which they feel called of God to perform; but such should remember the promises of God are sure, and if He wants us to do anything, we had better be about it and leave the result with Him.

Some are not fulfilling their mission for lack of interest in their fellowmen; others from selfishness; others from a love of ease; and a few are waiting to do some great thing. But be not deceived; God will never waste His grace upon us. We shall never have the ability to do great things until we prove ourselves capable by obedience in little things. But the cry is: "Where shall we work?"

The very best place is *just where you are.*

"What shall we do?"

Do the duty that lies nearest and you will be surprised how the way will open for other, and greater things.

"If ye know these things, happy are ye if ye do them."

D O all the good you can,
　　To all the people you can,
　　　In all the places you can,
By all the means you can,
At all the times you can,
And as long as ever you can."

ALMOST anybody can make a spurt, but only those who are soundly principled can stand the long stretch of heroic effort. "They that wait upon the Lord shall renew their strength," this language implies there is constant waste, wear and tear, making constant renewal necessary; and this is true alike of our physical, intellectual and religious nature. We need perpetually fresh impulses of power, or presently we shall come to a dead stop. And this is the meaning of that other Scripture, "He hath saved us by the washing of regeneration, and the renewing of the Holy Ghost." The first refers to the change that is wrought once for all, and the other to that constant impartation of fresh grace and strength to repair the loss of power that comes from contact with the world; this we must have, and this we may have, if we will only keep up our connection with our base of supplies.

"My grace is sufficient," saith the Lord. Only let the golden pipes be unobstructed, and the grace will flow steadily in; and steady flow is what we want. Enthusiasm is powerful, but "patient continuance in well-doing"—this, after all, is the thing that wins.

To "mount upon wings as eagles" is doubtless very fine, but to "run and not be weary" finer still; while to "walk and not faint" on the long, long tramp is the highest of all tests of true soldierly quality. There is no "hurrah" about that. Beautiful and enjoyable is the flush of feeling, but there will be times when feelings faint, and if we simply "go by our feelings" we shall presently cease to go at all.

LABOR BEFORE REST.

H sing to me not of the "Sweet by-and-by,"
   So long as there's work to be done;
  Sing not to me now of the mansions on high,
     So long as there's souls to be won.
    But, rather in clear and melodious strain,
    Let the songs of the reapers on mountain
      and plain
    The echoes awaken again and again,
     As we gather the sheaves one by one.

The mansions are glorious, I know very well,
  That the Savior has gone to prepare ;
I know that the angelic choruses swell
  Rich and sweet on the heavenly air ;
I know that the streets are of purest gold,
That the pearly white gates have a beauty untold,
That the green tree of life doth its blossoms unfold
  By the banks of the rivers so fair.

I know that in yon happy, heavenly land,
  The dear ones I loved here below
Await now my coming—a glorified band,
  In garments washed "whiter than snow."
Their trials are over, their triumphs complete,
They rest from their labors at Jesus' feet,
And join in a song of thanksgiving so sweet,
  For victories won here below.

But, so long as the world doth in wickedness lie,
  And time speeds so swiftly away,
And the children of men in their sinfulness die,
  And Satan claims souls for his prey ;
So long as there's one I can win "in His name,"
From a life of iniquity, sorrow or shame,
Or a poor wandering lost one, whom I can reclaim,
  Just so long in this world would I stay.

No, no! I'm not weary ; my soul is aflame ;
  The "strength of the Lord" is my stay ;
For "Lo, I am with you," his word doth proclaim,
  And I rest on that word every day.
With the light of his presence for my guiding star,
I shrink not nor falter in this holy war,
But, like the fresh horse that scents battle afar,
  I eagerly bound to the fray.

  Oh, glory! my soul doth exult in the thought
  That He gives me some fighting to do!
Awaken, my comrades! press out as you ought—
  There's a place in this conflict for you!
No longer sit singing of rest in the skies—
Till by scars you can show you have fought for
        the prize!
In the name of our King I entreat you, Arise!
  Press forward—the end is in view!

                              —-Mrs. E. E. Williams.

CHEERFULNESS.

CHEERFULNESS and contentment are small things in life, but they are not to be exchanged for the wisdom of Solomon, or the combined wealth of this entire nation, for they will not give the pleasure and happiness of a cheerful, contented spirit. What if our road be rough and scattered with thorns, does it better our condition to look sad and forlorn? Let us be thankful for our many undeserved mercies, then we shall have cheerful spirits, and our faces will be radient with smiles for all with whom we may meet— young and old, rich and poor.

It is but a little thing to do, but who can measure the good a smile may do? The little child will be the better and happier for it. The middle aged, burdened with the cares of this life, need it, as they toil up the mountain height; it will make their steps lighter. The aged need it, for in us they are living over their lives, now so near the close; and if we are cheerful and smiling light will be reflected upon their pathway, in the evening of their day from our cheerful countenances.

—M. A. C.

Climb not too high, lest the fall be greater.

Defer not till evening what the morning may accomplish.

Do not throw your opinions in everybody's teeth.

Don't measure other people's corn by your bushel.

Eagles fly alone, but sheep flock together.

WORTHY OF NOTE.

WE agree that the following is worthy a boy's no_tice. In fact, he cannot beat it into his head too thoroughly, if he hopes to make the fine-grained, solid man his mother expects him to be:

Every time I refuse a drink of liquor I improve my manhood.

Every time I spend a dollar foolishly I am opening a pauper's grave.

Every time I pay rent I am taking so much away from a home of my own.

Every time I speak a kind word I am adding a brick to my temple of manhood.

Every time I buy an article I am encouraging the manufacturer or producer.

Every time I pay a debt I am doing right and helping to put money in circulation.

Every time I refrain speaking in defense of a friend I prove that I am not a friend.

———————

EVERY day a self-denial. The thing that is difficult to do will be easy three hundred and sixty-five days hence, if each day it shall have been repeated. What power of self-mastery shall he enjoy, who, looking to God for graces, seeks every day to practice the grace he prays for!

—ANON.

156

HELP THAT COMES TOO LATE.

'TIS a wearisome world, this world of ours,
   With its tangles small and great,
  Its weeds that smother the springing flowers,
   And its hapless strifes with fate,
But the darkest day of its desolate days
  Sees the help that comes too late.

Ah! woe for the word that is never said
  Till the ear is deaf to hear,
And woe for the lack to the fainting head
  Of the ringing shout of cheer ;
Ah! woe for the laggard feet that tread
  In the mournful wake of the bier.

What booteth help when the heart is numb ?
  What booteth a broken spar
Of love thrown out when the lips are dumb,
  And life's bark drifteth far,
Oh ! far and fast from the alien past,
  Over the moaning bar ?

A pitiful thing the gift to-day
  That is dross and nothing worth,
Though if it had come but yesterday
  It had brimmed with sweet the earth.
A fading rose in a death-cold hand,
  That perished in want and dearth.

Who fain would help in this world of ours,
  Where sorrowful steps must fall,
Bring help in time to the waning powers,

Ere the bier is spread with the pall ;
Nor send reserves when the flags are furled,
And the dead beyond your call.

For baffling most in this dreary world,
With its tangles small and great,
Its lonesome nights and its weary days,
And its struggles forlorn with fate,
Is that bitterest grief, too deep for tears,
Of the help that comes to late.

—MARGARET E. SANGSTER.

GENTLENESS IS CHRIST-LIKENESS.

GENTLENESS is Christ-likeness. Jesus, our model in everything, is a most wonderful model here. He was rejected by "his own," and betrayed by his disciples; he was tried, mocked, scourged, crucified; and yet he bore all in gentleness and submission, never saying a harsh word or doing an unkind deed that would afterward need be repented of and forgiven; and when afterward he hung upon the cross, and was reviled, he reviled not again, but committed himself unto Him who judgeth righteously. At all times and everywhere He showed that His life was subject to the commanding power of the religion that He came to establish and to teach. Such gentleness is not to be confounded with weakness. It is not timidity or white-facedness. It is the truest courage, a Divine virtue, the consummate flower of a life filled with the power and spirit of love.

MISTAKES.

IT is a mistake to labor when you are not in a fit condition to do so. To think the more a person eats, the healthier and stronger he will become. To go to bed at night and rise at daybreak, and imagine that every hour taken from sleep is an hour gained. To imagine that if some work or exercise is good, violent or prolonged exercise is better. To conclude the smallest room in the house is large enough to sleep in. To eat as if you had only a minute to finish the meal in, or to eat without an appetite, or continue after it has been satisfied, merely to satisfy the taste. To believe that children can do as much work as grown people, and that the more hours they study the more they learn. To imagine whatever remedy causes one to feel immediately better (as alcoholic stimulants) is good for the system without regard to the after effects. To take off proper clothing out of season because you have become heated. To sleep exposed to a direct draft in any season. To think any nostrum or patent medicine is a specific for all of the diseases flesh is heir to.

LOOK UP.

NEVER give way to melancholy. Are you happy? Are you likely to remain so till evening, or next month, or next year? Then why destroy present happiness by a distant misery, which may never come at all? Every substantial grief has twenty shadows, and most of these shadows are of our own making.

IS LIFE WORTH LIVING?

IS life worth living?" Ask of him
  Who toils both day and night
  To make a little home for those
    So dear unto his sight.

"Is life worth living?" Ask of her
  Who, crowned with widow's weeds,
Doth find supremest happiness
  In kind and noble deeds.

"Is life worth living?" Ask again
  Of those whose highest aim
Is to assist their fellow-man,
  Without one thought of fame.

"Is life worth living?" Ah! dear friend,
  Let these good people tell;
A better question far is this—
  Is life worth living well?

THE NEW CHURCH.

IT was an humble church, no stately steeple
  Looked down upon the river and street;
An humble church, for humble, toiling people,
  Who hither came, with heavy, aching feet.

Outside there raged the city's ceaseless riot,
  And careless souls the path to ruin trod;
Within, amid a reverent Lord's Day quiet,
  The little church was set apart to God.

I saw another sight than those rapt faces ;
  I saw a vision of the years to be,
The throng of those whose forms shall fill these
      places,
  When time shall be no more with you and me.

More solemn than the solemn invocations,
  More joyful than these joyful notes of praise,
I heard the prayers of future generations,
  I heard the song of far-off future days.

I heard the wistful penitent's grieved sighing
  In memory of a sad and wasted past ;
And high above I heard the angels crying,
  "Rejoice ! the wanderer returns at last ! "

And then I heard the Master, softly saying,
  "O ye who reared this building for my sake,
Through toil and sacrifice and fervent praying—
  Most sweet to me the gift is that you make.

"For once I was exile, bowed with sadness,
  Unhoused, when birds straight to their nests
      might flee ;
And my remembering heart is filled with gladness
  When those that loved me built a church for me."

Sins are forgiven through repentance and faith in
Christ. Sinful nature is cleansed by the blood of Christ
through faith.

YOUR BEST ALWAYS.

SIR Joseph Reynolds was one of the most distinguished painters of his day, and, in answer to the inquiry, how he attained to such excellence, he replied: "By observing one simple rule, namely to make each painting the best." Depend upon it that the same thing is true in the service of God. He who wishes to preach well should endeavor each time to preach his best. The audience may be small, and the hearers illiterate, but the best possible sermon will not be thrown away upon them. It may be that the minister is invited to make one among several speakers at a tea-meeting. Never let him talk mere nonsense to fill up time, as so many have done in days past, but let him use the opportunity for quietly uttering some important truths. It is for the preacher's own good that he should never descend into mere dribble. Beyond all expectation, he may be accomplishing a great work, where his only idea is that he is doing a little one as well as he can. Our firm opinion is that he often accomplishes most when the occasion appears to be the least favorable.

Well do we remember a young man who was called to preach on a certain week-day morning at an anniversary of a village chapel. He was somewhat surprised to find that only eight persons were present in a spacious edifice; but he gave himself up, heart and soul, to service as thoroughly as if eight thousand had been gathered together. It was a time of refreshing to the eight, and to the preacher himself, and so nine were benefitted! What was the result? In the evening the audience filled the place; the rumor of the morning sermon had been industriously spread by the villagers, the scantiness of the audience being a factor in the singularity of the news; and every available person was mustered to cheer the poor young man, who was such a singular preacher. What was far better, there were memorials of good having been accomplished in the salvation of souls. A brother minister, who was present in the morning, because he was the preacher of the afternoon, remarked that if it had beeen his lot to conduct that morning service, the slender congregation would have taken all the life out of him, but that he saw the wisdom of always doing one's best under all sorts of circumstances; it would be sure to lead up to something larger by and by. Let every young speaker think of this, and throw all his energies into his discourse in a cottage to a dozen hearers.

—C. H. SPURGEON.

IT is not what men eat but what they digest, that makes them strong; not what we gain, but what we save that makes us rich; not what we read, but what we remember that makes us learned; and not what we preach, but what we practice that makes us christians. These are great but common truths, often forgotten by the glutton, the spendthrift, the book-worm and the hypocrite.

—LORD BACON.

A HAND SHAKE AT THE DOOR.

WE are very slow to understand the power of a hand shake at the door of a church, mission, or evangelistic service. In some churches there is a peculiar warmth pervading the whole place, and if we were to look about for the reason, we should find men and women at the door to welcome every one, both those who belonged to the church, and those who do not. A hand shake as they go, and a word of kindness for those who have trouble or sickness at home, a pressure of the hand for the strange young man as he comes for the first time, perhaps, into the city. A young man said not long since, "I go to such a church, went there when I first came to the city, and they seemed so glad to see me, that I was quite surprised. Two people shook hands with me as I went in, and a number as I came out. I felt at home right away, as if I had been among friends, and as I heard the sermon the pressure of the hand shake was still with me, and that sermon had a different impression upon me than it otherwise would. I believe the hand shake at the door was the instrument, in God's hand, of leading me to Christ." If we could read the testimony of those who have had similar experience, no doubt they would be along the same line. If in our church, mission, or evangelistic services that are being held in our town or city a hearty hand shake is not being given, let us see to it.

THE BURDEN.

TO every one on earth
    God gives a burden to be carried down
    The road that lies between the cross and
        crown,
        No lot is wholly free :
        He giveth one to thee.

Some carry it aloft,
Open and visible to any eyes :
And all may see its form and weight and size ;
    Some hide it in their breast,
    And deem it thus unguessed.

The burden is God's gift,
And it will make the bearer calm and strong,
Yet, lest it press too heavily and long,
    He says, "Cast it on Me,
    And it shall easy be."

And those who heed His voice,
And seek to give it back in trustful prayer,
Have quiet hearts that never can despair ;
    And hope lights up the way
    Upon the darkest day.

Take thou thy burden thus
Into thy hands, and lay it at His feet ;
And whether it be sorrow or defeat,
    Or pain, or sin, or care,
    Upon the darkest day.

It is the lonely load
That crushes out the light and life of heaven,
But born with Him, the soul restored, forgiven,
Sings out through all the days,
Her joy, and God's highest praise.

--MARIANNE FARNINGHAM.

LIVE FOR SOMETHING.

TOO many are living for nothing, and indeed worse
than nothing. Their lives are aimless. They
aim at nothing, and hit it. They desire to simply
have what they call a ''good time,'' as long as they live.
Only let them have what money they wish to spend, in
such ways as may gratify their uncultivated tastes, with
no serious cares on hand, no commanding responsibili-
ties laid upon them and no exhaustive drafts upon their
sympathies, and they seem to be contented with them-
selves. What a travesty this is on the true idea of
human life! How dwarfish and ''dudeish'' it is! On
the other hand, how noble and ennobling is the pur-
pose to live for something, something good, something
which will touch and impress other lives and enrich
them with blessings!

The eloquent Dr. Chalmers gave voice to these
weighty words: "Oh, man immortal, live for some-
thing, live for something! Do good and leave behind
you a monument of virtue that the storms of time can
never destroy. Write your name, by kindness, love
and mercy, on the hearts of thousands you come in con-

tact with, year by year, and you will never be forgotten. No, your name, your deeds will be as legible on the hearts you leave behind you, as the stars on the brow of the morning. Good deeds will shine as brightly on the earth as the stars of heaven." How such a life calls out and dignifies all of the better and finer elements of one's manhood! A young man or a young woman cannot live for something high and helpful without rapidly growing beautiful in moral character. Such a life gives tone and splendid quality to one's acts and whole career, and when he dies he leaves behind him impressions and fruits which will live on the lives of others with increasing power.

—C. H. WETHERBEE.

BROAD ROAD.

IT is hard to be charitable toward those who do not believe exactly as we do. Many times we are disposed to be very much put out with those who do not see the world just as we see it. Whether we are right or wrong, our best plan will not be to denounce and upbraid them, but rather to spend our time and energy in praying that we both may be able to see all things as God would have us. Unquestionably that is easier to talk about than to practice; but God will give to his children that spirit of love and tenderness toward all his creatures that will enable a child of God to be Christ-like even when he cannot agree with those with whom he comes in contact.

"GO FORWARD."

IN the spiritual life there is a great tendency to be content with mere beginnings. In ordinary affairs it is far otherwise. No mother would be content if her babe remained a mere babe; or if her child, though achieving straight strokes with great ability, and repeating the alphabet in a very skillful way, proceeded no further in the educational acquirements. No enterprising man of business would be satisfied with having duly completed his apprenticeship and opened on his own account in a small way. And no one would tell himself he had nothing further to care for who had placed the engaged ring on the hand of the fair object of his choice.

And yet, christians are sometimes inclined to feel fully satisfied now that they are really saved, and are professedly on the Lord's side. This done, they are ready to say to themselves, "I can now rest and be thankful!" What! A soldier resting at the very commencement of the campaign? A pilgrim resting as soon as his hand grasps the staff, and his feet stand in the King's highway? No! no! Rest? Why, he is just in position to march, to fight, to work for Him to whom he belongs! Being saved is but the merest beginning of the christian life. Now for the grand business of the man of God, the soldier of the cross, the servant of the King! There is the trumpet call! Who can mistake its ringing note? Advance! Advance!

REGKLESS FRANKNESS.

THERE is a class of people who pride themselves on their honesty and frankness, because, as they tell us, they "say just what they think," throwing out their opinions right and left, just as they happen to feel, no matter where they may strike, or whom they may wound. This boasted frankness, however, is not honesty, but is rather miserable impertinence and reckless cruelty.

We have no right to say what we think unless we think kindly, and lovingly, no right to unload our jealousies, envies, bad humor and miserable spites upon the hearts of our neighbors.

If we must be bad tempered, we should at least keep our ugliness locked up in our own breasts, and not let it wound the feelings and mar the happiness of others. If we must speak out our dislikes and prejudices and wretched feelings, let us go into our own rooms, and lock the door, and close the window, so that no ear but our own shall hear the hateful words.

If any man seemeth to be religious, or even morally decent, and bridleth not his tongue, that man's religion is vain and his character base.

—Selected.

~~~~~~~~~~

It is not so important for one to know when Christ will come again as to know that he is ready for His coming at any moment.

SOME KISSES AND SMILES.

THERE are beautiful songs that have never been sung—
That never were uttered by the pen or tongue.
They are waiting in silence a magical word
From the heart of the poet, that has not been heard.
Sometime they will come from the echoes in store
And thrill with their rapture a desolate shore.
Then, hearts that have languished in sorrow and grief
Shall spring from their ashes to happy relief.

There are kisses untaken, like beautiful gems,
That linger on lips like sweet fruit on the stems,
Those lips may grow pale in the whirlwind of time
And lose the sweet flushes of their young, sunny prime.
They may pass from our view like the rainbow's bright gleams,
But oft they'll return to our spirit in dreams,
And bring their sweet kisses, untasted before,
To thrill our sad hearts on this time-beaten shore.

Bright smiles have been wasted; their glory unseen,
Have lingered awhile like the bright sunny sheen
That falls on the mountains so hoary and old,
To lend them a mantle of glory and gold,
Transforming the faces of the dark gloomy sod
Into beauty and grace, like the smile of a god.
Those smiles that are wasted—by desert winds tossed—
Shall gladden our souls, for they have not been lost.

BEAR THE CROSS YOU HAVE.

LET us be satisfied with the cross we now have to carry. Too often we wish that we might exchange our present cross for one which lies beyond our reach. We know not what we ask, when we ask for an untried cross in the place of the one which we are wearing. We sometimes think if we only had the cross which another brother seems to be easily bearing, we could get along better; but very likely if we had his cross we would want to exchange it for still another. Mr. Spurgeon wisely says: "It is folly to imagine, as we have sometimes done, that we could bear anything except that which we are called upon to endure. We are like the young man who says he wants a situation. What can you do? He can do anything. . That man you never engage, because you know he can do nothing. So it is with us. If we say, 'I can bear anything but this,' we prove our universal impatience. If we had the choice of our crosses, the one we should choose would turn out to be more inconvenient than that which God appoints for us, and yet we will have it that our present cross is unsuitable and specially galling. I would say to any of that mind, 'if your burden does not fit your shoulder, bear it till it does.' Time will reconcile you to the yoke, if grace abides with you." Is not one great reason why Christians bear their cross with apparent ease and even satisfaction, because they do not chafe under it, but make the best use of the grace which God gives them to carry it? The ox that is always fretting under his yoke is the one which has a sore neck and a suffering head. The Christian who is constantly chafing under the burden he bears, is always sore and sour, and is also envious of the condition of those whom he supposes have an easier time than he has. He is always wishing that his condition was different from what it is. Poor unhappy man! He has a great deal yet to learn. He has not yet learned the blessed art of commanding sweet contentment in the ways of God. Let God choose your cross and then bear it with praise to him.

—REV. C. H. WETHERBEE.

AN ARAB SAYING.

REMEMBER, three things come not back :
The arrow sent upon its track—
It will not swerve, it will not stay
Its speed ; it flies to wound or slay.

The spoken word, so soon forgot
By thee ; yet it has perished not ;
In other hearts 'tis living still,
And doing work for good or ill.

And the lost opportunity,
That cometh back no more to thee ;
In vain thou weepest, in vain dost yearn,
These three will never more return.

THE ATMOSPHERE OF HOME,

HOUSEHOLD hygiene is by no means limited to sanitary dwellings and suitable diet and dress. It extends to what may be called the atmosphere of the home and includes the influence of thoughts and emotions upon the body. It is a physiological fact that a spirit of gloom or constant fault-finding in the family, beside depressing the spirits, actually reacts upon the vital forces. Morbid tendencies are strengthened and incipient diseases are held to develop in the homes which lack healthful stimulus of cheer and kindness. Violent emotions derange digestion. A child who is allowed to indulge in fits of anger receive harm in the physical as well as the moral nature. It is the exception, a misanthrope, a cynic or a chronic grumbler is in the possession of good health. For hygienic reasons alone, if there were no higher motives to influence parents, it pays to flood the home with the sunshine of love and the joy of religion.

GO ye into the world and preach the Gospel to every creature," means that you are to preach Christ to your milk-man, your servant girl, the man with whom you are doing business, your errand boy, your dressmaker, your next door neighbor, the workman next you in the shop, your letter-carrier, and the children you meet.

Preach ''Jesus saves'' to every-body.

173

STAND FOR THE RIGHT.

BE firm, be bold, be strong, be true,
   "And dare to stand alone;"
Strive for the right, what e'er you do,
   Though helpers there may be none.

Nay—bend not to the swelling surge
   Of fashion's sneers and wrong;
'Twill bear thee on to ruin's verge,
   With current wild and strong.

Stand to the right; though falsehood rail,
   And proud lips coldly sneer;
A poisoned arrow cannot wound
   A conscience pure and clear.

Stand for the right, and with clean hands
   Exalt the truth on high;
Thou 'lt find warm, sympathizing hearts
   Among the passers by.

Stand for the right; proclaim it loud,
   Thou 'lt find an answering tone
In honest hearts, and then no more
   Be doomed to stand alone.

WE talk about men's reaching nature up to nature's God. It is nothing to the way in which they may reach through the manhood up to manhood's God and learn the divine love by the human.
       —PHILLIP BROOKS.

174

WOMAN IS MAN'S BEST FRIEND.

BECAUSE she is his mother.

Because she is his wife.

Because without her he would be rude, rough and ungodly.

Because she can with him endure pain quietly and meet joy gladly.

Because she teaches him the value of gentle words, of kind thought and consideration.

Because she is patient with him in illness, and endures his fretfulness and "mothers" him.

Because she will stick to him through good and evil report, and always believe in him if she loves him.

OUR BEST.

WE have given of our best,
  And our merry days are done,"
Lisp the little leaves that fall
  Like rich jewels on the sun.
"Happy birds we've hushed to sleep,
  Snowy lambs have sought our shade,
Many weary ones have joyed
  In the shelter we have made."

"We have kept no songs of cheer
  In our wee hearts hid away,"
Chirp the birds. "To earth and sky
  We have told our joy all day.

Happily through the winter's gloom
　　Some sweet thought of us may glad
Eyes that watched the falling snow,
　　While the winds are keen and sad."

"We have glided, oft unseen,
　　Giving all the joy we could
To the parched and heated field,
　　To the silence of the woods,"
Softly chime the tinkling bells
　　Of the brooklets silver clear ;
"We have given of our best,
　　Since the Father led us there."

Have we sung our songs of joy
　　Unto some sad heart below ?
Kept some kindly word unsaid
　　In the year's quick ebb and flow ?
Have our cooling leaves of balm
　　Sheltered any weary guest ?
Like the birds and leaves and brooks,
　　Have we given of our best ?

　　　　　　　　　　—GEORGE COOPER.

GOOD HUMOR.

AMONG the rules of behavior which George Washington drew up for himself when but fourteen years of age, is one concerning cheerfulness at the table; for, he says, "Good humor makes one dish of meat a feast."

The daintiest meal can be spoiled by a frowning face. It is bad manners to carry ill-humor to the table, and it is bad economy besides; for bad humor makes bad digestion, and bad digestion calls for the doctor.

Who does not like sunshine better than cloud? A little sunshine on a face goes a long way toward lighting up a whole house. Never go to the table with a clouded face. The food will not be good if you do, no matter how carefully it has been prepared. Somebody will catch your cloudiness, and before you know it a thunder-storm may break over the table!

Cultivate good humor, and especially resolve that you will "eat no meal while the world stands" if it must be eaten in an ill humor.

IN getting rich remember that there are two questions which every rich man will be called upon to answer at the day of judgment. The first is, "how did you get your money?" and the second, "what did you do with it?"

CHILDHOOD.

OH, holy years untouched by fears,
  Oh, Life so fair and free,
When joy and love enwet by tears
  Crowned all the days for me ;
    I catch bright visions of the past
    Too happy and too bright too last.

Like sunny isles where summer smiles
  Through all the happy year,
Beyond the dusky tangled wilds
  Through which I walked in fear,
    Those early years so long and sweet,
    Are mirrored in life's ocean deep,

And as I gaze those gone by days
  Again their sweetness cast
Around me, as I catch the lays
  Of the long vanished past,
    And oft I fancy in my dreams
    I revel still in childhood scenes.

Oh, blessed life beyond the strife
  Of the storm-fretted years,
Thy music still is sweetly rife
  With hope, that to my ears
    Tells of a land where childhood stays
    And beauty crowns eternal days.
                    —Mrs. M. A. Holt.

178

CHILDHOOD.

WHAT GAME OF SMARTNESS.

A FEW mornings since, while waiting at the station of a large country town, I witnessed a little incident that I think will interest some young people.

The ticket agent had gone to breakfast, leaving the office in charge of a bright looking boy about fourteen or fifteen. The boy was reading what must have been a very interesting book, judging from the reluctant way in which he laid it aside to wait on the passengers.

Shortly after my arrival an old lady, oddly dressed and evidently not accustomed to traveling, came in; after depositing her bundles, and procuring her ticket, inquired civilly of the office boy, "What time is the up-train due?"

"There's a time table on the wall behind you," was the surly answer. "You can read I reckon."

Without a word the old woman put on her glasses, and after a long search gained the information the boy might have given her in less time than it had taken to give his ungracious answer.

"7:33—7:33? It must be most that time now," she soliloquized. "Young man, would you please tell me what time it is?" she asked timidly, glancing at the boy again.

"Why don't you look at the clock?" sneered the smart lad. "My business is to sell tickets, not to answer questions."

An old gentleman, very plainly dressed, who had been sitting in a corner with his hat pulled down over his eyes, looked up very quickly when he heard the boy's impolite response, but he said nothing, and after the lapse of a few minutes sauntered slowly across the room to the ticket window.

"What is your name my boy?" he said kindly, after nodding intelligently to the telegrapher.

"I do not know as it is any of your business; but if you have a fortune to leave, you can just name Dick Horton's kid Jack, and it will be O. K."

"Your father ought to be proud of such a promising boy," returned the gentleman dryly. "Is Mr. Johnson in?" he asked a little sharply.

"You can find out by making use of your eyes, I guess," said the boy, glancing around under tables and benches, apparently very much amused.

Just then another boy came in with some papers for the agent, and his smart friend said, loud enough to be heard all over the waiting room, "Here, Fred! don't go away till Johnson comes. Attend to the tickets if they are wanted. I have been bored to death answering questions, and I want to finish this book before the boss gets around."

The new-comer quietly hung up his hat and went to wait upon some ladies who were standing at the window.

A few minutes later the old gentleman asked somewhat sharply, "What time is the train due, Bub?"

"7:33." Was the prompt answer.

"And what time is it now?" demanded the same impatient voice that had spoken before.

"It is just fifteen minutes past seven," replyed the boy cheerfully.

"Ape," sneered smart Jack. "Why don't you bluff him off?"

"What is your name?" persisted the old gentleman, stepping up a little closer.

"Fred Myers," responded the boy politely.

"Is the boss in?" was the next inquiry in a much lower tone.

"No, sir, he has gone to breakfast, but will be back in a few minutes," was the quiet answer.

"Seeing that your master is not in, can't you give me cut rates to Wheeling?   I'll see that you are not found out."

"My Master is always in," was the boy's quick reply.

Just then Mr. Johnson, the agent, came in, and addressed the plain looking stranger as Mr. Hayes; and the boys both knew that the superintendent of the railroad had been talking to them, and before they recovered from their confusion they heard him say:

"Mr. Knok, your telegraph operator has been appointed to take charge of an office in the city, and I came down to look after a suitable boy to take his place here.   Remembering the information you gave me sometime ago, I had made up my mind concerning whom his successor should be, but after what I have witnessed this morning, I have come to the conclusion that Dick Horton's kid Jack is too smart for our use, and that this boy whose Master is always in can be trusted to take charge of the responsible position.

Smart Jack tried to mutter an excuse for his impoliteness when he realized what he had lost, but the indignant superintendent cooly informed him that his roughness toward passengers could not be tolerated, and that he must seek other employment until he learned to apply the small courtesies of life.

ORDER.

IT is such a little thing to keep your room in order—and such a great thing! It is such a little matter for you, and such a great one for your mother. It is such a little test of the resolution you make Sundays, to live more as you know you ought this week, and it is such great proof of that resolution. Try it, boys and girls. Rise early enough to say your prayer, and spend five minutes, even three, in "picking up" your room. You have no idea what a pleasant keynote that will be to the whole day.

ALL that Christ, our great teacher, delivers to us, is truth—truth unmixed with error, truth of the mightiest importance, truth that can make us free, truth that can make us holy, truth that can make us blessed forevermore.

THE REVENUE GAIN.

PROUD bird, so noble and free,
  Perched "mid the stripes and stars,"
    As ye sit with brave, outspreading wings,
      There's a stain your banner mars.
Oh! have ye no eyes to weep?
  See ye not the blood of the slain?
The blood of America's noblest sons,
  Poured out for revenue gain?

Proud eagle, fold your wings
  And hang your head with shame,
That the Christian nation ye symbolize
  Such murderous laws should frame!
O'er a dark and dreadful sea,
  The ensign of freedom waves,
While the "ship of state" is bearing down
  Brave sons to dishonored graves.

Sixty thousand a year are hurled
  . Neath the terrible flood,
While government fosters the fearful crime
  And pockets the price of blood!
And wives and children may wail,
  And "Rachels" may weep in vain;
For the "ship of state" with flaunting sail
  Must take her revenue gain!

Wrecked are bodies and souls of men;
  But what are human lives,   ·
What are prayers and groans and sighs and tears,
  What are broken-hearted wives,

183

Compared with revenue gain ?
  For the "ship of state" must sail
Though her noblest sons sink 'neath the flood,
  And widows and orphans wail!

Compassionate heavens, weep
  For the blood of the slain,
Till righteous laws shall sweep from the land
  This most accursed stain.
Ye rocks and stones break forth,
  Nor hold your peace, ye hills
So long as the nation for revenue gain
  The blood of her citizens spills.

      —NAIRJEAN AUDENRIED.

I WILL BE GOOD.

AT the age of twelve it was thought necessary to tell Victoria that she was nearest heir to the throne. It was done in a very quiet way. A genealogical table was put into her historical book. When the Princess opened it she read on to the end, and then remarked to her governess, "I see I am nearer the throne than I thought."

"So it is, madame," replied her teacher.

After some silent moments, Victoria very gravely said: "How many a child would boast, but they don't know the difficulty. There is much splendor, but there is more responsibility."

She then gave her hand to her governess, saying, "I will be good—I will be good."

HEROISM AT HOME.

HOW useless our lives seem to us sometimes! How we long for an opportunity to perform some great action! We become tired of the routine of home life, and imagine we would be far happier in other scenes. We forget that the world bestows no such titles as noble as father, mother, sister, or brother. In the sacred precincts of home we have many chances of heroism. The daily acts of self-denial for the good of a loved one, the gentle word of soothing for another's trouble, care for the sick, may all seem as nothing; yet who can tell the good they can accomplish! Our slightest word may have an influence over another for good or evil. We are daily sowing the seed which will bring forth some sort of harvest. Well it be for us if the harvest will be one we will be proud to garner. If some one in that dear home can look back in after years, and as he tenderly utters our name, says: "Her words and example prepared me for a life of usefulness, to her I owe my present happiness," we may well say, "I have not lived in vain."

WHERE do you stand?" is often asked concerning the opinions and lives of men. Oliver Wendell Holmes has said, "I find the great thing in this world is, not so much where we stand, as in what direction we are moving." A man might be standing on a ship that is drifting to destruction.

THE WAY TO REFORM IS TO REFORM.

A BAD habit is overcome by stifling it at once, not by gradually breaking away from it. Compromise is not complete reform; and then, too, where the change is not immediate, carelessness is likely to lead to laxity, and, finally, to an abandonment of the effort to reform. Lord Baconsfield said, "The way to succeed is to succeed," and the surest way to reform is to reform.

An interesting anecdote is told of the late James Harper, one of the founders of the great publishing house of Harper and Brothers. When he was a young publisher in Cliff Street, he tried hard to dissuade one of his neighbors from drinking. One day when he had talked earnestly on the subject, his friend turned upon him thus:

"Neighbor Harper you don't like the taste of liquor, but you are as much a slave to tobacco as I am to rum, and you couldn't break off that habit any more than I could break off from drinking."

To this retort Mr. Harper made no reply for a time, but it sunk deep into his mind. He thought it over all day, and finally made up his mind that no habit of his should be a snare to another. Before he slept that night he put his tobacco, his pipe and all the apparatus of smoking out of sight on the top shelf of his kitchen. To the day of his death he never used tobacco again.

It cost him a severe effort to keep his resolution, but he made it cheerfully, and did not mention the matter until the victory was complete.

EVERY DAY A LITTLE.

EVERY day a little knowledge. One fact in a day. How small is one fact! Ten years pass by. Three thousand six hundred and fifty facts are not a small thing.

Every day a little self-denial. A thing that is difficult to-day will be an easy thing to do three hundred and sixty days hence, if each day it shall have been repeated. What power of self-mastery shall he enjoy who, looking to God for grace, seeks every day to practice the grace he prays for.

Every day a little helpfulness. We live for the good of others, if our living is in any sense true living. It is not great deeds of kindness only in which the blessing is found. In little deeds of "kindness," repeated every day, we find true happiness. At home, at school, in the street, in the neighbor's house, on the playground, we shall find opportunity every day for usefulness.

Every day a little look into the Bible. One chapter a day. What a treasure of Bible knowledge one may acquire in ten years! Every day a verse committed to memory. What a volume in twenty-five years!

KIND words and pleasant smiles, are precious jewels that do not lose in value by giving others a view of them. Indeed, like precious stones, they become valuable only from the enjoyment they afford.

NOT ALONE.

NEVER mind where you work, care more how you work; never mind who sees, if God approves. If He smiles, be content. We cannot always be sure when we are most useful. It is not the acreage you sow, it is the multiplication which God gives the seed which makes up the harvest. You have less to do with being successful than with being faithful. Your main comfort is that in your labor you are not alone. For God, the eternal One, who guides the marches of the stars, is with you.

—REV. C. H. SPURGEON.

KEEP AT IT.

IN any business, art or undertaking, very little is accomplished without time and perseverance. It is not the man who rushes enthusiastically into anything for a few weeks, and easily gives up when he finds success is not immediately forthcoming, that makes his mark in the world; but it is the man, who, day after day, month after month steadily plods along confidently believing he will succeed, who does finally accomplish his end.

So it is in christian life. The man who becoming converted looks for an easy task before him in accomplishing the complete overthrow of his passions and

188

perverted inclinations, and becomes discouraged because he finds it so hard a task, has overlooked the fact that, though the blood of Christ will wash away all sin, each one must "work out his own salvation with fear and trembling."

Very little can be accomplished on the spur of the moment. A man must begin at the bottom and work up. This is the rule of business life, and the rule of christian life. Accepting this fact and trusting God for final success, no man will fall short of his desire, if he only keeps at it.

—W. M. S.

MAKING SUNSHINE.

WE can all brighten the world a little for others, if we will. Even a kind word will often scatter the clouds that enshroud some weary despondent heart. On the other hand, a petulant reply or a cruel criticism may deepen the darkness and drive the despondent one to despair. It is a solemn thing to live in a world where there is so much sorrow, and where Satan is tempting the unfortunate to "curse God and die." You and I, dear reader, may not be able to do much to help save the multitudes that are walking in darkness, but we are responsible for what we can do, small as it may seem. The thoughtful little girl who placed a candle in the window saved a ship from being wrecked. We can keep a tiny love-light burning wherever we go, and no one can tell how wide reaching and how blessed its influence may be.

GOD'S ARM IS LAW.

ANSWER me this question," says Dr. Guthrie; "Is it not as easy for the sea to carry the bulkiest ship as the sea-weed or foam it flings on the shore?" Is it not as easy for the affluent sun to battle a mountain as a mole-hill in the right? Is it not as easy for this vast earth to carry on its back an Alps as a grain of sand? Just so, believer, it is as easy for God to supply the greatest as the smallest needs, even as it was within His power to form a system as an atom—to create a blazing sun as to kindle a fire-fly's lamp.

IF WE KNEW.

COULD we but draw back the curtains
   That surround each others lives,
See the naked heart and spirit
   Know what spur the action gives,
Often we would find it better,
   Purer than we judge we should ;
We should love each other better
   If we only understood.

Could we judge all deeds by motives,
   See the good and bad within,
Often we should love the sinner
   All the while we loath the sin.
Could we know the powers working
   To o'erthrow integrity,
We should judge each other's errors
   With more patient charity.

If we knew the cares and trials,
  Knew the effort all in vain,
And the bitter disappointment,
  Understood the loss and gain—
Would the grim external roughness
  Seem, I wonder, just the same ?
Should we help where now we hinder?
  Should we pity where we blame ?

Ah ! we judge each other harshly,
  Knowing not life's hidden force ;
Knowing not the fount of action
  Is less turbid at its source.
Seeking not amid the evil
  All the golden grains of good ;
Oh ! we 'd love each other better
  If we only understood.

LET US HELP OURSELVES.

IT has been the rule of my life,'' said a successful and illustrious man, ''never to ask anyone to do anything for me which I could do myself.''

The spirit of mutual helpfulness is lovely and commendable, it is true. It bespeaks not only unselfishness, but generosity. But the continual expectancy of help, or the belief that certain obligations are due you from some person or member of your family, or from the world at large, is selfish and fosters weakness.

We have often wondered why it is Tom's duty to wait on Mary, and why Mary is expected to clean up Tom's litter, hang up his coat and hunt his hat. But children consider themselves martyrs. Would it not be much pleasanter for each to do his or her own work?

It would have the effect in after years, of making Tom a more orderly man, and a better husband—should he become one—and of making Mary a stronger woman.

We have often wondered why mother's memory and hands must serve for a dozen persons. Would it not be better for all concerned if mother's kindness contained more of self-assertion and less of self-sacrifice? Would not, at times, papa feel less disturbed, nay, wrathful, if he were careful to keep his own papers in order, and perform the twenty other trivial things he has time to do in leisure moments, but expects of some one else? Would it not be better for sister to teach baby, who is old enough to button his own shoes, than to do it for him each morning as a duty?

The teacher who takes the pencil from a child's hand, to work out a problem for him, does that child a grave injustice. The teacher should instruct, but the child should do the work. We know and remember how to do a thing only by doing it. We become strong only by self-assertion and self-dependence.

Trust self; depend upon self above all else. Within that self is all you desire to be, and it can only be evolved and made manifest by your effort. Help given you from outside forces is but momentary, but to have insisted on self for the execution of any task is to have gained strength and power which will be a future help for the accomplishment of greater things. Be sympathetic and responsive; be generous and just, but issue for yourself a declaration of independence, and stand by it as faithfully as did the patriots of old. And insist on those about you doing likewise. This is right.

A WIFE'S SOFT ANSWER.

"WE were married thirty-seven years," said Mr. Gardiner Andrews, "and in all that time my wife never gave me a cross word. But I shall never forget the time I chided her. It was on a Sunday morning, when we had been married about two years. I found a button off my shirt, and threw it across the room.

'Sew on a button,' I said, in a brutal voice. She was a good christian woman, and was preparing for church; but she got a button and sewed it on."

"And what did she say?" asked a little bristling woman, with snapping eyes.

"She said, 'Forgive me, husband, I had a great deal to do yesterday and forgot it, but it shall not happen again.'"

"Oh," said the man fixing his eyes on the picture of his dear wife, "her gentle words almost broke my heart. I could have gone down on my knees to ask her forgiveness. She made a different man of me, and the world has been a different place since she died."

There was silence as he finished speaking, interrupted by a general clearing of throats, and a confused snuffling, as if we all had bad colds, and the little woman's snapping eyes looked suspiciously dim.

LABOR.

PAUSE not to dream of the future before us ;
   Pause not to weep the wild cares that come o'er us !
  Hark, how creation's deep, musical chorus,
   Unintermitting, goes up to heaven !
Never the ocean wave falters in flowing ;
Never the little seed stops in its growing ;
More and more richly the rose-heart keeps glowing,
  Till from its nourishing stem it is riven.

"Labor is worship !" the robin is singing ;
"Labor is worship !" the wild bee is ringing ;
Listen ! that eloquent whisper, upspringing,
  Speaks to my soul from out Nature's great heart.
From the dark cloud flows the soft-breathing flower,
From the small insect the rich coral bower ;
  Only man, in his pain, ever shrinks from his part.

" Labor is life !"—'Tis the still water faileth ;
Idleness ever despaireth, bewaileth ;
•Keep the watch wound, for the dark rust assaileth !
  Flowers droop and die in the stillness of noon.
Labor is glory !—The flying cloud lightens ;
Only the waving wing changes and brightens ;
Idle hearts only the dark future frightens,
  Play the sweet keys would'st thou keep them in tune.

Labor is rest, from the sorrows that greet us ;
Rest from the petty vexations that meet us ;
Rest from the sin-promptings that ever entreat us ;
  Rest from the world-sirens that lure us to ill.

Work—and pure slumbers shall wait on thy pillow ;
Work—thou shalt ride over Care's coming billow ;
Lie not down wearied 'neath Woe's weeping willow ;
  Work with stout heart and resolute will.

Droop not, though shame, sin and anguish are round thee;
Bravely fling off the cold chain that has bound thee ;
Look to yon pure heaven smiling beyond thee ;
  Rest not content in thy darkness—a clod ;
Work for some good, be it ever so slow ;
Cherish some flower, be it ever so lowly ;
Labor !—all labor is noble and holy ;
  Let thy great deeds be thy prayer to thy God.

HAVE PATIENCE.

OH, the drudgery of this every day routine!" cries many a business man, and many a house-keeping woman. "To get through the day, and to have the same round to traverse to-morrow!" Yes, but how do you know what use the gracious Superintendent of your life is making of this humdrum, as you call it? A poor, blind mill-horse treads his beat, hour after hour, and it all seems to come to nothing. But the shaft he is turning, is geared into others, and they into wheels, that in other rooms, above him, far away beyond his hearing, are working out the results that he could never comprehend. Wait until you see no longer through a glass darkly, and see the unknown bearings and connections of your life-work with other generations, and may be with other worlds.

IN THE DAY OF TROUBLE.

THE day of trouble is very sure to come. "In my prosperity," says the Psalmist, "I said, I shall never be moved;" but how short-lived was that prosperity; how vain was that confidence. The day of trouble comes—sickness, affliction, sorrow, disgrace—all these come, and often they overtake us at times when we have no comforter, and when lover and friend are far from us. Those who have eaten our bread turn away, and look coldly upon us. Those whom we have befriended in hours of need forget the hand that helped them, and we think that all things are against us.

What then shall we do? "Call upon me in the day of trouble, and I will deliver thee, and thou shalt glorify me." How many have proved the truthfulness of this promise. How many a cry has gone up in hours of anguish and distress, and in how many ways God has sent deliverance to his chosen people!

Let us learn that in the day of trouble we have a sure refuge. "God is our refuge and strength, a present help in trouble. Therefore will not we fear though the earth be removed, and though the mountains be carried into the midst of the sea: though the waters thereof roar and be troubled, though the mountains shake with the swelling thereof." Above the storm and tumult, above the world's wild rush and rage, the Lord sitteth King forever, as the helper and trust of His people, the confidence of all who cast their cares and burdens on Him.

Let the day of trouble find us at the mercy-seat; let us not wait till the day of trouble comes to learn the way to that sacred refuge. They find most help in time of trouble who seek the Lord before the day of trouble comes. "Remember thy creator in the days of thy youth, BEFORE THE EVIL DAYS COME, when thou shalt say I have no pleasure in them." "Let us therefore come boldly to the throne of grace, that we may find grace to help in time of need."

JUST ONE THING.

"THERE is nothing like enthusiasm." Enthusiasm is a great thing; it has led many men to do wondrous deeds of valor, but there is one thing even greater.

The cold determination to fight on, because you are right, no matter how dark the surroundings.

There is plenty of enthusiasm in the charge of the light brigade, but the cold, hard courage of the men who fought and suffered and died in the trenches in front of Sebastopol all through that weary winter was something even grander.

It is a great thing to rush on with a crowd to victory, when victory is within reach.

It is a greater and grander thing to stand fast when the crowd has left you and victory seems afar off.

It is grand to be brave in battle; it is grander to be brave when there is nought we can do but to wait.

The highest charge Paul could give to the christian soldier was, "And having done all to stand."

Fellow comrades in this fight, remember that there are more who will throw up their hats and shout in charge than there are who will stand in the trench the season through.

Give us more soldiers who are willing to keep patiently, earnestly, faithfully at the work all the year round.

GOD'S WILL IS BEST.

LET nothing make thee sad or fretful,
      Or too regretful—
          Be still;
What God hath ordered must be right,
Then find in it thine own delight,
          My will.

Why shouldst thou fill to-day with sorrow
      About to-morrow,
          My heart?
One watches all with care most true,
Doubt not that He will give thee, too,
          Thy part.

Only be steadfast, never waver,
      Nor seek earth's favor,
          But rest;
Thou knowest what God wills must be
For all His creatures, so for thee,
          The best.

—PAUL FLEMMING.

WHEN A WISE WOMAN SMILES.

THAT is a wise woman who can smile at a compliment, be pleased and forget it.

That is a wise woman who can smile at an insult and never see it.

That is a wise woman who can smile when the little worries are coming about and make of them little bits of fun.

That is a wise woman who can smile when she gets up, and who can go to sleep with a smile, for in this way she greets the coming day, and at the end of it she has blotted out the disagreeables.

That is a wise woman who can smile for her friends and her enemies; it will keep the first, and it is the best weapon against the last.

That is a wise woman who can smile no matter how she feels. She is a woman who has learned to rule not only herself, but will gain domain over the cook; and that means that she governs comfort.

A WEALTHY man displaying one day his jewels to a philosopher, the latter said, "Thank you sir, for being willing to share such magnificent jewels with me."

"Share them with you, sir!" exclaimed the man. "What do you mean?"

"Why you allow me to look at them, and what more can you do with them yourself?" replied the philosopher.

MEMORIAL DAY.

WE garland their graves with flowers,
  We mingle our tears once more,
For those who have gone before us,
  For those we shall see no more.

They fell in the heat of the battle.
  They dropped in the morning ray,
They passed in glow of childhood,
  And we could not bid them nay.

They fell when the year were all garnered
  Allotted to man here below,
We followed them down to the crossing
  And felt it was well they should go.

We sigh, O we sigh for their presence,
  When sorrow like mountain waves roll,
When night, sable night settles o'er us,
  And there is no light for the soul.

O, sweet is their rest from all sorrow!
  O, sweet is their rest from all care!
In their beautiful home with the angels,
  Would God, O, would God we
    were there!

—ISAAC R. EMBREE.

GOOD MANNERS.

YESTERDAY I met one of my little friends on the street. I never forget to speak to my boys and girls, so I said, "Good morning." How do you think he replied? He looked up into my face and said, "Hallo!"

A little further on I met another little friend. I thought I would wait this time and see what he had to say. Just as he was near me, and I was expecting he would speak, he put his fingers between his teeth and whistled to a boy across the street, so sharp and shrill that it almost deafened me. That was all he said. Near the post-office I met a little boy, that we all know. He lifted his hat and said "Good morning, Mr. Johnson."

Now, which do you think was the best way—to "hallo," the rude whistle, or the lifted hat and cheery "good morning?" Which boy had the best manners?

Even girls do not all have good manners. The other day I saw two young ladies passing on opposite sides of the street. They were sixteen or seventeen years old. One called out, "Hallo, Mary!" The other replied, "Hallo, Sally!"

Now, I want to whisper to you that I do not expect that young ladies who are so rude as these two will ever improve much in their manners; but I do expect that all of you will cultivate good manners toward every one. You all know what good manners are. Be respectful to your parents and to all who are older than you. Be kind to your companions. Have too much respect for yourself to do a mean act or say a bad word. Treat your teacher in the public school and Sunday-school with the honor that is due to her.

Be quiet and attentive at church, and set an example to some young men and women, whom we all know, who never behave themselves anywhere.

DON'T LOOK BACK.

THE only way to succeed in a religious or any other kind of life, is to decide to do it. To map out a course that you intend to follow, and then stick to it, no matter how many obstacles may block the way. The man who says in his heart, "I will try it a little way, and if I like it I will go on," will never go to heaven. The devil will switch him off the line before he gets fairly started. It is like starting a steamboat up stream, with no coal on board except that under the boilers. As soon as the fire goes out the boat will stop and float back. The only way to make sure of the shining streets of glory is to say good-bye to the world forever when you start. The main reason why there are so many back-sliders in the church is because they never intended to make more than a short walk toward heaven to begin with. The only way to serve God is to cut the bridge behind you when you begin.

THE RIGHT ROAD.

I HAVE lost the road to happiness,
    Does any one know it, pray ?
I was dwelling there when the morn was fair,
    But somehow I wandered away.

"I saw rare treasures in scenes of pleasures,
    I ran to pursue them, when lo !
I had lost the path to happiness,
    And knew not whither to go.

"I have lost the way to happiness,
    Oh, who will lead me back ? "
"Turn off from the highway of selfishness
    To the right, up duty's track.

"Keep straight along, and you can't go wrong ;
    For as sure as you live, I say,
The fair lost fields of happiness
    Can only be found that way."

        —ELLA WHEELER WILCOX.

A CERTAIN amount of opposition is a great help to man. Kites rise against and not with the wind. Even a head wind is better than none. No man ever worked his passage in a dead calm. Let no man wax pale, therefore, because of opposition.

        —JOHN NEAL.

PREVENTIVE MERCIES.

GOD'S gifts to us often excite our gratitude and thankful praise, but how seldom do we remember to thank Him for the preventive mercies of our life. How often we have to bless God for hindering us in our plans, putting obstacles in our way, and preventing our self-will from triumphing, we can only judge by the escapes we make, and even then we do not begin to know it all.

We know the accidents that actually occur, but how many unsuspected ones have been warded off? What perils have been on our right and left, and only restrained by God's omnipotent hand! When a thousand fall at our side, and ten thousand at our right hand, and it does not come nigh us, then we understand God's preventive care, and praise Him for it. But is it not even more wonderful when we are kept from the very sight and sound of danger? Physiologists tell us that every day we have many narrow escapes from death. We do not know how often death may have passed by us so closely that it scarcely left room for a breath between it and ourselves; we only know the events that do take place, the accidents that did happen, the sudden death that did occur. The accidents that we were spared, the perils that were commanded to stand aside, who shall estimate of God's preventive mercies?

We remember the story of a minister who came, pale and trembling, into an assembly of his brethren to

ask them to join with him in grateful prayer for the
marvelous escape from death which had been vouch-
safed him. On the edge of a precipice his horse had
stumbled, but had recovered his footing in time to save
his rider from being dashed to pieces at the foot of the
cliff. Another minister arose, saying that he had just
had a still grecter manifestation of God's mercy; in com-
ing over the same place his horse had not even stumbled.
If we but remember, when we enumerate our blessings,
that God's preventive mercies towards us are more in
number than the sands of the seashore, our hearts will
overflow with constant thanksgiving for the love which
ever broods over us, unseen, and too often unrecogniz-
ed, protecting us from evil.

—M. E. KENNEY.

NEW EVERY MORNING.

EVERY day is a fresh beginning,
 Every morn is the world made new;
 Ye who are weary of sorrow and sinning,
  Here is a beautiful hope for you;
  A hope for me and a hope for you.

All the past things are past and over,
 The tasks are done and the tears are shed;
Yesterday's errors let yesterday cover;
 Yesterday's wounds which smarted and bled
 Are healed with the healing which night has shed.

Yesterday now is a part of forever,
 Bound up in a sheaf which God holds tight,

NEW EVERY MORNING.

With glad days, and sad days, and bad days which
      never
  Shall visit us more with their bloom and their
      blight,
  Their fulness of sunshine or sorrowful night.

Let them go, since we cannot re-live them,
  Cannot undo, and cannot atone ;
God in his mercy receive, forgive them ;
  Only the new days are our own ;
  To-day is ours, and to-day alone.

Here are the skies all burnished brightly,
  Here is the spent earth, all re-born,
Here are the tired limbs, springing lightly
  To face the sun and to share with the morn,
  In the chrism of dew and the cool of dawn.

Every day is a fresh beginning ;
  Listen, my soul, to the glad refrain,
And spite of old sorrow and older sinning,
  And puzzles forecasted, and possible pain,
  Take heart with the day and begin again.
               —SUSAN COOLIDGE.

A GENTLE VOICE.

PERHAPS our voice is not always as pleasant as it
ought to be, but we realize it the moment we hear
one that is soft and low and even modulated, and
instinctively we alter ours to correspond with it. Noth-
ing so quickly checks rising anger, or quick retort, as
a gentle voice. Well has the wise man said: "A soft
answer turneth away wrath; but grievous words stir up
anger."

Few of us can remember our mothers, now, perhaps,
passed away, as having had other than pleasant voices.
Harsh words were strangers to those lips. The children,
when they had done wrong, were corrected, but the
voice that chided their misdoings was a gentle one. Let
our children have like remembrances of us. Children
are quick to imitate. If the mother or father speaks
crossly, or, in a loud, commanding tone, the child soon
learns to speak so also, and among his younger com-
panions he will assume the tone that he has heard from
older lips.

Although a pleasant voice is not given to every-body,
culture can accomplish wonders in this as every thing
else. Let anyone strive to acquire a pleasant voice, per-
severing time after time, when in a moment of forgetful-
ness the old harsh notes escape the lips, and after a
time the voice will become changed to one at least soft
and well modulated, if not musical.

HOW TO GROW BEAUTIFUL.

WOMAN, famous as one of the most kindly and most lovable among leaders of the best American society, once said: "If I have accomplished anything in life, it is due to a word spoken to me in the right season, when I was a child, by my old teacher. I was the only homely, awkward girl in a class of exceptionly pretty ones, and being also dull in my books, became the butt of the school. I fell into a morose, despairing state, gave up study, withdrew into myself, and grew daily more bitter and vindictive.

"One day the French teacher, a gray-haired old woman, with keen eyes and a kind smile, found me crying.

" 'What ails you, my child?' she asked.

" 'Oh, Madame, I am so ugly!' I sobbed out.

"She soothed me, but did not contradict me.

"Presently she took me to her room, and after amusing me for some time said: 'I have a present for you,' handing a scaly coarse lump, covered with earth. 'It is rough and brown as you, "ugly," did you say? Very well! We will call it by your name, then. It is you! Now you shall plant it, and water it, and give it sun for a week or two.

"I planted it and watered it carefully; the green leaves came out first, and at last the golden Japanese lily, the first I had ever seen. Madame came to share my delight.

" 'Ah,' she said, significantly, 'who would believe so much beauty and fragrance were shut up in that little,

208

rough, ugly thing? But it took heart and came into the sun.'

"It was the first time it ever occurred to me that, in spite of my ugly face, I, too, might be able to win friends, and make myself beloved in the world."

FAITH'S REST.

A CHRISTIAN lady in one of the religious papers gives the following receipt for rest. "There is nothing will give a chance for rest to ever-tired nerves so surely as a simple religious faith in the overruling, wise and tender providence which has us in its keeping. It is in chafing against the conditions of our lives that we tire ourselves immeasurably. It is in being anxious about things which we cannot help that we often do the most of our speeding. A simple faith in God which practically and every moment, and not only theoretically and on Sundays, rests on the knowledge that He cares for us at least as much as we care for those who are the dearest to us, will do much to give the tired nerves the feeling of a bird in its nest. Do not spend what strength you have, like clematis, in climbing yourself, but lay hold on things that are eternal, and the peace of them will pass into your soul like a piece of healing balm. Put yourself in the great everlasting currents, and then you can rest on your oars, and let those currents bear you on their strength."

There is nothing in this world so beautiful and so blessed as the repose of faith.

A CURBSTONE SCENE.

IN the shade of a tree, by the street of a city,
  Lay a tired little boy, with a turf for his bed,
In rags, but no beggar appealing to pity,—
  A child of the lowly who toiled for his bread.
Beside him stood a handcart loaded with fuel,
  Bits of board he had gleaned in the lanes where he crept,
Till the wheels o'er the pavement dragged heavy and cruel,.
  And, spent with the strain of his burden, he slept.

Will any one care as the many pass nigh him ?—
  A threadbare wood-sawyer, bent, wrinkled and old
Caught sight of the sleeper, came near and stood by him,
  And read in the picture the story it told.
Hungry face, scanty raiment with barely a button,
  Hatless head, naked feet, fretted sore on the stone,—
He fished out a morsel of dry bread and mutton,
  And left him the dinner he'd brought for his own.

There were eyes bright and merry, eyes tearful and tender,
  On the watch ere the old man had tiptoed away,
And some, in that meek loan of love and its lender,
  Saw the angel that stopped where the little boy lay,
And the soul of that child, through the tatters that wound
        him,
  Drew the soul of the clad and the fed to his side ;
Young and old brought their blessing to scatter around him,
  And crumbs from the table of God to divide.

A boy and a man dropped a dime and a dollar,
  Women opened their purses by ones and by twos,
Willing hands from the mansions, both greater and smaller,
  Brought a hat, a jacket and a stout pair of shoes.

All stealthy and silent, with gentle conniving,
   They laid down their gifts with the wood-sawyer's crust,
And lingered to see at the sleeper's reviving,
   His bashful thanksgiving smile up from the dust.

Soon the little boy woke.   Was it bounty or plunder
   Spread out at his feet ?   Then a laugh in his ears
Turned his face where a glance gave the key to the wonder,
   And he clasped his new riches with blushes and tears.
And his helpers had joy which was tender and holy
   When they looked then and after, full many a day,
Down the street where the toil-ridden child of the lowly
   With his cart and his treasures had trotted away.

Oh, hearts that are human, are human forever !
   You may close them in caste, but they beat through the
        wall.
Wealth and want own a kinship no breeding can sever,
   And in sorrow the lowest are brothers of all.
Bound love needs the magic of pity to free it ;
   Men only are selfish because they are blind ;
When the poor help the poor, if the whole world could
        see it,
   The haughty would blush and the cruel grow kind.
                —Theron Brown.

A SERMONETTE ON ETIQUETTE.

IF you have company of your very own? Ah, then no no pains should be spared to give pleasure.

It is never proper, in her own house, for a girl to wear a dress so fine that any one bidden might feel her own clothes shabby or too plain. Neither is it well-bred to have or do anything simply for show.

To honor one's friends, the table should be set with the daintiest china and the brightest silver and glass. But if one has only plain crockery and pewter spoons, then the whiteness of the tablecloth, and the freshness of the napkins, and especially the cordial welcome, are all that is necessary.

Never apologize for anything on the table. If the bread is not quite as light as usual, or if the cake, alas! has a "heavy streak," do not call attention to it. It will make a bad matter no better, and apologies always put visitors in an awkward position.

Do not urge your guests to eat. It is proper for a friend to ask for any dish on the table. If so be he or she is shy, it may be allowable to say, "But are you sure I may not give you a bit of the turkey or a slice of the ham?"

If again your guest says, "No," do not insist.

If games be the evening's amusement, a hostess should be sure that every one is drawn into the fun.

If a visitor stands alone, quickly, before there is a chance for him to feel awkward, go yourself to talk with him, or ask some one else to do so. That anybody should find himself ill at ease in your home reflects discredit on you.

There is no wider field for unselfish tact than in ones own parlor, and the motto of every hostess should be: "Not to be ministered unto, but to minister."

—MARY S. McCOBB.

LEARNING A BUSINESS.

GENTLEMAN who had induced a large publishing-house to take his son in employ at a moderate rate of pay, not long since, was especially anxious in his request that the young man should be put to work and learn the business.

This instruction was needless, as although modern fashion has done away with much of the janitor and porterage of old times, yet the young man found the selection of stock for orders, packing the same, entering, charging ditto and occasional errands kept him actively employed for about ten hours a day, with an hour out for dinner.

At the end of three week's time he failed to put in an appearance, but the father walked in one morning with the information that John would not return to the position.

"Why not?" asked the publisher.

"Well, John has to have his breakfast early every morning to get here, and then he is not used to carrying bundles, and sometimes he's been sent with books right up to the houses of the people we know socially. My son hasn't been brought up that way, and I guess I won't have him learn this business.''

He did not, and what's more, has never learned any other business.

Now let us look at another picture, that of a son of a wealthy mill owner desiring to become a manager of the mill.

''But that is impossible,'' said the father, ''unless you practically learn the business.''

''That is what I would like to do,'' said the son.

''But to become a superintendent or manager we prefer a man who has risen from the ranks and understands the mechanical department and ways of employes.''

''Let me begin 'in the ranks' then,'' replied the young man.

To this the father assented, stipulating that no favor should be shown the son, but he should actually begin the work at regular labor in the mechanical department.

Not only was this done, but the young man went and boarded in the manufacturing town at a workman's boarding-house, and went in and out of the factory at bell call. In three years he was foreman of one of the departments, and a former classmate and well-known society man, calling there upon him, was surprised at meeting a stalwart fellow in blue overalls, with hands so soiled with machinery oil as to prevent the conventional hand-shake.

But this young man persevered, made and paid his own way himself, and his father concluded it would not

injure his future prospects. Judging from the fact that
he is now manager of mills (not his father's), at a salary
of ten thousand a year, with ability to command even
better compensation and partnership, is evidence that
"learning a business," even by a man of good educa-
tion and a rich father, pays a good return, both in mon-
ey and manly independence.

THE WORD SHE REMEMBERED.

"YOU remember the sermon you heard, my dear?"
 The little one blushed, and dropped her eyes,
 Then lifting them bravely, with look of cheer,
  Eyes that were blue as the morning skies.

"I'm afraid I forgot what the minister said,
 He said so much to the grown up men,
And the pulpit was 'way over my head;
 But I told mamma that he said 'Amen.'

"And 'Amen,' you know means 'Let it be,'
 Whatever our Lord may please to do;
And that is sermon enough for me,
 If I mind and feel so the whole week through."

I took the little one's word to heart;
 I wish I could carry it all day long,
The "Amen" spirit which hides the art
 To meet each cross with a happy song.
      —M. E. SANGSTER.

215

STRENGTH IN WEAKNESS.

"He giveth power to the faint; and to them that have
no might he increaseth strength."

IT is no dream Great Comforter,
 But very truth to me,
That all earth's strengthless, fainting ones
 May be made strong in Thee.

The years have taught me many things,
 But none so sure as this ;
That shelter, solace, joy, and strength,
 Are always where God is.

So now, when hope and courage fail,
 And only fear is strong,
My heart will sing, as in the past,
 An unforgotten song.

"God is my refuge and my strength,
 I will not be afraid ; "
And though the night be wild and dark,
 I'll meet it undismayed.
     —MARIANA FARNINGHAM.

DEATH is very uncertain as to the time of its com-
ing, therefore the injunction is to watch. "There-
fore be ye also ready; for in such an hour as ye
think not, the Son of man cometh." "But as the days
of Noah were, so shall also the coming of the Son of
man be." "Watch, therefore."

IF I WERE A GIRL.

I would take care of my health, by living out-doors as much as possible, and taking long walks in the sun-shine. English girls understand how necessary this is for good complexions and cheerful spirits. Wear simple clothing, that you may climb mountains and breathe freely.

I would secure the best education. Go to college, by all means, if it is possible. A woman, in these days, if she would be attractive as well as useful, must be intelligent. Educated men need educated wives. Children need educated mothers. Women themselves need a broad education, lest their thoughts become centered in clothes or in the small round of society gossip which belittles. Read books and thereby become intelligent.

I would cultivate cheerfulness. Discontent soon shows itself in the face. If you have some disappointments, so do others. If you are cramped for money, be thankful that your lot is no worse than it is. Learn to make the best of things. An unhappy woman is a perpetual cloud in a home. A fretful girl has few friends, and the number lessens year by year.

I would say kind things of others, especially of girls. A girl who makes unkind remarks about other girls had better be avoided by young men. She will not make an agreeable companion for life.

I would learn how to be self-supporting. Especially in this country, where fortunes change, it is wise for a woman to be able to care for herself. Helpless women are not a comfort to others, and usually not to themselves.

I would try to be polite everywhere. True courtesy is more winsome than a pretty face or fine dress. Loud talk or loud dress does not betoken the lady. Be appreciative and sympathetic, and you have two keys which will unlock almost all hearts.

I would learn self-control. To know when to speak and when to be silent, and have hateful things said about you and be able to answer pleasantly, to have people confide in you and be wise enough to keep it locked in your own heart, to be in poverty and not to be soured by it, to meet temptation and be strong before it, to be strong enough to perform any labor or duty that needs to be done—all this shows a noble mastery over self.

I would be punctual. Being late at meals, late at church, or late in meeting engagements, makes unnecessary friction in families. If we are willing to lose valuable time, we have no right to make others lose it.

I would not be careless about the affections. Girls too often think that young men are not easily hurt in love matters, or if they are, they soon recover. As a rule, probably, men love as deeply as women, and to play with hearts is a sin.

I have known girls engaged to two young men at the same time, thoughtless as to the effect upon those whom they could not marry. It is a pitiful thing to spoil a life, and it is not unfrequently done. The golden rule of doing unto others as we would that others should do unto us is especially applicable here.

—SARAH K. BOLTON.

AN AMERICAN IDEAL.

AN independent young man ;
 A right kind of stuff young man ;
  A deep, comprehensible,
  Plain spoken, sensible,
 Thoroughly self-made young man.

A not-to be-beaten young man ;
An up to the front young man ;
 A genuine, plucky,
 Happy-go-lucky,
Try it again young man.

A knowledge seeking young man ;
A real wide-awake young man ;
 A working in season,
 Find out the reason,
Not too smart to learn young man.

A look-out-for-others young man ;
A practice-not-preach young man ;
 Kind, sympathetic,
 Not all theoretic,
One-in-a-thousand young man.

Now-a-days scarce young man ;
A-hard-to-be-found young man ;
 A perfectly self possessed,
 Not always over-dressed,
Kind that I like young man.

BY FITS AND STARTS.

ONE of the hardest lessons to learn is that which teaches us to continue to labor zealously, even in the face of difficulties, and wait patiently for the reward that is tardy in its coming. But it is a lesson that the young man or woman cannot learn too early in life. The good, old-fashioned sermon on perseverance, though somewhat disregarded amid the hurry and bustle of the present, nevertheless holds a truth that will not be put down. Application is the prize of success to-day, as it ever has been.

Too often we hear young men declare that their business or profession is a failure, because it has not brought immediate wealth or honor, and find them leaving one occupation for another that appears more promising. In many cases the new calling is no more satisfactory than the one previously followed, and it in turn gives place to another. And so change follows change, the cause of failure always being ascribed to the occupation that has not been thoroughly tried by a continuous effort.

Good results come only to those who deserve them.

One day in winter a boy was engaged is shoveling snow from the pavement. The drift was a deep one, and he was quite a small boy with a very small shovel, and the task appeared like a large undertaking. But minute after minute the lad labored, for two whole hours, and the drift was removed from the walk.

When asked how he had accomplished so much with such a small tool, he replied:

"I had nothing but a little stove-shovel to work with, I know, but by keeping at it I got the job done."

And that is the secret behind many of the great achievements of life. By just "keeping at it" the greatest duties are performed, and success wrought from the most unpromising circumstances. The men who have done much have not been those who went from one calling to another, or who labored by fits and starts. They have been those who, having chosen an occupation, began their work earnestly and kept at it.

Spasmodic efforts amount to little or nothing. It is steady, continuous driving that counts. It is well to begin work; it is better to *finish* it. The lesson for all to learn is to do one thing at a time, and to follow that until it is *done.*

SOLID TRUTH.

TWO members of the church in Scotland were good friends till they took different sides at the time of the disruption. They were both thatchers by trade. When the dispute about the principles of kirks grew hot they ceased to speak to each other. But one day they were both employed at the same job. Each took one side of the roof and when they had worked up to the top they were face to face. They couldn't flee, so at last Andrew took off his cap, and scratching his head. said:

"Johnny, you and me, I think ha'e been very foolish to dispute as we have done concerning Christ's will about our kirks, until we ha'e clean forgotten his will about oor ain selves; and so we have fought and fought for what we call the truth, and it has ended in spite. What ever's wrang, it's perfectly certain that it never can be right to be uncivil, unneighborly, unkind,—in fact, to hate one anither. Na, na! That's the devil's work, and na God's. Noo, it strikes me that maybe it's wi' the kirk as with this house—ye'e working on a'e side and me o' tither, but if we only do our work weel, we will meet at the top at last. Gie's your han' neighbor." And so they shook hands and were the best of friends ever after.

CREEPING UP THE STAIRS.

IN the softly-falling twilight
　　Of a weary, weary day,
　With a quiet step I entered
　　Where the children were at play.
I was brooding o'er some trouble
　　That had met me unawares,
When a little voice came ringing,
　　" Me is creepin' up a stairs."

Oh! it touched the tenderest heart string
　　With a breath and force divine,
And such melodies awakened
　　As my words can ne'er define.

222

And I turned to see our darling,
   All forgetful of my cares,
When I saw the little creature
   Slowly creeping up the stairs.

Step by step she bravely clambered
   On her little hands and knees,
Keeping up a constant chatter
   Like a magpie in the trees ;
Till at last she reached the topmost,
   When o'er all the world's affairs
She, delighted, stood a victor,
   After creeping up the stairs.

Fainting heart, behold an image
   Of man's brief and struggling life,
Whose best prizes must be captured
   With an earnest, noble strife ;
Onward, upward, reaching ever,
   Bending to the weight of cares,
Hoping, fearing, still expecting,
   We go creeping up the stairs.

On their steps may be no carpet,
   By their sides may be no rail,
Hands and knees may often pain us,
   And the heart may almost fail;
Still above there is a glory
   Which no weariness impairs,
With its rest and joy forever,
   After creeping up the stairs.

A FEW weeks since I saw a touching and beautiful sight. Driving through a rugged part of the country my attention was directed to an elderly lady trying to pick her way over a rough hillside. She came very slowly and carefully. The hill was quite steep, and I was pitying her and thinking if it would not be well to offer my services, when I heard a whistling boy coming up behind my carriage. He bounded past, and running up the hill put his arms around the lady and steadied her steps, saying pleasant words, I know, for the face incased in the warm hood looked beaming and bright with happiness. As we passed I heard these words: "It is so nice to have a boy to come and help a mother down a hill." They passed on and went into a farm house at the foot of the hill; I knew they were mother and son. There was a sermon in those few words. I thought, I wish every boy could have heard them.

You boys are all of you here to help mother down the hill of life. You don't all do it though; more's the pity. Some of you make it harder for her; she is anxious about you, and then she has to pick her way over places a thousand times rougher than walking down a steep hill. Perhaps you are getting into bad habits, and will not obey her council. Her heart is bruised and torn by your conduct. She knows what the results of evil doing are: that if a boy begins habits that he only considers light as cobwebs in his youth, by and by they may become iron chains around him, and when he is a man he will be a slave to them.

Now, boys, if you would help the dear mother down the hill of life and make the path smooth for her, do the things she wishes you to do. And if you are all right as regards bad habits, perhaps you are not as thoughtful of the "little things" that make up life as you might be. Be as polite in waiting upon your mother as you are in waiting on other boys' mothers. Don't speak in rough tones to her. Be always gentle when you speak to her, and careful to remember what she wishes you to be particular to do at different times and different places.

"It's so nice to have a boy to help a mother down the hill." Yes, when weary and worn with life's hard work, and age begins to come, it is a great satisfaction and a source of gratitude to know that a strong, upright boy is coming to help mother down.

And you boys who have gone from home all together, you cannot literally put your arms around mother and steady her steps, and yet you can write good, long letters, and tell her you wish you were in the old home again, so you could hug her and kiss her as you did when you was a little fellow and loved to climb up in her lap. One of the greatest blessings in the world is that of having a praying mother. Make yourselves worthy of the good mothers God has given you, and take your mother's God for your God in the days of your youth.

POVERTY AND AMBITION.

ISTORY has taught us that no circumstances are too humble for a child born into them to rise to eminence. It has also taught us that poverty is frequently a help rather than a hindrance, and the right kind of a man will make circumstances bend to his purpose and not let circumstances bend him. There is a breed of heroes, which is never extinct in any age of the world; who delight in obstacles, and who make poverty, disadvantages and youthful deprivations only serve as the rounds of the ladder by which they climb to greatness. They do not sit down and whine because others are more fortunate than they. They take fortune as it comes, unmurmuringly, and by a kind of mysterious alchemy, as it were, transmute misfortunes into benefits.

STRUGGLE.

REAT strength is bought with pain
From out the strife—
From out the storms that sweep the human soul—
Comes forth the lofty calm of self-control.

Peace after war. Although the heart may be
Trampled and plowed like a torn battle-field,
Rich are the fruits that follow victory,
And battle-grounds the fullest harvests yield.

LABOR.

Strong grows his arm who breasts a downward stream,.
    And stems with steady stroke the mighty tide
Of his own passions. Sore the wrench may seem,
    Yet only he is strong whose strength is tried.

To toil is hard. To lay aside the oar—
    To softly rise and fall with passion's swell—
Is easier far, but when the dream is o'er,
    The bitterness of waking none can tell.

To float at ease, by sleepy zephyrs fanned,
    Is but to grow more feeble, day by day,
While slips life's little hour out, sand by sand,
    And strength and hope together waste away.

He only wins who sets his thews of steel
    With tighter tension for the prick of pain ;
Who wearies, yet stands fast ; whose patient zeal
    Welcomes the present loss for future gain.

Toil before ease : the cross before the crown.
    Who covets rest, he first must earn the boon.
He who at night in peace would lay him down,
    Must bear his load amid the heats of noon.

How can we expect a harvest of thought who have
not had the seed time of character?

A nice wife and a back door often make a rich man
poor.

THE HUMAN MOUTH.

THE next time you are on a street car or in a crowd, notice attentively the faces about you and see if I am not right in saying the expression of the mouth gives you the key to the whole character.

"You will find the women better subjected than the men. In the latter, mustaches adroitly conceal much that might otherwise mar a good-looking face, for it is true that a very few mouths wear the graceful curves nature cast them in. Take the woman who sat opposite you to-night.

"She was beautifully dressed, but how you pitied the people who had to live with her, for every time the car gave a lurch or someone rubbed against her, she scowled in the face of the poor unfortunate beside her as if he was presumably responsible for the discomforts she suffered, and you shuddered to think what that woman's face would be were the coffee cold or the cakes white.

"You secretly adored the gracious looking woman sitting next the door, who caught all the draughts and was crowded and jostled by every passer, but still maintained that gentle equilibrium so delightful to look upon.

"Yes, I know it requires immense courage and fortitude to look cheerful when your dainty patent tips are being ruthlessly trodden on, but there is your chance to be truly heroic; besides, if you will allow yourself to be annoyed and show it, someone is sure to observe it.

"Study yourselves, if you will, some day when the world seems clouded, from the day outside to the domestic atmosphere inside, when the indigo tints predominate everywhere, hunt out the best mirror you can find and take a good square look at yourself.

"Does the reflection please you? How quickly you pull up the corners of the mouth (you didn't know you could look so ugly,) for most of us, no matter how readily we inflict discontented expressions on the world at large, dislike to confront the same of ourselves."

WHAT A SMILE DID.

LADY of position and property, anxious about her neighbors, provided religious services for them. She was very deaf—could scarcely hear at all. On one occasion one of her preachers managed to make her understand him, and at the close of the conversation asked: "But what part do you take in the work?" "Oh," she replied, "*I smile them in and smile them out!*" Very soon the preacher saw the result of her generous, loving sympathy in a multitude of broad-shouldered, hard-fisted men, who entered the place of worship, delighted to get a smile from her as she used to stand in the door-way to receive them. Why do not the working class attend the house of God? They would in great numbers, if self-denying, Christ-loving christians would smile them in and smile them out.

PATIENCE.

BE patient! Easy words to speak
 While plenty fills the cup of life,
 While health brings roses to the cheek,
  And far removed our cares and strife.

Falling so glibly from the tongue
 Of those—I often think of this—
Whom suffering has never wrung,
 Who scarcely know what patience is.

Be patient! when the suff'rer lies
 Prostrate beneath some fell disease,
And longs, through torturing agonies,
 Only for one short hour of ease.

Be patient when the weary brain
 Is racked with thought and anxious care,
And troubles in an endless train
 Seem almost more than it can bear.

To feel the torture of delay,
 The agony of hope deferred;
To labor still from day to day,
 The prize unwon, the prayer unheard.

And still to hope and strive and wait
 The due reward for fortune's kiss;
This is to almost conquer fate,
 This is to learn what patience is.

Despair not ! though the clouds are dark,
  And storm and danger veil the sky ;
Let fate and courage guide thy barque,
  The storm will pass, the port is nigh.

Be patient, and the tide will turn,
  Shadows will flee before the sun ;
These are the hopes that live and burn
  To light us till our work is done.

KEEP IT TO YOURSELF.

YOU have trouble, your feelings are injured, your husband is unkind, your wife frets, your home is not pleasant, your friends do not treat you fairly, and things generally move unpleasantly. Well, what of it? Keep it to yourself. A smothering fire can be found and extinguished; but, when coals are scattered, you cannot pick them up. Bury your sorrow. The place for sad disgusting things is under the ground. A cut finger is not benefited by pulling off the plaster and exposing it to somebody's eye. Charity covereth a multitude of sins. Things thus covered are cured without a scar; but, once published and confided to meddling friends, there is no end to the trouble they may cause. Keep it to yourself. Troubles are trancient; and when a sorrow is healed and passed, what a comfort it is to say, "No one ever knew it till it was over."

PRAY FOR POWER.

THE worlding may succeed in life by carefulness, by skill, by intelligence and by force, but in the work of God no man can succeed without prayer. No human power can effect the changes and accomplish the work required in the service of God. There is a superhuman work to be done, and a superhuman energy is required for its accomplishment.

To be prayerless is to be powerless. No matter what other qualifications men may have for the work, unless they have the power of God, they will never succeed in accomplishing the service of God.

YOUR NEIGHBOR'S MOTES.

LEARN to seal your lips forever on the wretched, miserable habit of telling the world about the motes in your neighbor's eye. Who made you a judge over him? Go, if you will, and personally tell him his faults between you and him alone. Tell him with love and sympathy in your heart because you want to help him to become nobler and better, because you cannot bear to see a stain on him, and not because you would humble him or glory over him, and in the end he will bless you for it, and you will have done a good work. But never tell the world of his faults.

A RECONCILIATION.

I DO not know
  If I were wrong or you ;
It grieves me so
  To think I gave you pain,
That I my gift must rue,
  And take it back again.

I do not know
  If you or I were right ;
Your tears have caused me woe,
  And if you weep again
I shall grow more contrite,
  And covet all your pain.

I do not know
  Nor care which one was right ;
For when your dear eyes flow
  I cannot speak for pain,
And tear-mists blind my sight
  Until you smile again.

So let it go—
  We may both have been wrong,
Or partly so ;
  But sin is purged by pain,
And royal souls are strong
  To wound and heal again.

—ELLA D. CLYMER.

I DON'T love you, Auntie, you have spoiled my paper," said little Nell as she began to cry and held up a paper from which I had just clipped a choice bit for a scrap-book I am making for her.

Although she is scarcely four years old, I am laying plans for her future happiness, and I believe she will fully appreciate and be grateful for it all when she is old enough to understand how it is.

But at present, she sees only that something has been taken that she wants now, although it would do her no good if she had it.

She no longer enjoys the pictures and the rest of the paper but makes herself miserable for the little bit seemingly taken from her.

But she is no more unreasonable than many of us who are older.

How many times we *act*, if not *say* "I don't love you God," when he has withheld this or that anticipated object or pleasure from us. As we grow older we see God's wisdom in withholding many things that we once thought necessary to our happiness.

Let us learn to fully trust Him in all things, believing He knows what is best for us, and so loves us as to withhold what we ought not to have, although we earnestly desire it. Let us leave the choice to Him, for He will surely give us the best.

234

BE UP AND DOING.

"ARE you not wearying for the heavenly rest?" said Whitfield to an old minister one day.

"No, certainly not!" he replied.

"Why not?" was the surprised rejoinder of Whitfield.

"Why, my good brother," said the aged saint, "if you were to send your servant into the fields to do a certain portion of work for you, and promised to give him refreshments in the evening, what would you say if you found him languid and discontented in the middle of the day, and murmuring, 'Would to God it were evening!' Would you not bid him be up and doing, and finish the work, and then go home and enjoy the promised rest? Just so does God require of you and me, that instead of looking for Saturday night, we do our day's work in the day."

HOW TO MAKE CHILDREN LOVELY.

THERE is just one way; that is to surround them by day and night with an atmosphere of love. Restraint and reproof may be mingled with love, but love must be a constant element. "I found my little girl was growing unamiable and plain," said a mother to us the other day, "and, reflecting on it sadly, I could only accuse myself as the cause thereof. So I changed my management, and improved every opportunity to praise and encourage her; to assure her of my unbounded affection for her, and my earnest desire that she should grow up to lovely and harmonious womanhood. As a rose opens to the sunshine, so the child opened in the warmth of the constant affection and caresses I showered upon her; her peevishness passed away, her face grew beautiful; and now one look from me brings her to my side, obedient to my will, and happiest when she is near me." Is not this a lesson for all parents? Not all the plowing or weeding or cultivation of every sort we can give our growing crops, will do for them what the steady shining of the sun can affect. Love is the sun-shine of the family; without it, not character, or morality, or virtue, can be brought to perfection.

TELL JESUS.

WHEN thou wakest in the morning,
 Ere thou tread the untried way
Of the lot that lies before thee,
 Through the coming busy day ;
Whether sunbeams promise brightness,
 Whether dim forebodings fall,
Be the dawning glad or gloomy,
 Go to Jesus—tell Him all.

In the calm of sweet communion
 Let the daily work be done ;
In the peace of soul out-pouring
 Care be banished, patience won ;

236

And if earth, with its enchantments,
  Seeks the spirit to enthrall,
Ere thou listen, ere thou answer,
  Turn to Jesus—tell Him all !

Then, as hour by hour glides by thee,
  Thou wilt blessed guidance know ;
Thine own burdens being lightened,
  Thou can'st bear another's woe ;
Thou can'st help the weak ones onward,
  Thou can'st raise up those that fall ;
But remember, while thou servest,
  Still tell Jesus—tell him all !

And if weariness creep o'er thee,
  As the day wears to its close,
Or if sudden fierce temptation
  Bring thee face to face with foes,
In thy weakness, in thy peril,
  Raise to heaven a trustful call ;
Strength and calm for every crisis
  Come—in telling Jesus all.

—GEORGIANA TAYLOR.

"IF I WERE A BOY."

IF I were a boy again I would look on the cheerful side of everything, for almost everything has a cheerful side. Life is very much like a mirror; if you smile upon it, it smiles back upon you; but if you frown and look doubtful upon it, you will be sure to get a similar look in return. I once heard it said of a grumbling, unthankful person: ''He would have made an uncommonly fine sour apple, if he had happened to have been born in that station." Inner sunshine not only warms the heart of the owner, but all those who come in contact with it. Indifference begets indifference. "Who shuts love out, in turn shall be shut out from love."

If I were a boy again, I would school myself to say "No," oftener. I might write pages on the importance of learning very early in life to gain that point where a young man can stand erect and decline doing an unworthy thing because it is unworthy.

If I were a boy again, I would demand of myself more courtesy toward my companions and friends. Indeed, I would rigorously exact it of myself to strangers as well. The smallest courtesies interspersed along the rough roads of life are like the English sparrows singing to us all the winter long, and making that season of ice and snow more endurable to everybody.

But I have talked long enough, and this shall be my parting paragraph. Instead of trying so hard as some of us do to be happy, as if that was the soul purpose of life, I would, if I were a boy again, try still harder to deserve happiness.

—JAMES T. FIELDS.

AN OPEN STAND.

YOU will not be able to go through life without being discovered; a lighted candle cannot be hid. There is a feeling among some good people that it will be wise to be very reticent and hide their light under a -bushel. They intend to lie low all the war time, and come out when the palms are being distributed. They hope to travel to Heaven by the back lanes, and skulk into glory by disguise. Rest assured, my fellow christians, that at some period or other, in the most quiet lives, there will come a moment for open decision. Days will come wben we must speak out, or próve traitors to our Lord and to his truth. You cannot long hold fire in the hollow of your hand, or keep a candle under the bed. Godliness, like murder, will out. You will not always be able to travel to Heaven *incog.—Spurgeon.*

A WIFE'S LUCKY ACCIDENT.

SOMETIMES what seems to be a very unfortunate accident will turn out to be a blessing in disguis e. It is said that tinted paper was first made by accident, in this way: Mrs. East, the wife of an English paper maker, working on a wash day near a large vat which had in it the pulp from which the paper was to be made, accidentally dropped her bluing bag into it.

She thought the paper would be ruined, and was too frightened to tell her husband what she had done.

When the paper came out, it had a peculiar tinge, but the workmen could not explain it, so the paper maker sent the whole batch to London; with instructions to sell it for whatever they could get for it. But when the buyers saw it they thought it pretty, called it "something new," and orders poured in upon the astonished manufacturer for more of the same sort. The wife confessed what she had done, and we may be sure she was forgiven readily, for by her lucky accident her husband's fortune was made; and that is the history of the very simple origin of tinted paper.

A BRIGHTER MORROW.

DARK cloud-folds wave above us,
  The squadrons of the rain
Bear down upon the forest,
  And sweep along the plain ;
They break their shining lances
  Against our loved retreat,
And trample our sweet blossoms
  With swift, unsparing feet ;
Yet will our hearts be joyous,
  Nor grief nor trouble borrow,
There cometh peace, the storm will cease—
  There'll be a brighter morrow.

So, when our lives are darkened,
  And clouds of ill hang o'er,
We'll never fear the sunshine
  Will find the earth no more.

"Let not your hearts be troubled!"
   Still kindly sayeth He
Whose mandate hushed the waters
   Of stormy Galilee.
He brings the balm of Gilead
   To heal the wounds of sorrow;
At His behest, there cometh rest—
   There'll be a brighter morrow.

Brave brother, art thou weary
   And is the journey long?
Dear sisters, do'st thou falter,
   Hath sorrow stilled thy song?
Rejoice! the sunset reddens,
   The clouds are rolling by,
The glorious "bow of promise"
   Hangs in the eastern sky!
Thy Heaven will be sweeter
   For days of earthly sorrow;
The storm will cease, there cometh peace—
   There'll be a brighter morrow.
              —ANDREW DOWNING.

DO not be discouraged at the difficulties that seem so great before you. They may seem great a little way off, but they always diminish or vanish altogether as we come near them. Some one has said duties and difficulties are like the nightmare; as soon as you stir, they vanish. Learn to look on the bright side and you will be surprised at the number of things that will turn up to help.

WHEN SILENCE IS GOLDEN.

THAT there is a time to speak and a time to keep silent, seems to be an idea which some very good people have failed to grasp. The Mongols illustrate this thought in a story that runs thus:

Two geese, when about to start southward on their autumn migration, were entreated by a frog to take him with them. On the geese expressing their willingness to do so if a means of conveyance could be devised, the frog produced a stock of strong grass,got the two geese to take it one by each end, while he clung to it with his mouth in the middle.

In this manner the three were making the journey successfully when they were noticed from below by some men, who loudly expressed their admiration of the device, and wondered who had been clever enough to discover it. The frog opened his mouth to say, "It was I," lost his hold, fell to the earth, and was dashed to pieces.

MORAL:—Do not let pride induce you to speak when safety requires you to be silent.

TRUST AND REST.

TRUST God implicitly, submit to Him cheerfully, and you will find that all shall be well; that more grace will be given you; that the heavier the trial, the larger will be the blessed measure of the strength. The shepherd is leading you in the right way to his own blessed fold. Leave it all to Him.

NO MONEY IN IT.

MY mother gets me up, builds the fire, and gets my breakfast, and sends me off," said a bright youth. "Then she gets my father up and gets his breakfast and sends him off. Then she gives the other children their breakfast, and sends them to school; and then she and the baby have their breakfast."

"How old is the baby?" asked the reporter.

"Oh, she is 'most two, but she can talk and walk as well as any of us."

"Are you well paid?"

"I get two dollars a week, and father gets two dollars a day."

"How much does your mother get?"

With a bewildered look the boy said, "Mother, why she don't work for anybody."

"I thought you said she worked for all of you."

"Oh, yes, for us, she does; but there ain't no money in it."

WHEN SHALL WE WIN.

WHEN shall we win? Why, when we fire
Straight to the mark and never tire;
When we hold fast, as we've begun
And still work on till all is done.

LEARN TO TALK.

AMONG the fascinations of a beautiful woman, none exceed that of a cultivated voice. Every woman cannot learn to sing, but she can learn to practice alluring intonations of the voice. Good speech is tuneful though it be not song. Modulation in talking is a sort of harmony. Lack of a pretty face may be entirely counteracted by a well-trained voice united with an ease of manner.

CHARITY.

CHARITY opens her door to need,
Without regard to faith or creed ;
Spreads her mantle of love and grace
Without regard to time or place.

She does not ask applause of men,
The blatant voice of tongue or pen ;
But sheds her blessings soft and still,
As sweet and pure as mountain rill.

Where'er distress and sorrows are,
She bends her love and gives her care ;
Lifts up the sad and sorrowing heart,
With mercy's charm and pity's part.

She spreads her mantle free and fair,
As Nature's gifts—the light and air,
With hand and purse, alike she's free,
And boundless as the heaving sea.

244

When called to meet some special case,
She does not ask whereof the place ;
She bends her strength to give relief,
Assuage their sorrow, care and grief.

Spreads her mantle, o'er every ill,
Her mercy as the dews distill ;
Seeks not for pomp or proud array,
But simply asks the means, the way.

The orphan's prayer, the widow's cry,
Whenever souls in anguish sigh,
She turns her feet to help and bless,
And joyous gives her kind caress.

All hail sweet charity ! all hail ! all hail !
When here on earth all else shall fail,
Thy breast all free, and pure and bright,
Shall glow with Heaven's brightest light.

—A. F. Scott.

WITHOUT earnestness no man is ever great, or really does great things. He may be the cleverest man; he may be brilliant, entertaining, popular, but he will want weight. No soul moving picture was ever painted that had not in its depths a shadow.

If you can see nothing but the bad, shut your eyes. Better be blind than unable to see the beautiful and the good.

NICE DISCRIMINATION OF WORDS.

PRETTY, refers to external beauty on a small scale. Grace of manner, is a natural gift; elegance, implies cultivation. Well-bred, refers to general conduct rather than individual actions. Beautiful, is the strongest word of its class, implying softness and delicacy in addition to everything that is in similar words. Courtesy has reference to others, politeness, to ourselves. The former is a duty or privilege to others, the latter is behavior assumed from proper self-respect. Benevolent, refers to the character of the agent acting, benificent, to the act performed. Charitable, is restricted to almsgiving except when used in reference to judgment of others. Lovely is used where there is something more than external beauty—when there is a combination of personal beauty and pleasing manner. Faultless features do not make a lady lovely who is disagreeable in disposition.

EVERY ONE CAN HELP.

A GENTLEMAN related once that a traveler stood outside a splendid cathedral in Germany, expressing his admiration of its beauty. "Yes," said a laborer who happened to hear him, "it's a fine building and took us many years to finish it." "Took you," exclaimed the gentleman, "why what had you to do with it?" "I mixed the mortar that's in it sir," was the modest reply. That laborer had a right to feel he had some share in the grand work now complete; his part though humble, had been well done, and he was not ashamed of it. In the struggle of right against wrong, every one can help; your place dear reader may be lowly, but if you are diligent and trustworthy, if you fulfill your daily work as in the Master's sight, you are a fellow laborer with Him, you will yet hear Him say to you, "Well done, good and faithful servant."

GROWING OLD.

THEY call it "going down the hill!" when we are growing old,
And speak with mournful accents when our tale is nearly told;
They sigh when talking of the past, the days that used to be,
As if the future were not bright with immortality.

But 'tis not going down—'tis climbing higher and higher,
Until we almost see the mountains that our souls desire;
For if the natural eye grows dim, it is but dim to the earth,
While the eye of faith grows keener to discern the Savior's worth.

Who would exchange for shooting blade, the waving golden grain,
Or when the corn is fully ripe, would wish it green again?
And who would wish the hoary head, found in the way of truth,
To be again encircled with the sunny locks of youth?

For though in truth the outward man must perish and
    decay,
The inward man shall be renewed by grace from day to
    day ;
Those who are planted by the Lord, unshaken in the root,
Shall in their old age flourish, and bring forth choicest
    fruit.

It is not years that make old men ; the spirit may be
    young,
Though fully three score years and ten the wheels of life
    have run;
God has Himself recorded, in His blessed word of truth
That they who wait upon the Lord, they shall e'en renew
    their youth.

And when the eyes now dim shall open to behold the
    king,
And ears now dull with age shall hear the harps of Heaven
    ring—
And on the head now hoary shall be placed the crown of
    gold,
Then shall be known the lasting joy of never growing old.

OUR human duties are faithfully and joyfully per-
formed only when we feel that they are not of our
own choosing, but tasks divinely ordered and at-
tuned to that high purpose which "through the ages
runs."

                                 —H. G. SPAULDING.

SYSTEMATIC SAVING.

SMALL savings are the foundation of great wealth. Most of the successful men of America practiced economy to secure a foothold in the commercial or financial world. Many of the professional celebrities of our day and age began life at the foot of the ladder and rose step by step, each advance made possible by self-denial and frugality. The late Daniel Dougherty, whose fame as an orator, author and lawyer was world-wide, saved enough out of his pitifully small wages as a messenger boy to pay for the laying of the foundation of his education.

No thoughtless spendthrift can ever hope to win fame or fortune. Many a genius has ended his career in the gutter because he failed to understand the first principle of business life. The man who is generous before being just is a useless, and often dangerous, member of society.

Systematic saving is the keynote to success. Dickens has illustrated the truth of this statement by drawing the character of Micawber. Every city and hamlet in the United States has its Micawbers—good fellows, jovial and generous, but forever living on the work and charity of their friends. Chronic impecuniosity always ends in a total loss of self-respect, and man who cannot respect himself is on the road to the poor house or the penitentiary.

Every able-bodied man in the United States can save something out of his weekly wages or his monthly salary. The self-denial which may be required to become a capitalist on a small scale may lead to better things. It trains the mind and develops confidence in self. Five dollars per month placed in a building association is equivalent to one thousand dollars in nine years. Five dollars deposited each month in a reliable savings bank amounts to sixty dollars at the close of each year and four per cent. interest.

Labor organizations would do well to instruct their members in the rudiments of practical financiering.

Every dollar saved, if properly invested in a home, building association or bank, earns another dollar in the course of a few months and eventually makes the investor a free man who can look forward to sickness and old age with perfect equanimity.

Every dollar wasted is a wasted opportunity. The spendthrift has no friends when his substance is squandered. The last days of his life are invariably days of misery and vain regrets.

Look upon both sides of the picture before it is too late. Habits of economy and vicious traits are alike formed early in life. Every man must at an early period decide for himself whether it is better to be a useful citizen or a drone, a man or a parasite.

BROKEN HEARTS.

THERE are broken hearts in the world to-day
  Though smiling faces hide them ;
They pass and repass on the old highway,
  With stifled grief beside them.
The wan, white face of the woman who knows
  That she must wander apart
From the soul where not even pity glows,
  With a proud and broken heart.

There are broken hearts in the world to-day,
  Beneath warm furs and laces ;
Bleak December gnaws at those hearts, though May
  Smiles in the dauntless faces.
The resolute eyes of the man we see
  By day in the busy mart ;
Look down in the night through his soul, and he
  Looks into a broken heart.

There are broken hearts in the world to-day,
  For all the cynic's laughter;
The warm hearts that were red and growing gray,
  Hope fled and Youth went after.
But the sun comes up and the world goes round
  And all of us play our parts,
But over as well as under the ground
  There are dead and broken hearts.

—JOHN ERNEST MCCANN.

KEEPING HIS WORD.

EMPLOYEES are often very particular not to over-
step their own duties, or to do work neglected by
others. It would be well, however, for every
young man just starting in life to remember that the
man who succeeds, is the one who is ready to turn his
hand to anything that will advance the interest of his
employer, as he would be were he in business for him-
self.

Mr. Wilder, the first president of the American Tract
Society, and widely known for his large benevolence in
this country and in Europe, was once head clerk for a
large firm in Charlestown, Mass. He sold a customer
a ball of Russian duck, to be delivered at one o'clock.
The firm was out of duck and he went over to Boston
to buy it. No cart-man was at hand, and he engaged
a porter to take it over in a wheel-barrow.

Returning soon after, he found the porter on the
bridge, sitting on the wheel-barrow, half dead with
heat. It was half-past twelve, and the duck was prom-
ised at one. Without hesitation, Mr. Wilder, in spite
of heat and dust, started with the wheel-barrow.

A wealthy merchant on horseback met him and said,
with a smile, "Turned truckman, Wilder?"

"These goods are due at one o'clock," said Mr.
Wilder, "and my porter has given out, so I must de-
liver them myself to keep my word."

"Good, good!" said the gentleman, and went

directly to Mr. Wilder's employer to tell what he had seen, and to add, ''Tell Wilder when he wishes to go into business for himself, my name is at his service for thirty thousand dollars.''

No work is too menial if it is necessary to keep an engagement.

* * *

THE GIRL WHO WORKS.

HERE is a girl, and I love to think of her and talk of her, who comes in late when there is company who wears a pretty little air of mingled responsibility and anxiety with her youth, whom the others seem to depend upon and look to her for many comforts. She is the girl who helps mother.

In her own home she is a blessed little saint and comforter. She takes unfinished tasks from the tired, stiff fingers that falter at their work; her strong young figure is a staff upon which the gray-haired, white-faced mother leans and is rested. She helps mother with the spring's sewing, the week's mending, with a cheerful conversation and congenial companionship that some girls do not think worth while on only mother. And when there comes a day when she must bend over the old worn-out body of mother lying unheedful in her coffin, rough hands folded, her long disquiet merged in rest, something very sweet will be mingled with her loss, and the girl who helped mother will find a benediction of peace upon her head.

THE GRUMBLER,

HIS YOUTH.

HIS cap was too thick and his coat was too thin ;
He couldn't be quiet, he hated a din ;
He hated to write, and he hated to read;
He was certainly very much injured indeed ;
He must study and toil ; overwork he detested ;
His parents were strict and he never was rested ;
He knew he was wretched as wretched could be,
There was no one so wretchedly wretched as he.

HIS MANHOOD.

His farm was too small and his taxes too big ;
He was selfish and lazy and as cross as a pig ;
His wife was too silly, his children too rude,
And just because he was uncommonly good !
He hadn't got money enough to spare ;
He had nothing at all fit to eat or to wear ;
He knew he was wretched as wretched could·be,
There was no one so wretchedly wretched as he.

HIS OLD AGE.

He finds he has sorrows more deep than his fears ;
He grumbles to think he has grumbled for years ;
He grumbles to think he has grumbled away
His home and his children, his life's little day.
But alas ! 'tis too late ! it is no use to say
That his eyes are too dim and his hair too gray;
He knows he is wretched as wretched can be ;
There is no one so wretchedly wretched as he.

OUR NEIGHBOR'S AFFAIRS.

WHY discuss them at all. It is such a temptation to add details and distort meanings in order to produce a piquant story, that even good people sometimes yield to it; so beware danger and eschew gossips entirely A word spoken out of season, even the truth badly told, or at an improper time, may inflict an injury which it is not in the power of anyone to repair. The motives of the individual are quite a secondary matter; the gun-shot wound inflicted by the man who "didn't know his gun was loaded" is as fatal as the murderer's shot. When a cruel wrong has been done an innocent person, it only adds fuel to one's indignation to have the gossip retailer expostulate with tears in her eyes, that she meant no harm; she only told what she heard; she did not know it would do harm. The harm that has been wrought is a matter which chiefly concerns us, in such a case, not the motives. It is a good rule not only to refrain from all evil criticism of persons, but from listening to such criticism. It should be systematically enfo$_{rc}$ed on children that such conversation is beneath them and indicative of low breeding. The writer remembers seeing a mite of eight years old withdraw herself when such conversation which was distasteful was taking place. "Mamma has always told me," she said, "never to gossip about my friends, or to go with anyone who did, and I don't want to hear anything mean of people I don't know." And this should be the creed of everyone.

If you hear a bad story on anyone, remember that, if it is true, by repeating it you put an obstacle in the way of the guilty man to prevent his doing better in the future, and if it is not true, you do him a greater injury than can be done in any other way. There are so many good reasons why you should not repeat gossip, and not one good one why you should, that if you stop and reflect you will never be guilty of it. You know that after you have said it you cannot unsay it nor limit the number to whom your words will be repeated.

KEEP SWEET.

CAN it be gainsaid, that there is no duty more largely neglected by the average, every-day christian than the duty of being pleasant? One reason may be because so few people ever look upon it in the light of a duty. But are we not under just as much obligation to be pleasant as to be honest, or truthful, or just, or pure, or generous? Parents who punish children severely for other faults will often excuse a fit of moroseness or sulleness by saying, "Oh, it is only his natural disposition!" as if that settled the whole question. Pleasantness of speech and manner can be cultivated like any other grace of character. To be sweet when everything seems to be going wrong, and when everybody around is cross, as well as when the domestic skies are free from clouds; then it is that the pleasant member of the family is appreciated.

IF I HAD KNOWN.

IF I had known when last I touched the fingers
  Of him I loved so well,
That ne'er again their clinging clasp would thrill me
  With love's strange spell,
I had not been so careless in my greeting
  So free to say farewell—
    If I had known !

If I had known that low voice, sad and tender,
  That pleaded for one word,
One little word to carry as love's token,
  Would ne'er be heard
Till life were past, my heart, then cold and careless,
  How might it have been stirred—
    If I had known !

If I had known ! Ah ! hopeless, sad reflection ;
  Thus late, it brings no cheer.
If I had known how soon cold death would silence
  The voice so dear :
Had shown some of the little love I cherished,
  Life were not now so drear—
    If I had known ! ·

                                    —M. C. BROWN.

LITTLE Harry had seen some older boys fly their kites from the tops of houses, and he thought it would be nice fun if he could do so too—so he came to his aunt and said:

"Aunt Mary, can I go up to the top of the house and fly my kite?"

His aunt wished to do everything that was proper to please him, but she thought this was very unsafe, so she said:

"No, Harry, my boy; I think that is very dangerous sort of play. I'd rather you wouldn't go."

"All right. Then I'll go out on the bridge," said Harry.

His aunt smiled, and said she hoped he would always be as obedient as that.

"Harry, what are you doing?" said his mother on one occasion.

"Spinning my new top, mother."

"Can't you take the baby out to ride? Get the carriage, and I'll bring him down."

"All right!" shouted the boy, as he put his top away in his pocket, and hastened to obey his mother.

"Uncle William, may I go over to the store this morning?" said Harry one day at breakfast. "I want to see those baskets again that I was looking at yesterday."

"O yes, Harry," said his uncle; "I shall be very glad to have you."

"But I cannot spare you to-day, Harry," said his mother; "I want you to go with me; you shall go to the store another time."

"All right," said Harry, and went on eating.

No matter what Harry was asked to do, or what refusal he met with when asking for anything, his constant answer was "All right." He never asked, "Why can't I?" or "Why musn't I?" Harry not only learned to obey, but he learned to obey in good humor.

THE BONDAGE OF LOVE.

 SWEET will of God, thou hast girded me round,
    Like the deep moving currents that girdle the sea;
    With omnipotent love is my poor nature bound,
    And this bondage of love sets me perfectly free.

For years my will wrestled with vague discontent,
    That like a sad angel o'ershadowed my way;
    God's light in my soul oft with darkness was blent;
    And my heart ever longed for an unclouded day.

My wild will was captured, yet under the yoke
    There was pain, and not peace, at the press of the
        load,
Till the glorious burden the last fiber broke,
    And I melted like wax in the furnace of God.

And now I have flung myself recklessly out,
    Like a chip on the stream of the Infinite will;
    I pass the rough rocks with a smile and a shout,
    And I just let my God His dear purpose fulfill.

I care not for self ; all my blisses and pains
　　I gladly yield up to the mandate above ;
My crosses and triumphs, my losses and gains,
　　I bury them all in the vortex of love.

And now my King Jesus has all his own way,
　　I wait but to catch his low whispering word ;
'Tis my bliss to lie low 'neath his scepter's bright sway,
　　For my triumph I see in each step of my Lord.

Forever I choose the good will of my God,
　　Its holy, deep riches to love and to know ;
The serfdom of love doth so sweeten my rod,
　　That its touch maketh rivers of honey to flow.

Roll on, checkered seasons, bring smiles or bring tears,
　　My soul sweetly sails on an infinite tide ;
I shall soon touch the shore of eternity's years,
　　And near the white throne of my Savior abide.
　　　　　　　　　　　　　—George D. Watson.

THE little I have seen in the world teaches me to
look upon the errors of others in sorrow, not in
anger. When I take the history of one poor
heart that has sinned and suffered, and represent to my-
self the struggles and temptations it has passed through,
the brief pulsation of joy, the feverish inquietude of
friends, I would fain leave the erring soul of my fellow
man with Him from whose hand it came.
　　　　　　　　　　　　　—*Longfellow.*

260

A CUSTOMER SECURED.

A YOUNG man in a dry goods store in Boston was endeavoring to sell a customer some goods. He had a quantity on hand which he much desired to dispose of, as they were not of the freshest style, and the man seemed inclined to take them.

When the goods had been examined, and the bargain was about to be concluded, the customer inquired:

"Are these goods the latest style?"

The young man hesitated. He wanted to sell the goods, and it appeared evident that if he said they were the latest style the man would take them. But he could not tell a lie and he replied:

"They are not the latest style, but they are very good style."

The man looked at him, examined some other goods of later styles, and said:

"I will take those of the older style, and some of the new also. Your honesty in stating the facts will fasten me to this place."

The man not only sold his goods and kept a good conscience, but he also retained a good customer whom he might never have seen again if he had not spoken to him the exact truth. There is no permanent gain in falsehood and deception.

Righteousness and truth are a sure foundation.

GIVE A HAND TO YOUR BROTHER.

GIVE a hand to your brother
   Wrestling with wind and wave,
Eagerly help another—
   You are saved that you may save!

Heavily seas are breaking
   O'er his drooping form,
Hope, is his heart forsaking,
   Help! warriors of the storm!

Out of the depths of sorrow
   Calls he with bitter cry,
Wait for no other morrow,
   But grasp him ere he die!

Cometh no shining angel
   In swift unwearied flight,
With the voice of the glad evangel
   Down from the courts of light?

Hearts and hands that are human
   In pitying haste must move ;
Throw out the rope of promise,
   Draw him with cords of love!

Give a hand to your brother
   Wrestling with wind and wave,
Eagerly help another
   You are saved that you may save !
                  —C. T. CARISBROOKE.

A N English embassador to one of the great eastern
empires had the misfortune to lose his wife while
she was performing the gracious duties of her high
office. The bereaved nobleman—one of the most dis-
tinguished of living diplomatists—was so stricken
by his loss that he felt the need of having his two
daughters by his side ; but these were young girls in
school in far-off England. Unable to endure the
gloom cast over the magnificent embassy by the death
of its mistress, the embassador sailed for home to bring
his daughters eastward.

On the eve of their departure from England for the
country in which her father held official position, the
elder of the girls was surprised by an invitation to lunch
with Queen Victoria.

Lady Mary—as we will call her—was a true-hearted
English girl, and had many of the high ideals of her
dead mother.

After the lunch the queen led her into a private room,
and taking her hands said :

"Lady Mary, you are leaving England to take at your
father's side your mother's place in the high position
which he holds."

The girl flushed with surprise, for this was the first
intimation she had received of the real nature of her
future. That she must fulfill the difficult and delicate
public duties falling to the wife of an embassador had

not been explained to her. She made a gesture of appeal, which the queen checked.

"You are the same age I was," continued the queen, gravely, "when I was called to the duties of a queen of England. I do not expect you at once to do all that your mother was able to do. She was one of the rarest flowers of England, I shall not advise you about this duty or that in detail. Knowledge will come with the every-day requirements of the position. But I wish you to carry out with you one suggestion from me, which I hope you will not forget. You will meet many people, my dear, whom you will not understand, and many whom you cannot love. Bury the bad in people, and always seek for the good. Do this, and with the intelligence and good judgment which I am sure you have, England will soon honor you as she has honored your mother."

The queen kissed the girl gently upon her forehead, and the interview was soon closed.

It is not hard to understand why the people of England love their queen, when we hear such true incidents of her life as this.

Lady Mary went forth with her father to her high duties and large opportunities for doing good or ill. A recent resident of the empire, who has had every social opportunity for acquaintance with the embassador's family and with the most exclusive drawing-rooms of its capital, lately told the writer that the career of this young girl in embassadorial circles had been a remarkable one. The queen's personal advice had evidently done much toward crystalizing a naturally fine character

into one of uncommon strength and usefulness.   Such
an earnest and devout young life in diplomatic society
made it natural for men and women brought into con-
tact with it to be the best, and to do the best.   Even
the most unpromising attache became a better man for
meeting her.   He had to, for her white hands "buried
the bad," and kept alive the " good" in him.

Victoria's advice was both queenly and womanly.   It
touched the sources of a royal truth.   The christian
queen knew well the power of a pure, divinely-influ-
enced life, that seeks in human hearts only that which
is good and true.   Her own life has exemplified it.

CUMBERED WITH SERVING.

HE was cumbered with serving ;—the household, the
    board,
  The meal to be mingled, the feast to be spread,—
So she could not sit still at the feet of the Lord
  Though her spirit was faint for the heavenly bread.

She was cumbered with serving ; the quick tones grew
    sharp;
There were lines on her brow, there was grief in her eyes ;
  And no time could she spare for the sweet thrilling harp,
Or the hymn that should gently as incense arise.

She was cumbered with serving ; she marveled indeed
  That any could rest while the work must be done,
The work that was pressing, since days with such speed
  Fled on till night and the fall of the sun.

She was cumbered with serving ; the dear Lord was there,—
   She could touch Him, could call Him, could bend at
      His knee ;
Yet this was the whole of her querulous prayer :
   "O Master, my sister, wilt Thou bid her help me ?"

Ah ! Martha of Bethany, many there be
   Who are cumbered like thee with earth's service this day.
And fettered and weary and fretted like thee
   They go to the master and bitterly pray.

And some of them, matrons, are tired of steps
   All over the house from morn till the eve,
And some of them, mothers, are pale to the lips,
   With the tasks they must do or the tasks they must leave.

And their comfort it is, when the great tears well up,
   And the soul with endeavor and longing is spent,
That the Lord has compassion, who sees their life's cup
   So dark with the brewing of hot discontent.

And his "Cumbered with serving," although it reprove,
   And stir them with shame, hath a pitiful tone,
And they hear through its tender reproach the Christ's love
   That never lets slip from its clasping, his own.
                —MARGARET E. SANGSTER.

Doing, not dreaming, is the secret of success.   Thinking out plans will not amount to anything unless the thought be followed by a determined will to execute.

266

CHILD OF SORROW.

CHILD of sorrow, murmur not,
  Thy sorrow soon will cease ;
Angels are waiting for thy soul
  At that celestial place.

I know thy burden has been great,
  Thy body sore oppressed,
But Christ is waiting at the gate
  To call thee to thy rest.

God wants his jewels bright,
  All polished bright and fine ;
He will not give one stroke too much,
  His love is all divine.

"Dear Lord, I murmur not,
  Thy blessed will be done ;
I know my burden has been great,
  But not like thy dear Son.

He died that I might live,
  And there with Him abide ;
O, precious Jesus, holy name,
  My soul is satisfied.

I know that I am His,
  He fills my soul with love ;
I know my name is written there,
  In those bright realms above. "

A COMMONPLACE CHILD.

"MARY'S a commonplace child," they say,
   Praising Roberta, Robert and Ray ;
   "Maurice and Ellen are smart as steel ;
Bertha is handsome, and so is Neal ;
The baby's a cherub, so sweet and mild !
But Mary is such a commonplace child !"

Yet mirth and brilliancy seldom heed
A dusty chair or a button's need,
And beauty oft times wears a frown
If given the task of mending a gown ;
And the mother sighs, in a disheartened way,
Thinking the children grow worse each day.

But the freckle-faced girl, who at books is slow,
Runs upstairs, downstairs, to and fro,
Dresses the baby, the table sets,
Washes the dishes and feeds the pets ;
And mother, resting, from cares beguiled,
Thanks God for Mary her commonplace child.
              —EMMA C. DOWD.

WHAT A LITTLE GIRL DID.

A GOOD many years ago a little girl of twelve
years of age was passing an old brick prison in
the city of Chicago, on her way to school, when
she saw a hand beckoning from behind a cell window

and heard a voice asking her to please bring him something to read.

For many weeks after she went to the prison every Sunday, carrying the poor prisoner a book to read from her father's library. At last one day she was called to his death-bed.

"Little girl," said he, "you have saved my soul; promise me that you will do all your life for the poor people in prison what you have done for me."

The little girl promised, and she kept her promise. Linda Gilbert has been all her life the steadfast friend of the prisoner. She has established good libraries in many prisons, and visited and helped hundreds of prisoners; and from the great number whom she has helped, six hundred are now, to her certain knowledge, leading honest lives. Prisoners from all parts of the country know and love her name, and surely the God of prisoners must look upon her work with interest.

And all this because a little girl heard and heeded the call to help a suffering soul.

THE HIDDEN TALENT.

"THOU wicked and slothful servant," the text,
And then it was lost, what he said next,
For well I knew the whole of that tale,
How the master had come, and my heart did quail
As I thought of my own talent hidden away
Where it had lain for many a day.
I had tenderly wrapped, and laid it with care
Away from my sight, and then, without prayer,
Had gone on my way, and entirely forgot;

Though at the time I intended not
To leave it so long :   Oh, what if my Master
Should suddenly come, and my heart beat faster
As the solemn thought with awful fear
Came to my mind, perhaps he is near !
I knew full well when I laid it down,
And I little thought I should lose my crown.
But now I could see with awful force
The folly of such a foolish course.
Oh, preachers be true !   The whole truth teach,
Thou knowest not what heart it may reach.
God's judgments, and justice, help make up the whole,
And the faithful watchman delivers his soul.

~~~~~~~~~~

THE PRICE OF A DRINK.

IVE cents a glass !"   Does anyone think
That is really the price of a drink ?
"Five cents a glass," I heard you say,
"Why, *that* isn't very much to pay."
Ah, no, indeed, 'tis a very small sum
You are passing over 'twixt finger and thumb,
And if that were all you gave away
It wouldn't be very much to pay.

The price of a drink ! let him decide
Who has lost his courage, and manhood's pride ;
And lies a groveling heap of clay,
Not far removed from a beast to-day.
The price of a drink ! let that one tell
Who sleeps to-night in a murderer's cell,
And feels within the fires of hell.

Honor and virtue, love and truth,
All the glory and pride of youth,

Hopes and manhood, the wreath of fame,
High endeavor and noble aim.
These are the treasures thrown away
For the price of a drink from day to day.

" Five cents a glass !" How Satan laughed
As over the bar the young man quaffed
The beaded liquor, for the demon knew
The terrible work that drink would do !
And before morning the victim lay
With his life-blood swiftly ebbing away,
And that was the price *he* paid, alas !
For the pleasure of taking a social glass.

The price of a drink ! If you care to know
What some are willing to pay for it, go
Through that wretched tenement over there,
With dingy windows and broken stair,
Where foul disease like a vampire crawls
With out-stretched wings o'er the mouldy walls.

There poverty dwells with her hungry brood
Wild-eyed as demons, for lack of food ;
There shame, in a corner crouches low ;
There violence deals its cruel blow ;
The innocent ones are thus accursed
To pay the price of this endless thirst.

" Five cents a glass !" Oh, if that were all,
The sacrifice would indeed be small !
But the cost in coin is the least amount
We pay ; and whoever will keep account
Will learn the terrible waste and blight
That follows this ruinous appetite.
" Five cents a glass ! Does any one think
That *this is all* one pays for a drink ?"

271

NO COMMON PEOPLE.

SOMEONE remarked in the hearing of Abraham Lincoln, when he was President of the United States, that he was quite a common-looking man. "Friend," he replied, gently, "the Lord loves common-looking people best. That is why he made so many of them." We read that the "Common-people" heard Jesus gladly. He made his teaching so plain and attractive to them that the uneducated masses fully understood, and appreciated it accordingly. Never, however, did the Saviour speak of his brothers and sisters as common-people. He knew not only what was in man generally, but what was in each individual. He does not think of men in masses and crowds, but as individuals, each having a precious soul with joys and sorrows all its own, and a most interesting and quite a unique life-history. "What God has cleansed call not thou common." If there are any "common people" it is the thoughtless ones who use this phrase when speaking of others.

MY CROWN.

MY crown is in my heart, and not my head ;
Not deck'd with diamonds and Indian stones,
Nor to be seen ; my crown is called content ;
A crown it is that seldom kings enjoy.
—SHAKESPEAR.

WHAT TO TEACH OUR DAUGHTERS.

T a social gathering some one proposed this question, "What shall I teach my daughter?" The following replies were handed in:

Teach her that one hundred cents make a dollar.

Teach her to arrange both parlor and library.

Teach her to say "no" and mean it, or "yes" and stick to it.

Teach her to wear a calico dress and wear it like a queen.

Teach her how to sew on buttons, darn stockings and mend gloves.

Teach her to dress for health and comfort as well as for appearance.

Teach her to cultivate flowers and to keep the kitchen garden—combining the useful and ornamental.

Teach her to make her room the neatest room in the house.

Teach her to have nothing to do with intemperate or dissolute young men.

Teach her that tight-lacing is uncomely, as well as injurious to the health.

Teach her to regard the morals and habits, and not money, in selecting her associates.

Teach her to observe the old rule—"A place for everything, and everything in its place."

Teach her that music, drawing and painting are real accomplishments in the home, and are not to be neglected if there be time and money for their use.

Teach her that a good, steady, church-going mechanic, farmer, clerk or teacher, without a cent, is worth more than forty loafers or non-producers in broadcloth.

Teach her to embrace every opportunity for reading, and to select such books as will give her the most useful and practical information in order to make the best progress in earlier as well as in later home and school life.

LET GOD CONTROL.

I NEED some oil, said an ancient Monk, so he planted an olive sapling.

"Lord," he prayed, "it needs rain that its tender roots may drink and swell. Send gentle showers." And the Lord sent a gentle shower.

"Lord," prayed the Monk, "My tree needs sun. Send sun, I pray Thee." And the sun shone, gilding the dripping clouds.

"Now frost, my Lord, to brace its tissues," cried the Monk. And behold the little tree stood sparkling with frost. But at evening it died. Then the Monk sought the cell of a brother Monk and told his strange experience.

"I too have planted a little tree," he said, "and see! it thrives well. But I entrust my tree to its God. He who made it knows better what it needs than a man like me. I laid no condition. I fixed not ways or means. "Lord send it what it needs," I prayed,— "storm or sunshine, wind, rain, or frost. Thou hast made it and Thou dost know."

FEELING RESPONSIBILITY.

THE work of a great many men and women is impaired in quality and diminished in force by an excessive sense of responsibility. There are a great many people whose work lies in a department, but whose sense of responsibility is extended to cover the whole sphere of action. Their specific duty is to do a particular thing, and to do it with all the power and skill they possess, but they spend their strength in nervous anxiety with regard to the work in other departments for which they have no direct responsibility. It is very easy to make the sense of responsibility tyrannical, and to defeat the very end for which it is given. When this sense becomes so intense and pressing that it no longer leaves the man or woman free to do the best work in the best way, it is abnormal. There are hosts of men and women to-day whose power of doing good is seriously diminished by their painful solicitude for their fellow-men. They bear the whole burden of the world upon their shoulders; all the misery of humanity rests upon their hearts and they are saddened and sickened by a sense of their own inability to deal with great problems, to right great wrongs, and to lift great burdens. This is not only a great mistake, but, in a way, it shows a taint of skepticism, it involves a distrust of God. George MacDonald has portrayed this state of mind in one of his best-known stories, in which a man of great earnestness and of heroic temper is so overcome by his consciousness of human misery and of the crying needs of the world that he is really unfitted for duty. It is pointed out to him at last that he is not only doing his own work, but trying to do God's work also; that God is responsible for the universe, and not man; and all that any man is responsible for, is the work that he personally can do under the most favorable conditions. To do that work thoroughly one must have cheer, courage and the entire command of one's forces. To waste these precious things, through a general feeling of the vastness of the problem and the inadequacy of a man to deal with it, is to call God's judgment into question and to doubt His power to direct His own world. Life is made up, not only of works, but of faith, and no man can do the work of this day with the highest efficiency who does not surround his own special task with an invigorating and exhaustible atmosphere of faith. If we perform the duty laid before us, and do the work assigned us, God will take care of the rest of the world. We have no right to paralyze ourselves by attempting to add His work to our own.

IF a civil word or two will render a man happy, he must be wretched indeed who will not give them to him. Such a disposition is like lighting another man's candle by one's own, which loses none of its brilliancy by what the other gains.

"HE DOETH ALL THINGS WELL."

YES, blessed Lord, thou doest,
  Thou doest all things well;
Thou maketh both the deaf to hear,
  The dumb thy goodness tell.

Unloose our tongues, dear Lord,
  Help us to speak for thee ;
Help us to speak, and plainly speak
  Of the love that makes us free.

Open our ears, dear Lord,
  The dullness all remove ;
May we thy slightest whisper hear,
  The whispers of thy love.

He doeth all things well,
  Lord, help us to believe,
That what is best for us to have
  Thou wilt freely give.

And though we cannot see it now,
  We shall hereafter know
All that the Lord has done for us,
  It was best it should be so.

         —A. M. YOUGH.

THE FOLLY OF FLATTERY.

TO seek through the flattery of another to win them to friendship, is both unchristian in its religious phases, and unwise as an attempted stroke of worldly policy. It is something like a heart sickening and really disgusting fact that some professed christians descend to these seriously questioned methods which appeal to the pride and vanity of another as a means of courting their approval. This is done when the gifts and graces of another are over-rated in order to enlist his personal favor. To deliberately present to another that his abilities are of a high order, and that there must, from that fact, be a sublime future before him, when, in the judgment of the flatterer, his capacities are no higher than the average, is before the Lord but bare-faced falsification, prompted by a debased and sordid selfishness. Such friends won by such falsehood are very sure to prove false. It is well to express honest appreciation of merit where there is merit, and where there is evident grace to bear the commendation, but this unhallowed method of flattering conceits into an increase of pride and pomp, when their need is the crucifixion of the inordinate elements of pride still remaining, is a snare in which the devil befools by twos— the flattered and the flatterer.

What is really best for us lies always in our reach, though often overlooked.

THE MORTGAGE ON THE FARM.

TIS gone at last, and I am glad; it stayed a fearful
   while,
   And when the world was light and gay, I could not
      even smile ;
It stood before me like a giant, outstretched its iron arm ;
No matter where I looked, I saw the mortgage on the farm.

I'll tell you how it happened, for I want the world to know,
How glad I am this winter day whilst earth is white as
      snow ;
I'm just as happy as a lark.   No cause for rude alarm
Confronts us now, for lifted is the mortgage on the farm.

The children they were growing up and they were smart
      and trim,
To some big college in the east we'd sent our youngest,
      Jim ;
And every time he wrote us, at the bottom of his screed
He'd tack some Latin fol-de-rol which none of us could
      read.

The girls they ran to music, and to painting and to rhymes,
They said the house was out of style and far behind the
      times ;
They suddenly diskivered that it didn't keep 'em warm—
Another step, of course, toward a mortgage on the farm.

We took a cranky notion, Hannah Jane and me, one day,
While we were coming home from town, talking all the
      way ;

The old house wasn't big enough for us, although for years
Beneath its humble roof we'd shared each others joys and
    tears.

We built it o'er, and when 'twas done, I wish you could
    have seen it,
It was a most tremendous thing—I really didn't mean it ;
Why, it was big enough to hold the people of the town,
And not half as cozy as the old one we pulled down.

I bought a fine pianner and it shortened still the pile,
But, then, it pleased the children and they banged it all
    the while ;
No matter what they played for me, their music had no
    charm,
For every tune said plainly : ":There's a mortgage on the
    farm ! "

I worked from morn till eve, toiled as often toils the slave,
To meet the grizzly interest ; I tried hard to be brave,
And oft when I came home at night, with tired brain and
    arm,
The chickens hung their heads : they felt the mortgage on
    the farm.

We saved a penny now and then ; we laid them in a row,
The girls they played the same old tunes, and let the new
    ones go ;
And when from college came our Jim, with laurels on his
    brow,
I led him to the stumpy field and put him to the plow.

He something said in Latin, but I didn't understand.
It did me good to see his plow turn up the dewy land ;

And when the year had ended and empty were the cribs,
We found we'd hit that mortgage, sir, a blow between the
ribs.

To-day I harnessed up the team and thundered off to town,
And in the lawyer's sight I planked the last bright dollar
down ;
And when I trotted up the lane, a feelin' good and warm,
The old red rooster crowed his best : " No mortgage on
the farm !"

I'll sleep almighty good to-night, the best for many a day,
The skeleton that haunted us has passed fore'er away ;
The girls can play the brand new tunes with no fears to
alarm,
And Jim can go to congress with no mortgage on the farm.
                                        —T. C. HARBAUGH.

GOD'S LOVE.

STANDING on the top of the Cheviot Hills, a little
son's hand enclosed in his, a father taught the
measure of the measureless love of God.   Point-
ing northward over Scotland, then southward over
England, then eastward over the German Ocean, then
westward over the limitless hill and dale, and then
sweeping his hand around the whole circling horizon,
he said: "Johnny, my boy, God's love is as big as all
that!"

"Why, father," the boy cheerily replied, with spark-
ling eyes, "then we must be in the very middle of it."

THEY FAILED TO OBSERVE.

ENTLEMEN, you do not use your faculties of ob-
servation," said an old professor, addressing his
class. Here he pushed forward a gallipot contain-
ing a chemical of exceedingly offensive smell. "When
I was a student," he continued, "I used my sense of
taste," and with that he dipped his finger in the galli-
pot and then put his finger in his mouth. "Taste it,
gentlemen; taste it," said the professor, "and exercise
your preceptive faculties." The gallipot was pushed
toward the reluctant class, one by one. The students
resolutely dipped their fingers into the concoction, and,
with many a wry face, sucked the abomination from
their fingers. "Gentlemen, gentlemen," said the pro-
fessor, "I must repeat that you do not use your facul-
ties of observation, for if you had looked more closely
at what I was doing, you would have seen that the
finger I put in my mouth, was not the finger I dip-
ped in the gallipot."

THE HIGHLY FINISHED AX.

HERE are you going with that fine ax my boy?"
"Going out chopping." "You have got your
ax in pretty nice shape?" "Yes, I have polish-
ed the handle until it is as smooth as glass. On
one side of the blade you see I have an exquisite oil
painting. The end of the handle, as you see, is ex-

quisitely carved, and all together, I flatter myself I have a very highly finished ax."

"Then I suppose you have ground it so that it has a fine cutting edge?"

"N—no—I didn't have time to sharpen it." "But how do you expect to cut wood with it, if you haven't sharpened it?" "Why, I expect it will wear itself sharp." "So it may, but it will wear you out at the same time. Why on earth didn't you prepare your ax for the use you intended to make of it instead of putting in so much time polishing and ornamenting it?"

"Well, if you must know, I prepared my ax for its work on the same plan that I prepared myself for my work in life."

"I devoted six years of my life to the study of branches that would polish and refine, and when I graduated I could call myself an educated idiot in six different languages, but I couldn't write legibly, couldn't draw up a receipt in proper form, and didn't know the first principle of book-keeping."

"I expect to get some practical ideas pounded into me by the hard knocks of experience, but I don't know but I made a mistake in not grinding my talents in a practical school where, when I graduated I would be qualified for the actual work of life. As it is, I am a polished, decorated, edgeless ax; but one consolation is I've got lots of company, for the world is full of us."

Not bad luck, but bad judgment; not ill conditions, but ill thinking make life a failure.

HAS IT.

HAS the liquor traffic ever built a church, asylum, or endowed a college?

Has it ever set a standard of business character which is recognized in banks and counting-rooms?

Has it ever made a wife happier than she would be with a sober husband?

Has it ever led a youth up into noble manhood?

Has it ever paid its own way as a revenue returner?

Has it ever lessened crimes and criminals?

No, no! Then has it not been weighed and found wanting, and condemned as a malfactor?

Dare you sustain such an agency, and claim to be a good citizen?

BE TRUE.

O FRIEND, or foe, or lover,
        Be true!
Though none thy faith discover,
        Be true!
Though men should mock thee for thy pains
And wreck thy work and wrest thy gains,
        Be true, be true!

'Mid youth's seducing pleasures
        Be true!
'Mid manhood's golden treasures
        Be true!

When age is dulling every sense,
And tempting to indifference,
  Be true, be true!

When all is fair around thee,
  Be true!
When health and hope have crowned thee,
  Be true!
When quick the pulse and full the life,
And strength rejoices in the strife,
  Be true, be true!

When doubt and dread o'ertake thee,
  Be true!
Though all the world forsake thee,
  Be true!
Should sickness smite thee in thy bed,
Or speed thy dearest to the dead,
  Be true, be true!

When night is blackest o'er thee,
  Be true!
When yawns the grave before thee,
  Be true!
When God gleams downward from the height,
And opens out the infinite,
  Be true, be true!

     —JOHN HALL INGHAM.

One good act done to-day is worth a thousand in contemplation for some future time.

THE DEVIL'S FOUR SERVANTS.

THE Devil has a great many servants. They are all busy and in all places. Some are so vile looking that one instinctively turns from them in disgust; but some are so sociable, insinuating and plausible, that they almost deceive at times the very elect. Among this latter class are to be found the Devil's four chief servants. Here are their names:

"There's no Danger!"

"Only this Once."

"Everybody Does So."

"By and By."

All four are cheats and liars. They mean to deceive you and cheat you out of Heaven, and they will do it if you will listen to them.

FEAR.

FEAR hath torment," saith the apostle. Some christians are paralyzed for life by the mono-mania of fear. They fear to pray in public. They fear to be singular for right. They are afraid to give to the Lord's cause lest they come to want. They fear to rebuke a brother for his fault. They fear to confess Christ before men. They are afraid to leave the old church or party that has left the truth. They are afraid to espouse a good cause where it is not popular. They fear shadows and fail to secure the substance. They are like the invalid afflicted with the delusion that he was made of brittle clay, and if struck, would snap into fragments. He was cured by a friend deliberately up-setting him from his carriage, when he arose from the ground sound in mind as well as body. The cure for a foolish fear is faith and a forced obedience of duty. Just as there is one cure for selfishness—self-sacrifice; as there is one cure for spiritual laziness—work, there is one cure for timidity, and that is to plunge into a dis-agreeable duty before the ague shiver has time to come on. "Whatsoever thy hand findeth to do, do it with thy might."

WHAT I LOVE.

I LOVE the Lord with all my heart ;
　　I love to do his will ;
I love the gentle voice which says,
　　In trouble, "Peace be still."

I love to walk as Jesus walked,
　　Along the narrow way ;
I love to know his Spirit guides
　　My footsteps day by day.

I love to follow where he leads ;
　　I love the truth, the light ;
I love to bring His kingdom nigh ;
　　I love for God to fight.

287

I love to hear the sinner's cry—
   "Oh Lord, my sins forgive !"
I love to hear them testify,
   When pardon they receive.

My life is love; I'll tell you why,
   Perhaps you think it strange,
But God is love, He dwells within,
   'Twas He who wrought the change.

For once I loved the world and sin ;
   I love them now no more ;
My love is changed to higher things,
   My Saviour I adore.

Oh, ye who live for self and ease,
   There's something nobler far ;
Come, cast your all at Jesus' feet,
   He'll help you love the war.

He'll give you grace just as you need ;
   He'll help you all the way ;
And victory's sure if only you
   Let perfect love have sway.

            —LUCY M. DEWS.

GOOD resolutions are often like loosely tied cords —on the first strain of temptation they slip. They should be tied in a hard knot of prayer. And they should be kept tight; tight and firm by constant stretching Godward. If they slip, or break, tie them again.

LIFE.

IF we have divine life within us we can easily recover from all wounds the world can give us. Wear the skin from your hand and it grows on again, but wear a hole in your glove and it needs a patch to cover it. When christians are killed by persecution it is not of ill-treatment they die, but from lack of vitality. Christ within us readily repairs all the damage Satan can do us from without. Winter strips the trees of their beauty; but if they are full of life, spring covers them with leaves and blossoms. We may, by false accusation, be robbed of reputation and of friends for a season; but if Christ's throne is mantained in our hearts, his royal courtiers will rally around it again. It does not promise us exemption from trials, but victory over trials.

If the heart is weak all the motions are slow. When the pulse of the athlete fails, it does not require a blow to prostrate him, but he falls of his own weight.

One who gets inward vigor does not need to be urged by others. A little boy, full of life, confined for the first time in the schoolroom, when asked by the teacher why he whistled, said, "It whistled itself." Have the mind of Christ and you will do the work of Christ. When the works of a clock are in order you are not obliged every few minutes to put the hands in the right place. Take more pains to have the heart right with God, and you will have less trouble in keeping the life right. "Out of the abundance of the heart the mouth speaketh."

Hate vain thoughts and you will not utter vain words. Have tender love for your brethren and you will not hold them up to ridicule. Keep alive to God and you will not lay the foundation for repentance from dead works.

WHAT AN UNHEALTHY BOOK WILL DO.

NOW, I ask why will women buy these books? I will not say that they are doing it intentionally; most likely it is due to thoughtlessness. But in nothing can thoughtlessness work more injury than in the selection of books. Our whole natures are moulded by what we read. Let a woman read books of an unhealthy character, and she is bound to be influenced by them. No person living ever escaped the memory of a bad book. I know a woman who in girlhood read a novel in which sin was the predominant characteristic. Since then she has read hundreds of books by the masters of literature, and filled her mind with their best and most elevating thoughts.

But has the impression made by that one book, read when she was a girl, ever been effaced? I quote her own words to me: "Although I have lived nearly sixty years since I read that book, and have associated continually through all that subsequent period with the purest minds in literature, I have never been able to forget that book. Day after day it comes back to me, and I would give to-day half of my fortune if the impression left by that story could be removed from my mind." And in countless hearts will this statement find a responsive echo. The mind will oft times throw off the impression made by an indecent picture, for in art we see vice only in outline; but in a book where vice is told us in words—our own instrument of expression—the impression is lasting, and its influences will be felt through generations.

THE PRESENT NEED.

THE crying need of the time is not money, not prayer, not preaching, not evangelistic effort; it is men, men and women, saturated with the spirit of Christ; not a few, or even a great many, to go out as missionaries and evangelists, but men and women by the tens of thousands, by the million, *to be Christians*, to open heart and life to the Spirit's grace; enough of them to create an atmosphere absorbing, and retaining, and diffusing the light and heat streaming from the Sun of Righteousness, to carry in every direction by innumerable channels of irrigation the Water of Life, to take up and distribute the vast unused Niagara force, the mighty tidal energy which would accomplish all the church's work before this generation passed away.

—J. Munro Gibson.

PRESS ON!

PRESS on ! surmount the rocky steeps,
    Climb boldly o'er the torrent's arch :
He fails alone who feebly creeps,
    He wins who dares the hero's march.
Be thou a hero ! let thy might
    Tramp on eternal snows its way,
And, through the ebon walls of night,
    Hew down a passage unto day.

Press on ! if once and twice thy feet
    Slip back and stumble, harder try ;
From him who never dreads to meet
    Danger and death, they'er sure to fly.
To coward's ranks the bullet speeds,
    While on their breast who never quail,
Gleams guardian of chivalric deeds,
    Bright courage, like a coat of mail.

Press on ! if fortune play thee false
    To-day, to-morrow she'll be true ;
Whom now she sinks, she now exalts,—
    Taking old gifts and granting new,
The wisdom of the present hour
    Makes up for follies past and gone :
To weakness strength succeeds, and power
    From frailty springs—Press on ! press on !

Therefore, press on ! and reach the goal,
    And gain the prize and wear the crown :
Faint not ! for to the steadfast soul
    Come wealth, and honor, and renown.
To thine own self be true, and keep
    Thy mind from sloth, thy heart from soil ;
Press on ! and thou shalt surely reap
    A heavenly harvest for thy toil.

"GRANDMA I MEAN TO THREAD YOUR NEEDLES EVER SO NICELY TO-DAY."

TIRESOME.

I HATE threading needles," said Millicent to herself as she undressed one night, "and yet grandma is always wanting me to do it! I believe she uses all these threads on purpose. I wish there were some one else beside me to do things. Its Milly here and Milly there, all day long."

The little grumbling girl pulled off her dress with vexed fingers, and a button went flying under the chest of drawers; and then, instead of looking for it, she turned to the table and began to brush her hair.

Then her eyes fell on the text-book, with her text for the day, and she started when she thought how little she had remembered it: "Whatsoever ye do, do it heartily, as unto the Lord!"

"Threading needles?" she questioned, blushing as she remembered how far from heartily she had performed that little task that dull afternoon.

" 'As to the Lord!' I never thought of that!" she exclaimed. "How could I be so horrid? and grandma, too! Why, I ought to have done it out of love to her, to say nothing of Jesus!"

She hid her face with her hands. Millicent did love Jesus, but, somehow, it was so much easier to please herself.

The next day the little girl stole up to the patient, aged one, who had so few pleasures, and, in a little gentle voice, said· . "Grandma, I mean to thread your needles ever so nicely to-day."

THANKFULNESS.

FOR all that God in mercy sends;
　　For health and parents, home and friends,
　　For comfort in the time of need,
For every kindly word and deed,
For happy thoughts and holy talk,
For guidance in our daily walk,
　　For everything give thanks!

For beauty in this world of ours,
For verdant grass and lovely flowers,
For songs of birds, and hum of bees,
For the refreshing summer breeze,
For hill and plain, for streams and wood,
For the great ocean's mighty flood,
　　In everything give thanks!

For the sweet sleep which comes with night,
For the returning morning's light,
For the bright sun that shines on high,
For the stars glittering in the sky,
For these, and everything we see,
O Lord, our hearts we lift to Thee,
　　For everything give thanks!
　　　　　　　　—ELLEN ISABELL TUPPER.

~~~~~~~~~~

THE truest test of civilization is not the census, nor
the size of the cities, nor the crops; no, but the
kind of men the country turns out.

HUMILITY—WHAT IS IT.

THE first step in religion is humility; the second step in religion is humility; the third step in religion is humility. . How can a man repent without humility? How càn a person be obedient to Christ without humility? The humble penitent in perseverance is sure to find the mercy of Jesus. Humility, O thou gem of pure christianity! Without it our religion is headstrong, fierce, uncontrollable, and vain. All our church and personal difficulties arise in the absence of humility.

~~~~~~~~~~

HOW TO DO THE MOST GOOD.

THE TACT OF TRUE AND CHRISTIAN LOVE IN SERVICE.

LOVE not only wants to serve, but love will find a way of serving. Love is not satisfied until it has persevered and planned and changed its ways of working indefinitely, to secure success in its purpose of helping the loved one. It may be that one can better be helped by indirect suggestions than by plain spoken counsel. Finding this to be so, the loving one will avoid directness of speech in the line of sound advice, and will work with tact and caution and considerateness, so as to help the other without disturbing him. It may be, again, that the positive and earnest advocacy of a truth in discussion between two friends tends to set all the firmer against it the one who would like to learn the merits of that question, but who can not be taught in that way. In such a case the positive and earnest man will curb himself in the expression of his convictions to the friend whom he loves, lest he so jar upon him as to prevent his gaining the good of a discussion which is to be desired from it. It is not enough to say that both parties ought to study each others ways, and come to a common standard of fairness—he who truly loves will be glad to go over to the other's standpoint of thought and feeling in order to help him, instead of claiming the right of meeting halfway. Love is more than willing to do all that is needed on both sides in a friendship, and true love will find a way of doing it; for it is a necessity of love to be the mother of invention in the proof and expression of its all-prevailing potency.

IT is a great mercy to enjoy the gospel of peace, but a greater joy to enjoy the peace of the gospel.

Did you ever feel the joy of winning a soul for Christ? I tell you there is no joy out of heaven which excels it—the grasp of the hand of one who says, "By your means I was turned from darkness."

—C. H. Spurgeon.

The lower down a christian gets the higher up he looks.

UNSATISFIED.

WE long for things beyond our reach,
    And waste in sighs and tears
The golden hours fraught with good
    While listning to our fears.

We sigh for fame, position, wealth,
    For comfort, and for ease,
For houses fine adorned with art,
    With everything to please.

We long for gold for daily use,
    Enough to satisfy
Real or imagined wants of ours,
    As day by day goes by.

We fail to see the sunny lights
    Which glint across our way,
We see not all the golden rays,
    Which brighten every day.

We fail to gather of life's sweets
    Because of life's unrest ;
Forget, we see but dimly now,
    God's ways are always best.

In every path there's something bright,
    Some joy in every cross ;
And what poor mortal's count as gain
    Is often greatest loss.

                —MARY B. CARTER.

WORDS OF COUNSEL TO YOUNG CONVERTS.

DON'T think you have lost all your religion because you find you have made a mistake in something, or conclude that God is dead because the sky turns black sometimes.

God is in the storm as much as he is in the sunshine. Make up your mind that you are going to believe in God always, no matter what happens. No sensible man will tear up his railroad ticket because the train runs through a tunnel.

Determine to be a happy christian whether you have a cent in your pocket or not. With God's grace it won't take much money to make you rich.

Don't be a wobbling christian. Keep your eye on Christ and you won't have a bit of trouble in keeping even in your experience. Adopt a platform that will mean loyalty to God always and stand on it.

Get in the habit of feeling what concerns you. Keep in the closest communion with Him by asking and trusting Him constantly to manage you.

Never make a plan and leave God out. Make Him first in all your undertakings. If you make a mistake, instead of sitting down to cry and fret about it, tell God all about it, and ask him to overlook it for good.

Maintain habits of secret prayer, and pray and praise while you work, or rest, or think. Ask God to help you to love people you don't like.

KEEP STEADILY ON.

SATAN never surrenders. We may think he is defeated. The sound of battle may die away, and all may seem calm and peaceful, but the enemy still lives. When we do not hear the lion's roar it is time to guard against the serpent's wiles. In the high day of our prosperity he may be planning some surprise which shall result in our overthrow. Our only security is constant vigilance, constant fidelity, constant activity, constant trust. We must watch and pray, and fight and pray, and if we do this we have the help of Him who said: "I will never leave thee nor forsake thee."

Above all, let us not be diverted from our work. Beware of Satan's feints and stratagems. Keep at what the Lord has given you to do. Never leave the Lord's work to chase the Devil's rabbits. Let them run. It is safer than to undertake to follow them. Do not stone the Devil's dogs, let them bark; keep in the middle of the road and march boldly on. Many things which may seem to demand our instant attention are possibly only the tricks and devices of the great deceiver, who chuckles as he turns us from our proper work, and proceeds to accomplish his own evil purposes. If you work the work of God, men will hate you. If you fail, men will despise you. If you succeed, they will envy you. If you prosper, they will try to supplant you. Be sober ; be vigilant ; keep a firm hand, and keep steadily on. The dust will clear by and by. Lies will die, liars will find their level, and the man who keeps steadily on will reach the goal at last.

AS YOU GO THROUGH LIFE.

DON'T look for flaws as you go through life ;
  And even when you find them,
It is wise and kind to be somewhat blind,
  And look for the virtue behind them ;
For the cloudiest night has a hint of light
  Somewhere in its shadowy hiding ;
It is better far to hunt for a star,
  Than the spots on the sun abiding.

The current of life runs ever away
  To the bosom of God's great ocean.
Don't waste your force 'gainst the river's course
  And think to alter its motion.
Don't waste a curse on the universe—
  Remember, it lived before you.
Don't butt at the storm with your puny form—
  But bend and let it go o'er you.

The world will never adjust itself
  To suit your whims to the letter.
Some things must go wrong your whole life long,
  And the sooner you know it the better.
It is folly to fight with the infinite,
  And go under at last in the wrestle.
The wiser man shapes himself in God's plan
  As the water shapes into a vessel.

—ELLA WHEELER WILCOX.

A CHANGE FOR ALL TO WORK.

IT does not require a giant to sow a seed, nor a steam shovel or trip-hammer to bury it in the ground. A little child can drop corn as well as Goliath, and it only needs to be covered lightly and gently patted down, and then the sunshine and the rain does the rest.

Just so the good seed of God does not need giants, orators or great men to sow it. A word may be spoken by a little child; a tract may be dropped by the wayside, or enclosed and sent through the mail; a letter may be written, and papers may be distributed by the feeblest, and so in a multitude of ways, humble, insignificant and unknown persons may do work, the importance of which none but the Lord can measure.

A few pennies for scriptures or tracts is all the capital or stock in trade required to begin, and when these are carefully distributed, with prayer for a blessing, then a new supply can be obtained, and the work can be further extended. Here is something for everyone to do, and when once done only the Lord can tell how vast and how blessed the results may be. How many are there who stand ready to undertake such work as this? How many who are saying, "Lord, what wilt thou have me to do?" and yet neglecting work which is clearly within their reach, within their means, within their power, and which can do no hurt, and may do great good?

A BELIEF IN GOD.

I WILL frankly tell you that my experience in the prolonged scientific investigations convince me that a belief in God—a God that is behind and within the chaos of vanishing points of human knowledge—adds a wonderful stimulus to the man who attempts to penetrate into the regions of the unknown. Of myself, I may say that I never take the preparations for penetrating into some small province of nature hitherto undiscovered, without breathing a prayer to the Being who hides his secrets only to allure me graciously on to the unfolding of them.

—PROF. AGASSIE.

THE SUN AND THE WIND.

THE Sun and the Wind laid a wager one day
Which would take from a man his cloak away.
"I've only to blow right strong," said the Wind,
"And his cloak will go flying far behind."

"That trick will not work at all," said the Sun ;
"I know that the wager by me will be won.
But do your own way, you blust'ring fellow,
Then I will shine out so warm and yellow,
I'm sure I will have the best of the joke,
For quickly the man will drop his old cloak."

The man jogged along, just humming a song,
His cloak fast buttoned to keep him warm,
When, sudden, the Wind blew loud and strong :
" Whe-ugh ! Hello ! why, here is a storm !"
Then closer around him his cloak was drawn—
Still closer and closer ! With head bent down
He galloped off fast for the nearest town.

Then the Sun shone out with its golden smiles ;
And though it's away up—millions of miles—
Yet it heard the traveler laugh and say :
" Good horse, don't hurry the rest of the way !

" We'll take it more easy this lovely day ;
But first let me put this hot cloak away."
And the cloak came off ! And the rest of the ride
It hung and swung at the horse's side.

And the Wind hushed down, ashamed to blow,
But the Sun shone on in a happy glow
A-singing a song that seemed to say :
"In a game where it takes the two to play,
Sunshine gets the better of Wind any day !"

MORAL.

So, boys, and girls too, when you find yourself rusty,
And fretty and fussy and cross-grained and gusty,
Just remember the tale of the Wind and the Sun,
The man and the cloak, and the way it was done !

Talk little of your own grievances, or of other's mis-
doings.

THE GENIUS OF APPRECIATION.

THERE are men and women who have a genius for drawing the very best out of all their associates.

A sensitive nature feels unconsciously the personal atmosphere of another, and a cynic or a satirist shuts up such a nature as completely as the cold or the night closes a sensitive flower. In the presence of a cynic or satirist, a sensitive person is dumb and helpless. In a genial and appreciative atmosphere, however, such a nature opens as a closed flower at the touch of the sun.

There can be no happier function in life than to so act upon people that they think their best, as there can be nothing more unfortunate than to silence, paralyze, and discourage others.

This faculty of evoking the best in another is, in its way, as rare a kind of genius as the genius of expression. It has happened more than once in the history of art, that a turbulent, eager, and dumb spirit, struggling with itself, has suddenly become clarified and found expression in the hope, faith, and love of these appreciative natures; and so appreciation has become the mother of creation.

To possess this quality of appreciation, one must have a certain purity and elevation of nature. It is impossible to awaken the ideal in others unless we first possess it in ourselves; impossible to make others believe in the best and highest things, unless we ourselves believe in those things. Unconscious influence is, after all, the greatest and most subtle form of expression.

To inspire others when we are not conscious of it, by the mere expression of ourselves, has an element of the divine in it. It is the overflow of a high nature, which, by its mere contact with lesser natures, inspires, builds, and enlarges.

Nothing was more beautiful in Mr. Emerson's character than the respect which he paid to every human being. It seemed as if he always expected to receive from every one he met some new message of life, something which should lay him under perpetual obligation. He treated everyone not only with courtesy, but with the profound respect which one would accord to the message of a king. It was very inspiring to others, this sort of attention ; but it was preeminently beautiful in the man himself, and was the lasting evidence of the nobility of his soul.

AY well is good, but *do well* is better ;
  Do well seems spirit, *say well* the letter.
  Say well is Godly, and helpeth to please,
- But *do well* lives Godly, and gives the world ease.
Say well to silence sometimes is bound,
But *do well* is free on every ground.
Say well has friends, some here, some there,
But *do well* is welcome everywhere.
But *say well* to many God's word cleaves,
But for lack of *do well* it often leaves.
If *say well* and *do well* were bound in one frame,
Then all were done, all were won, and gotten were
       gain.

DANGER SIGNALS.

ONE evening not long since as I was coming home from town on a different street, I noticed men had been digging deep trenches for sewer-pipes, and as the work was yet incomplete, they had put up danger signals everywhere it seemed people would have any trouble in regard to them.

Of course it is the custom to put up these signals of danger wherever a place is known to be unsafe, and I had seen a great many of them in my life, but they never impressed me like this before. I thought if every place in the United States that was known to be unsafe, should have a danger signal, it would save not only boys and young men, but whole families.

Every one knows the saloon is unsafe, they know the billiard, and card-table, and gambling house is unsafe; but because the workmen have failed to put up the danger signals, many have fallen in, and are so bruised it is impossible for them to rise without help.

Dear reader will you not help to hold the light that shall reveal the deep trenches of sin ere some of your loved ones are lost?

MOTHER'S GOOD-BYE.

SIT down by the side of your mother, my boy,
　　You have only a moment, I know,
　　But you will stay till I give my parting advice,
　　　'Tis all I have to bestow.
You leave us to seek for employment, my boy,
　　By the world you have yet to be tried ;
But in all the temptations and struggles you meet,
　　May your heart in your Savior confide.

Hold fast to the right, hold fast to the right,
　　Wherever your footsteps may roam ;
Oh, forsake not the way of salvation, my boy,
　　That you learned from your mother at home.

You'll find in your satchel a Bible, my boy,
　　'Tis a book of all others the best ;
It will teach you to live, it will help you to die,
　　And lead to the gates of the blest.
I gave you to God, in your cradle, my boy,
　　I have taught you the best that I knew ;
As long as his mercy permits me to live,
　　I shall never cease praying for you.

Your father is coming to bid you good-bye ;
　　Oh, how lonely and sad we shall be !
But when far from the scenes of your childhood and
　　　youth,
　　You'll think of your father and me.
I want you to feel ev'ry word I have said,
　　For it came from the depths of my love ;
And, my boy, if we never behold you on earth,
　　Will you promise to meet us above ?"

"IF IT DEPENDS ON YOU."

A HASTY glance and our eyes caught these words; and they went direct to the heart. For days the startling contingency has sounded in every voice, and gleamed or glared from every page.

We have heard a father talking to his children; a mother praying for her darlings; a wife pleading for an unsaved husband; a pastor for his flock; and again for the sinful and erring of his parish, and we have said: "If it depends on these, all is well."

We have heard a father's careless and profane words, accompanied with a sneer at Christ and His love, and all these in the presence of his son; a mother's giddy and foolish talk of society and pleasure; a husband's bitter fling of words at the gentle and prayerful wife; a pastor's neglect of the sheep of the great Shepherd, and disregard of the perishing and dying, and we have said: Alas! If it depends on these, how sad is the fate of souls.

We have seen the rumseller and the pastor stand side by side at the ballot-box and each go his way. Meeting a noble youth we could but say: If it depends on that ballot, whether you are sober or drunken, how sad and uncertain must be your fate.

Men love money, and lust for power, and plot for unholy gain; and if it depends on such as these where will the State and nation be a hundred years from now?

MY boy, do you realize that each year the grave is nearer you than ever before—that unless you are active, the season of life will close before even half of your self-allotted contract will have been performed, unless, like too many people, you have no aim, no hope, no ambition beyond picking your teeth after dinner? Half of the world, yes, more than half, go to the reception room of eternity without any object in life—as driftwood floats down the stream, guided by the current, and lodging against the first obstruction. And what is driftwood, my boy? Once in a while a good stick of timber is found therein but it is generally more work to haul it out, clean off the sand and mud, than it is worth; and more time and tools are spoiled in making it into what you wish than the stick will ever bring, even in an active market.

Have a purpose, my boy. Live for something. Make up your mind what you will be, and come to the mark, or die in the attempt. This is a land where there is no stint to ambition. All have an equal chance. Blood tells, pluck wins, honor and integrity well directed will scale the highest rock, and bear a heavy load to its top. Do not start off in life without knowing where you are going. Load for the game you are hunting. It is as easy to be a man, as to be a mouse. It is as easy to have friends as enemies—it is easier to have them both than to go through life like a tar bucket under a wagon, bumping over stumps, or swinging right and left, without a will of your own. Everyone can be something. There is enough to do. There are forests to fell, rivers to explore, cities to build, railroads to construct, inventions yet to be studied out, ideas to advance, men to convert, countries to conquer, women to love, offices to be filled, wealth and position to acquire, a name to win, a Heaven to reach. Yes, my boy, there is lots of work to do, and you and I must do our share."

DON'T GIVE IN.

BOYS, when troubles crowd upon you
   (You'll find plenty in this life),
And when fortune seems to flout you,
   And you're weary with the strife ;
Then's the time to show your metal ;
   Keep your heads up ; don't give in ;
Face the trouble, grasp the nettle,
   And determine you will win.

What's the good of turning craven ?
   That will never gain the fight,
That will bring you to no haven
   Of success and calm delight.
No, boys, no ! Be up and doing,
   Put your shoulder to the task !
Fortune's shy, and needs pursuing
   If within her smile you'd bask.

          —SOMERVILLE GIBNEY.

GOD'S WORD.

VERY sincere laborer in God's vineyard has a sense of responsibility in gathering the spiritual harvest. Jesus, when upon earth, never relieved his true followers of their burden. He said : "Go work to-day in my vineyard." If the early christians had disregarded this command, holding that the salvation of the world was not a human task, but was exclusively a divine work, the kingdom of Christ would have been a failure. God's plan for the recovery of the world through regenerated souls would have been set aside through men's obduracy and disobedience.

But there may come an hour in the believer's history when he can say : "After all, this is God's work, not mine ; " "I have followed the Lord my God ; " " Now, therefore, give me this mountain." ' When the conditions have been all fulfilled on the human side, as they were in the case of believing Caleb, then the soul may rest in the divine promise, in the blessed assurance that God will bring results to pass in his own time and way.

~~~~~~~~

"In all thy gettings get understanding.
If you would kill a slander, let it alone.
No man repents of having done his duty.
Threatening a bad habit does not kill it.
Write benefits on marble, injuries on sand.
The more a man swears, the easier he is whipped.
Better break thy word than do worse in keeping it.'"

AGAINST LICENSE, HIGH OR LOW.

WE agitate the question against license high or low,
And oppose the liquor traffic, the Nation's direst foe;
With printing press and telegraph as agencies for
    Right,
The moral people of this land will rally for the fight.

We'll educate the people as the numbers multiply,
'Till a vote for any party with a license, low or high,
Will be against the Master, his betrayal as of old,
Though the thirty silver pieces may increase a hundred
    fold.

We'll legislate the traffic from the list of lawful trade,
When the pulpit with the platform will join the new cru-
    sade,
When a million loyal voters, on whom we can rely,
Shall stamp with infamy and shame the license, low or
    high.

We'll exterminate intemperance when we tear the breweries
    down,
And every liquor seller is driven from the town,
When beneath our unfurled banner and the vaulted starry
    sky,
No man can slay his neighbor with a license low or high.
—GEORGE G. ANNABLE.

~~~~~~~~~~

"Home is one thing sweet on earth. But homes are
built, not of stones, but of hearts."

312

CHARACTER IS CAPITAL.

THE man who is known to be honest, and of sound judgment, commands the confidence and resources of others. While men will not trust a rogue out of their sight, they confide in the integrity of an honest, upright man. He may be in debt ; he may have need to borrow ; he may be dependent on the help and good will of others ; but so long as he will tell the truth, and honestly try to fulfill his engagements, his character counts for thousands, and is worth to him more than silver or gold.

A good name is rather to be chosen than great riches; and a man who does business year after year prudently, honestly, and uprightly, will not often lack for helpers in time of need or straits. But the man who, for some present advantage condescends to cheating, falsehood and rascality, will soon find that for a temporary gain he has suffered an irreparable loss. His character gone, society watches him as it does a thief, and long years may elapse before he can recover from the effects of his own suicidal act.

Young man, old man, be honest, faithful and true, and if you have no other wealth, let your character be your own capital.

While a word is yet unspoken you are master of it; when once it is spoken it is master of you.

A BRAVE BOY.

YOU may come now, Harry! It's seven o'clock, and snowing fast," called his mother from the foot of the stairs.

"Yes, mother, why didn't you call me before? There'll be the paths to sweep before school, and I like to do them before breakfast."

"I thought you were tired, dear, and needed a morning nap."

"Please do not humor me that way, mother. You know I am the one to take care of you."

It did not take Harry long to dress that morning, although he did not slight his simple toilet; neither did he forget to kneel down and ask God's help upon the beginning of the new day; but he was out of bed with a bound, and his fingers flew fast.

"No drones in this hive, are there, mamma?" he said, running down stairs and giving his mother a resounding kiss. "Shall I have time to do anything before breakfast?"

"No, dear; the bell is just going to ring."

"Excuse me, please, mother this morning," Harry said, as he finished before the rest. "I want everything easy for you before I go to school."

A happy smile was her only answer, but she said as the door closed behind him:

"Dear boy! I believe that is the motto of his life— I want to make things easy for mother. He's never too tired or busy to help me. He's solid comfort."

"He's solid gold, a boy worth having," said uncle Ned. "I wish there were more of them."

Harry found the broom and began sweeping the snow away on either side of the path with a will. Suddenly looking up, he saw a lady watching him across the way.

"Good morning, Mrs. Martin," he said, raising his cap. "Isn't this a royal morning for work?"

"I should think so, my dear," she replied. "You seem to make easy work of everything. How does it happen?"

"Oh, I don't know, ma'am. Boys ought to be ready for anything, I think. Work comes easy to me. I'm young and strong, you know."

"So is Jamie; but he makes a fuss over everything he does. I wish he could catch some of your spirit. You'll make your mark in the world, if you keep on as you've begun, Harry."

"And I mean to, Mrs. Martin, if God spares my life. I must make things easy for mother, you know."

Mrs. Martin sighed. "I wish Jamie felt so," she said.

"Perhaps he doesn't feel the need of doing, because you're rich, Mrs. Martin. We're poor, you know; but we sha'n't always be so." And Harry's broom flew faster and faster over the frozen ground.

"Excuse me if I talk and work too," he said. "Mother needs me in the house before school. I have to be a girl and boy, too, you see."

"Don't you find that pretty hard my child?"

"Oh, no! I don't like wiping dishes as well as sweeping snow, to be sure; but that's no matter. I never stop to think what I like; it's what's got to be done to save mother."

"Bless you, my boy! Don't you ever think of yourself?"

"Oh, yes, indeed; I'm a selfish cub, anyway; but I'm trying to do better every day, and it's easier, since I ask God to help me before I begin."

"Are you a Christian, Harry?"

"Oh, yes'm! I've belonged to the army of the Lord just a year, and it's been the happiest year of my life. Fighting Satan and sin is great fun when a boy sets about it. I don't mean he shall conquer, Mrs. Martin. I like to knock him a blow whenever I can. Good morning."

Mrs. Martin stood looking after the brave, bright boy, who had already begun to be a blessing to the world, until he disappeared from sight.

"These are the boys who are wanted," she said, "these are the boys who are wanted."

Yes, yes, my dear readers, there are a great many such boys in the world. They are not wanted merely as snow sweepers, but the merchant and the banker want them in their counting houses.

Disregard or excuse your small fault, and you commit a greater one.

The man who works for God gets his pay in advance.

OUR DAILY BREAD.

GIVE us our daily bread, we say;
And look no farther than to-day;
    And be to-morrow gray or gold,
    Or plenty, or pinched with cold:
Thine be to-morrow as to-day!

Even as the small bird shall receive
The food its mother gives, nor grieve
    Lest that to-morrow fail; so we
    Lifting our lips and hearts to Thee
Trust Thee for all the days we live.

Keep us within Thy heart that's wide,
Thy love our nest in which we hide;
    Thy thought the wing to fold us in
    All night till the new day begin—
The day for which Thou wilt provide.

—KATHARINE TYNAN.

IN ME YE SHALL HAVE PEACE.

IN me, in me." O, souls for whom Christ died,
    Why will ye restless roam unsatisfied,
    O'er barren wastes and mountains dark and wide?

All day, behold the blessed shepherd stand
In pastures green, and stretch his pierced hand,
Unto the sheep he bought, in every land.

"Ye will not come!" the waters flow so still,
Ye are so thirsty and might drink your fill—
And still he sayeth—"whosoever will."

317

What is your life? Complaints that never cease!
Sad, weary moanings for far distant peace!
'And deeper darkness as the years increase.

Fears in the way!—and sometimes well ye know,
The golden bowl shall break, and ye must go
Out into utter gloom, from all below.

Then shall the soul return to him who gave—
Too late! Too late! the sweet Christ who can save
And welcome now—sits Judge beyond the grave.

O foolish virgins—buy fresh oil and wait
With girded garments at the Bridegroom's gate.
Soon will he come!—a king in royal state.

If thou wilt love him, in his happy train
Shalt thou pass in and part no more again
From those bright mansions where there is no pain.

"In me, in me," hear how the blessed word,
Flee as unto its nest the swift winged bird—
Thine shall be the shelter by no fear e'er stirred.

Hungry, thou shalt be fed, and weary rest
Upon his bosom, naked thou shalt be drest
In his own righteousness—wilt thou be blest.

—Mrs. L. F. Baker.

God heeds not so much what we say, as what we are
and what we do. Because if we are true and good, and
do well we shall doubtless speak right.

THE NEXT ONE IS MINE.

 FEW years ago a fire broke out in a little village, destroying several business places, and a large number of dwellings.

Brave men fought the flames even at the peril of their lives, but many were homeless before the cruel flames were extinguished.

During the fire a certain man was noticed to take a sudden interest in preventing the spread of it, and began directing all his energies to the saving of an old house that no one else seemed to care to save when so many better ones were in danger.

How hard he worked, carrying wet carpets, blankets, and water, doing everything he could to prevent it from burning, and begged others to help save it. He was told to let it alone, it could not be saved, but he told them it must be saved.

At last one called out in a reproving voice to know why he was so foolish!

The answer came in a tone never to be forgotten by those who heard it.

"*The next one is mine.*"

Oh, I thought, how interested people get when such things come so near home!

How unconcerned they are when some mother's heart is crushed over the son who comes reeling home! How they laugh when one boy cheats another, or one man knocks another down; when somebody's daughter has fallen, or someone who has held a high position suddenly meets with reverses!

How is it when it comes home?

How little some seem to care for the evils of the saloon in their midst so long as their son has not yet been drawn in, or the house of ill-fame, so long as their daughter has not been enticed.

Oh that men would wake up to their responsibility of the evils in their midst, and help prevent the spread of it before they have to exclaim in anguish, *"the next one is mine."*

DO SOMETHING.

YOU cannot set the world right, or the times, but you can do something for the truth, and all you can do will certainly tell if the work is for the Master, who gives you your share, and so the burden of responsibility is lifted off. This assurance makes peace, satisfaction, and repose possible even in the partial work done upon the earth. Go to a man who is carving a stone for a building; ask him where is that stone going, to what part of the temple, and how he is going to get it in its place; and what does he do? He points you to the builder's plans. So, when men shall ask where and how is your little achievement going into God's great plan, point them to the Master, who keeps the plans, and then go on doing your little service as faithfully as if the whole temple were yours to build.

—PHILIP BROOKS.

A ROYAL SERVICE.

AMONG the Master's callings of high honor,
    One oftentimes we miss,
Because our hearts in their impatient yearning,
    Fail to perceive its bliss ;
Fail to perceive the grandeur of its service,
    The deep, sweet joy it brings,
And deem some other easier or nobler,
    With richer harvestings.

And so we may not choose, but Christ appoints us
    The work of sitting still,
And saith, "My child, in quietness and patience
    This service now fulfill.
Since all these hours of weariness and waiting
    Are precious unto me,
Each one must needs be freighted with some blessing ;
    Love's perfect choice for thee.

"Then think not thou art kept within the shadow
    Of long, inactive years,
Without some purpose infinitely glorious,
    Some harvest, sown in tears."
And so there comes a glory and a gladness
    Into the weary days,
And in our hearts there shines a solemn radiance,
    Inwrought with quiet praise.

We learn that we are given this sweet service,
    Because the Master sees
That thus his delegates must oft be fitted
    For higher embassies.

We praise him for these lonely hours of waiting,
    And trusting look above,
Till all the hush and silence of their service
    Grows luminous with love.

We muse upon that ministry at Nazareth,
    Until it seems to be
A fellowship most sweet, a royal honor,
    To wait, O Christ ! with thee.
And even as we stand within the shadow
    Of these long years of thine,
Our waiting days grow better, holier, grander,
    Their service more sublime ;

Until at last we hear thy dear voice saying,
    "Child, I have need of thee
To fill this vacant place of trust and honor,
    To do this work for me."
And then, as fellow-workers with the Master,
    We shall arise and go
Forth to the harvest fields of earth, may be,
    The reaper's joy to know ;
Or to some perfect, wondrous service yonder,
    Within that Holy Place,
Where, veilless, in its full, transfigured glory,
    His servants see His face.

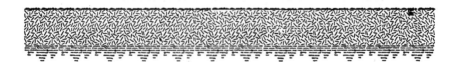

AN ILLUSION AND A TRUTH.

AMONG the passengers of a crowded steamboat there was a man who, in consequence of excesses with convivial companions, was seized with that terrible curse of intemperance, delirium tremens. In the midst of his frightful visions, and their expression in cries for help, he suddenly turned to his attendants and begged piteously for a Bible.

Immediately the inquiry was started for a copy, and without success, till a passenger recollected that he had the neglected volume packed away in his trunk. It was carried to the state room of the frantic sufferer and eagerly seized by him.

Then laying it on the bed above his breast, with a wild laugh, he exclaimed, "There, devils! you are beaten now; you can't get over that book."

A strange calm came over him as he lay with his wild eyes fixed intently on the word of God. The scene was one not to be forgotten; that frenzied inebriate, gazing with a smile of triumph upon that Bible, because in his imaginary conflict with fiends it lay between them and him, an impassable barrier.

A strange illusion was this, yet at the same time, it was an illustration of a mighty truth. Had the unfortunate man kept the precepts of God between his tempted soul and the enemy that wrought its destruction, ruin would have been avoided. There is safety in the Bible,

323

NOT QUITE READY, BUT ALMOST.

IN a short talk to our girls, Mary L. Palmer, very truthfully mirrors the young maiden who is never *quite* ready, and who is to be seen flying along the way making a partial toilet as she goes.

I actually know of one who combed her hair in a carriage on the way to a concert.

I always feel like asking such a one some questions about her home life, and the kind of books and papers she reads; if she has never seen an article on the subject of being ready that impressed her sufficiently to follow.

The maiden or lady who is ready, who has attended to her small belongings and appointments, has no further need to think of herself on entering a railway car, or setting out for a walk or drive, therefore has eyes and thoughts for what may be around her. She sees more, hears more, exercises her powers of observation more than one who must complete her readiness after starting. Grace of manner is thereby acquired, and an ease in appearance quite in contrast to the fidgety movements of the chronic fixer. Again, it is very annoying to accompany such a person.

"Tie my veil, please," is perhaps the first request. Presently, "Oh, do button my glove," and you act as a glove buttoner.

"Is my hat on even?"

You may be studying a fine bit of landscape, but you turn your eyes.

"Not quite," and a gentle push is given.

A little further on, "Are my bangs blown about? I ought to have combed them. Can't you smooth them a little with your hand?"

Your hand is gloved, but you oblige your friend.

Other requests are in order. Will you put a pin where the draping of her overskirt is down, or arrange her dolman, or lend a hair-pin to stay her falling locks? and by the time she is ready your interest in the walk is abating, or the journey nearly through, or—let us hope this last—your good nature has endured to the end.

A girl who is never ready will probably develop into a woman of the same mold. She will try her life long to catch up with herself and never seem to get there.

A good soldier is trained to habits of precision. Method marks his movements. Military drill is sometimes considered severe, but such drill is doubtless needed to form habits that will build good soldiers, doing good service for their country.

Now girls need to be good soldiers, doing service for themselves and each other. How can this be accomplished without habits that will form strong character, for back of the foundation lies character, and promptness and neatness are elements more desirable than fly-away qualities.

Every girl can mend her ways in the little matter of being ready at the start, and habits so strong that they can become second nature, are worth building on the right basis.

JUDGE NOT.

HOW do we know what hearts have vilest sin?
　　　How do we know?
　Many, like sepulchers, are foul within,
　　Whose outward garb is spotless as the snow,
　　And many may be pure we think not so.
How near to God the souls of such have been,
What mercy secret penitence may win—
　　　How do we know?

How can we tell who sinned more than we?
　　　How can we tell?
We think our brother walked guiltily,
　　Judging him in self-righteousness. Ah, well!
　　Perhaps had we been driven through the hell
Of his untold temptations, we might be
　　Less upright in our daily walk than he—
　　　How can we tell?

Dare we condemn the ills that others do?
　　　Dare we condemn?
Their strength is small, their trials not a few,
　　The tide of wrong is difficult to stem.
　　And if to us more clearly than to them
Is given knowledge of the great and true,
More do they need our help and pity, too—
　　　Dare we condemn?

God help us all and lead us day by day—
　　　God help us all!
We cannot walk alone the perfect way.
　　Evil allures us, tempts us, and we fall.
　　We are but human, and our power is small;
Not one of us may boast, and not a day
Rolls o'er our heads but each hath need to say
　　　God bless us all!

PRAYING FOR MORE FAITH.

THESE words from that much loved man, Phillips Brooks, are worthy serious thought.

"I hear men praying everywhere for more faith, but when I listen to them carefully and get at the real heart of their prayer, it is no more faith at all that they are wanting, but a change from faith to sight."

"What shall I do with this sorrow that God has sent me?"

"Take it up and bear it, and get strength and blessing out of it."

"Ah, if I only knew what blessing there was in it. If I saw how it would help me, then I could bear it."

"What shall I do with this hard hateful duty which Christ has laid right in my way?"

"Do it, and grow by doing it."

"Ah, yes, if I could only see that it would make me grow."

In both those cases do you not see that what you are begging for is not more faith, although you think it is, but sight.

You want to see for yourself the blessing in the sorrow, the strength in the hard hateful task.

Faith says not, "I see that it is good for me, and so God must have sent it," but, "God sent it, and so it must be good for me." Faith walking in the dark with God only prays Him to clasp its hand more closely, does not even ask Him for the lighting of the darkness, so that the man may find the way himself.

WHY WILL YOU.

WHY will you keep caring for what the world says? Try, oh, try, to be no longer a slave to it! You can have little idea of the comfort of the freedom from it—it is bliss! All this caring for what people will say is from pride, hoist your flag and abide by it. In an infinitely short space of time all secrets will be divulged. Therefore, if you are misjudged, why trouble to put yourself right? You have no idea what a great deal of trouble it will save you. Roll your burden to Him and he will make straight your mistakes. He will set you right with those with whom you have set yourself wrong. "Here I am a lump of clay; Thou art the potter. Mold me as Thou in thy wisdom wilt. Never mind my cries. Cut my life off—so be it ; prolong it—so be it. Just as Thou wilt, but I rely on thy unchanging guidance during the trial."

Oh, the comfort that comes from this!

—GEN. GORDON.

LET me truly feel that in myself I am nothing, and at once through every inlet of my soul God comes in and is everything to me. And as soon as I feel this, the almightiness of God pours through my spirit like a stream, and I can do all things through him that strengthens me.

—WILLIAM MOUNTFORD.

328

"HOME" AND HEAVEN.

Y boy was going away from home,
In a foreign land for a year to roam ;
His plans were many, his hopes were light,
His heart beat gayly, his eyes shone bright,
So eager he for the untried way
Which for twelve whole months before him lay.

" But you may be homesick, dear, " we said.
He merrily tossed his bright young head—
"Homesick ? Never ! Don't fear for me,
I'll welcome a change of scene," laughed he.
And off he started without a tear,
(Though we knew full well how he held us dear.)

The days went by till to months they grew ;
Letters were frequent and happy too.
Our boy was " here," and again was " there,"
Joyous and glad and without a care.
" Change of scene " he was having indeed,
And freedom to go where his choice might lead.

Six month had vanished, and I—ah, me !
With a mother's longing I pined to see
My "wandering boy" as the days crawled past,
Ere the time of return could come at last ;
But there came a letter so full of joy,
That I thought, " I am selfish to want my boy !"

He wrote to tell me of his standing high
On a mountain-top 'neath a sunrise sky,
Of the wonderful view before him spread,

And the glorious canopy o'er his head.
And I wrote him back—with steady pen,
Tho' tears of longing would flow again—

My pleasure because of his happiness ;
(And I wondered much, I will here confess,
If in all his absence he did not miss
His mother's touch and his mother's kiss,)
And added, "The higher your steps may go,
The nearer to Heaven you stand, you know."

His answer came o'er the weary miles,
And it brought us comfort and brought us smiles ;
For the heart of the boy was bared at last,
(And my doubts of his love flew quickly past.)
" Dear mother," it said, " wherever I roam,
There is no place nearer Heaven than home !"

And now my boy has returned to me.
Traveled and wise no doubt is he ;
But he sits with his dear young hand in mine,
And he looks at me with his eyes ashine,
And he whispers, "No matter where one may go,
It is home and mother make heaven below."
                              —Mary D. Brine.

WE will give our young readers a few rules by
which they may live at peace among themselves.
1. Mind your own business. 2. Keep your
tongue from evil. 3. Do not contend for every trifle,
whether it be a matter of right or opinion. 4. If others
neglect their duty to you, be sure you perform yours to
them. To return evil is wrong.

330

SHE GAINED A CUSTOMER.

I DON'T seem to find just what I want," said a lady to a clerk in one of the large Boston stores.

"I'm sorry," said the clerk, politely; "perhaps another time we may have a better supply."

"Possibly;" and the lady picked up her hand-bag and walked away, without even a word of thanks, although the saleswoman had been showing her laces for an hour, and taken down box after box for her examination.

"Well, Helen," said the companion clerk, as the customer passed out of hearing, "if I'd been in your place I'd given the fussy old thing a snub; bothering so long and not buying after all!"

"I wish she had bought," said Helen, "but at any rate I did my duty."

"Duty! yes, and very likely got a black mark from the floor-walker for not making a sale. I detest shoppers!"

"But another time she may buy something. Who knows? So I tried to be polite to her, though it does seem too bad to spend so much time and sell nothing."

"Yes; and it shows so on your books," answered her companion. "You ought to have sent her off long ago. You might have sold to two or three customers, for we had quite a rush one while."

A week later the same lady came again to the lace counter, and declining to be served by one of the other clerks, waited several minutes for Helen to get through with another customer, then she asked to see laces again. Helen was attentive and courteous; the customer made a small purchase and went out.

"Sold again by Madam Fussiness?" said one of the other clerks, laughing.

"Not quite," smiled Helen; "and I hope she'll come again."

Within a few days she did come again, this time bringing a friend with her; and to Helen's great satisfaction, both of them bought liberally.

When they had gone the floor-walker came to Helen and said:

"You've done well. That lady dressed so plainly was Mrs. S———. She's immensely rich and awfully fussy. Her patronage will be worth a good deal to the store. The superintendent shall hear how well you got along with her."

Patience and politeness had their reward, and it is to be hoped that the other clerks learned a lesson.

IT ISN'T FAR TO JESUS.

IT isn't far to Jesus;
    If you only knew how near,
You would reach Him in a moment,
    And banish all your fear.

He is standing close beside you,
    If only you could see,
And is saying, could you hear Him,
    "Let the children come to Me."

332

Don't you know He never changes,
   As your little friends do here?
He is always kind and ready
   For to comfort and to cheer;

And the very best about it is,
   He's always close at hand,
And will always listen to you,
   And always understand.

It matters not how little,
   Or how very young or weak;
And if you have been sinful,
   It was you He came to seek.

There is nothing that need hinder
   Your coming to Him now,
So you surely will not linger
   Until you older grow.

You really must love Jesus
   When you think of all His love
In coming down from heaven,
   That happy home above;

And lying in a manger,
   And suffering so much woe,
That you and all dear children
   To that bright world might go.

"Know thyself," is good advice, but "know about
your neighbors," is the general practice.

A HOUSE TO LET.

ONE day an old man met a business friend on the street and suddenly said to him, "John you have a house to let?"

"A house to let?" repeated the younger man. "Who told you so? I have no house to let."

"I think you have, John. You are not preparing to live in it yourself, I see. I mean your house not made with hands, eternal in the heavens. You have not made arrangements to move in, have you? It's to let, then."

The young man walked away as though a hornet had stung him, and he did not let the sun go down on his head without taking steps to inhabit that house himself.

COME TO CHRIST.

DEAR Friend, why don't you come to Christ
When all are pleading so;
Your Pastor, friends and neighbors,
Your wife and children too.
Dear Jesus stands with out-stretched arms,
And angels breathless wait
To bear your penitential prayer
Up to the golden gate.

Long in dreadful condemnation
You have suffered on,
Your sense of guilt and load of sin
Have well nigh crushed you down;

334

But Satan laughs at your distress,
He scoffs at your dispair!
And tries to keep you on his side
With, "bravo! Do and dare!"

Think of the fearful day when you
Before the Judge shall stand,
In speechless horror and dismay,
No one can help a hand
When God shall say, "Your day is past,
Away, it is no use,
You did not take the Son I gave,
You are without excuse."

I ask again, will you not come
While mercy pleads for you,
And let the Savior in his love
Give you a heart all new?
Oh do not let that wicked one
Rob you of heaven's joys,
And drag you down to endless woe
Into the fiendish noise.

Break the bands that sin has fastened,
Break them now and rise;
Behold the bleeding Lamb of God,
Accept the sacrifice.

"Do to-day's duty, fight to-day's temptation; do not
weaken and distract yourself by looking forward to
things you cannot see, and could not understand if you
saw them."

335

THE SECRET OF LIFE.

THE secret of life,—it is giving ;
　　To minister and to serve ;
　　Love's law binds the man to the angel,
　　And ruin befalls, if we swerve.
There are breadths of celestial horizons
　　Overhanging the commonest way ;
The cloud and the star share the glory,
　　And to breathe is an ecstacy.

Life dawns on us, wakes us, by glimpses ;
　　In heaven there is opened a door !—
That flash lit up vistas eternal ;
　　The dead are the living once more !·
To illumine the scroll of creation,
　　One swift, sudden vision sufficed :
Every riddle of life worth the reading
　　Has found its interpreter—Christ !

　　　　　　　　　　　　—LUCY LARCOM.

REAL POWER.

WEALTH, we are told is power; talent is power,
and knowledge is power. But there is a
mightier force in the world than either of these,
—a power which wealth is not rich enough to purchase,
nor genius subtle enough to refute, nor knowledge wise
enough to over-reach, nor authority imposing enough
to silence. They all tremble in its presence. It is
TRUTH—really the most potent element of social or

336

individual life. Though tossed on the billows of popular commotion, or cast into the seven-fold heated furnace of persecution, or trampled into the dust by the iron heel of power, TRUTH is the one indestructible thing in this world, that loses in no conflict, suffers from no abuse, and maintains its vitality and completeness after every assault. All kinds of conspiracies have been exhausted to crush it, and all kinds of seductions been employed to viciate and poison it; but none have succeeded, and none ever will. We can be confident of nothing else in this world, but the safety and imperishability of truth—for it is a part of the divine nature, and invested with eternity and omnipotence of its authority and source. It may often seem to be in danger; it is as much set upon and assaulted now after eighteen hundred years of successful resistance, as ever; but history and experience ought to reassure our faith. It has never yet failed, and it never will. We may rest serenely upon it, and feel no alarm: we may anticipate its success, and enjoy its triumphs in advance. In this struggling life, what encouragement and comfort there is in this thought—that the man of truth and the cause of truth, are connected with the most potent element in the world, and have all the certainty of succeeding which God's immutable nature and decree affords.

It won't help your own crop to sit · on the fence and count the weeds in your neighbor's field.

BE CAREFUL WHAT YOU SAY.

IN speaking of a person's faults,
    Pray don't forget your own ;
Remember, those in homes of glass
    Should seldom throw a stone.
If we have nothing else to do
    But talk of those who sin,
'Tis better we commence at home,
    And from that point begin.

We have no right to judge a man
    Until he's fairly tried ;
Should we not like his company,
    We know the world is wide.
Some may have faults—and who have not ?
    The old as well as young ;
Perhaps we may, for aught we know,
    Have fifty to their one.

I'll tell you of a better plan,
    And find it works full well ;
To try my own defects to cure
    Before of others tell ;
And though I sometimes hope to be
    No worse than some I know,
My own shortcomings bid me let
    .The faults of others go.

Then let us all when we commence
    To slander friend or foe,
Think of the harm one word may do
    To those we little know.
Remember, curses sometimes, like
    Our chickens, " roost at home."
Don't speak of other's faults until
    We have none of our own.

338

TWO SIDES.

TWO SIDES TO A QUESTION.

DO you know what you're doing, young lady,
    When you're trying to capture a beau ?
When you dress you in fancy apparel
    And go on the streets for a show ?
Will you be quite content with the mortal
    You are trying so faithful to get ?
Or, after the bargain is over,
    Will you have a dissatisfied fit ?

There are fits which are painful and lasting,
    But physicians the end may foretell,
But with this kind of fit, I am fearful,
    You will have all your life to get well.
I have learned by a slight observation
    There are sometimes two sides to a thing ;
I've noticed that sometimes young ladies
    Are apt to cry after they sing.

You say you love him for his beauty !
    Do you know he takes you for your dress ?
Do you know love is proved in the homestead,
    And that this will not stand the sad test ?
You will have few hours for the ball-room,
    And household duties to shirk,
For 'tis plain he will never be able
    To provide should you fail in the work.

And when there's no time for the frizzes,
    And bustles are things of the past,
And he sees that the beauty he married
    When confined to the home fails to last,

Remember, this is not false Scripture,
    And should you doubt now time will tell,—
He will go where he finds these attractions,
    And home will be next to a hell!

You will fade, and your husband will notice
    You are not the fair miss that he wed,
And, though he may try to conceal it,
    For his home there arises a dread ;
And he'll spend his spare time by the fireside
    Where fashion and beauty abound,
For he tires of the cares of the homestead,
    And goes where old pleasures are found.

Nor can I quite call him a scoundrel
    And say that he meant to deceive,
For that would be harshly affirming
    What I myself hardly believe.
He was full of ambition, you called it,
    And liked all the fun he could get ;
'Tis but the old life you admired,
    And he's not got over it yet.

Then remember, your building in folly
    The nest where you'll have to abide ;
You are giving your truth and your honor,
    And selling your Master beside.
And when you have found his heart roving
    From the one he has power to bless,
Say not he is false, for he clings to
    What he married—just beauty and dress.
        —Mrs. Nellie Mearns Weaver.

THE SECRET.

PROFESSOR Drummond, in an address, once told this story: "I know of a very beautiful character —one of the loveliest characters which ever bloomed on this earth. It was the character of a young girl. She always wore about her neck a little locket, but nobody was ever allowed to open it None of her companions ever knew what it contained. until one day she was laid up with a dangerous illness. Then one of them was granted permission to look into the locket, and she saw written there: 'Whom not having seen I love.' That was the secret of her beautiful life. She had changed into the beautiful life."

~~~~~~~~~~

"I KNOW SOMETHING NICE OF YOU."

AUNT Esther, won't you tell me how to climb over the misty mountains cousin Prudence is always placing across my way? She compares me to the *Union Signal*, and says I'm too effusive, I say too many pleasant things to people. I must be less demonstrative; always say good things of people behind their backs, so to speak, but never, never to their faces. She calls all my try-to-be-gentle speeches 'flattery,' and says that my friends will think me insincere, and that it is sure to make people *ego-ish* to hear nice things of themselves."

341

"You poor dear; come over on this cozy couch while I tell you a story of years—yes, years and years ago."

"But, aunt Esther, you are not so awful old as that, are you? You seem so nice and youthful to me? What nice, soft pillows these are—where did they come from?"

"From Alaska—filled with the soft, white down of the mountain goat."

"How nice of the goat to be so downy!" said Amy.

" Now, child, first tell me how you come to use that word *nice* so often? "

" Why, aunt Esther, that's your very own word ; you always used it so charmingly. The happiest voice of my childhood was yours as you whispered, ' I know something nice of you,' and I felt a foot taller that day, for I knew I had your approbation."

The tears filled Aunt Esther's brown eyes as she said, " It is nice of you to remember that, but that's another story; I will tell you of long ago, when my 'fairy canoe rode like foam o'er the wave.' I was a careless, happy girl ; I liked everybody, and thought everybody liked me ; I was not selfish, but I never thought to go out of my way to be thoughtful or generous ; anything for fun ; anything to have a good time. I was sent to a boarding school. The building was a great gloomy bastilish kind of a place. The energetic professor had been sent by President Lincoln as minister to China. The steward seemed to think it was war times, prices high, and he must stint and scrimp in every way to keep his exchequer on the top wave till the ' master should come back o'er the mighty deep.' The girls were often hungry and ill at ease ; wood was not cut as it ought to have been, and the rooms were always cold. My little room-mate, Mollie Brackett, was a sweet-faced, lovable girl, whose dear, generous ways have never faded from my memory. That old steward seemed to buy cheap, illuminating fluid, not oderless, however, for the butter was always impregnated with the oil which was lacking in the halls. No lamps were allowed to be lighted between tea-time and devotions, so there was a half hour or more after tea, before cheap lamp light when the younger girls were out in search of fun.

" One night, after a tealess 'tea,' Mollie and I wandered up and down in hopes some thrifty senior, who had laid in a store of wood, might ask us to spend a while with her ; but seniors were not good to little girls and we hoped in vain. The fifth story of this mansion was reputed to be haunted. We dared each the other to creep to the top of the narrow stairway and listen for the ' swish ' of the ghostly garments. We mounted, courage freezing in our veins ; we ran down, forgetting Lady McFarland's blue paper, 'Rule No. 35. No young lady allowed in the fifth story.'

"A door opened as we landed at the bottom of the stairs. A teacher, pale, fair, youthful, with auburn hair and clear brow that seemed crowned with a halo to us, as she said, not sternly as we deserved, ' Well, comrades, what seek you ? '

" Her pleasant voice inspired confidence and we instantly told her, 'We are hungry and cold and so lonesome that there is nothing to live for ; we have been up to get the ghost to scare us to death.'

" She said, 'come into my room.' Dear heart, if she

had known how afraid we were to go in. For teachers always invited us in to tell us some unpleasant thing 'for our good' and we didn't care to discuss those sub-jects ; we entered gingerly. Oh, that fire ! I can see the glimmer all across the years. A stove like an old-fashioned ' deestrick meetin' school house,' long, narrow —but, oh, such a wealth of red-hot coals ! She excused herself a moment, telling us to make ourselves 'nice' and comfortable.

" She returned with a half loaf of bread, some de-odorized butter from the teachers' table, one knife and three forks ; opening the stove door she gave us each a fork, and cut the bread thin. We sat on the floor and toasted it, burned our hands and warmed our souls with happy laughter. Not a word of rebuke for that lost chemistry lesson, not a whisper of mental or moral phi-losophy. And this was a teacher whom we had been afraid of ! The bell for prayers sounded—she took her little Bible and read the verses she would have us re-peat in devotions, ' He leadeth me beside still waters, he restoreth my soul.' How those verses always bring back her loving voice.

"She whispered: ' Come to-morrow evening. I know something nice of you.'

" The next twilight found us at her door.

" Thus began a little class that widened in numbers, whose motto was, ' I know something nice of somebody, I must surely tell her ; she will be encouraged.' If a girl were wearied she wandered into this dear room for this teacher's helpful 'something.' If our rooms were unusually ' nice,' we were sure to be told of it. It was like wearing a school medal of the older days. Each tried to be kind and generous to the other and to deserve praise.

"In all the passing years I have never seen a gentle deed, a self-forgetful act, but I have felt that I would like to whisper, ' I know something nice of you.' "

" Who was that fair-faced teacher, Aunt Esther? Did she keep the promise of her youth?"

"Aye, more, Amy; who was that fair-faced girl teacher? A woman to-day more widely known for her good that has grown by her influence than any other woman in the world. The halo that shone for us has lighted many a foreign shore, for everybody knows something 'nice' of Frances E. Willard, the best loved woman in the world!

"Don't save all your flowers for me till I am dead! Give me a few daisies each day. When I land on the other shore—if I have been faithful—I should like to have Miss Willard's 'sister Mary' meet me on the bank and say, 'I know something nice of you that my sister Frank taught you in dear old Evanston.'"

—M.

Converse with those that will do you good, or to whom you may do good.

He who cannot hold his peace until the true time comes for acting is no right man.

NOW AND THEN.

YES, study away, my dearies, and learn your lessons
      well,
For grandmother is not too old or stupid yet to
      tell
How faithful, thoughtful study makes the young eyes
      clear and bright,
And gives the bonny faces such a glow of inner light.

" Things were very different in my younger days, you
      know,
Some forty, no, say fifty—bless me ! sixty years ago !
What did we do ?   Why, children, if you only could
      have seen
How many skeins of wool I spun before I was sixteen !

" We learned to read the Bible without stopping once
      to spell,
To write a letter plain enough for one to read it well,
With just enough of ciphering our own accounts to
      keep ;
Of geography and history, perhaps a little peep.

" Your French and your Italian we never learned to
      speak,
And only parsons ever thought of Latin or of Greek.
Geology—geometry—to me they're much the same,
And every science that you talk of, nothing but a
      name.

346

" The beauties of the world around I see with simple
    eyes ;
Far different from a gaze like yours, so learned and so
    wise.
And I'm proud of you, my darlings, when I come
    about and see
Your books and books, the like of which were never
    made for me.

" For in all your life-long journey it must be that you
    will find
This knowledge of the Father's gifts, these treasures
    of the mind,
Will surely bring you nearer to him now, and, some
    bright day,
Will give you higher places in the home that's far
    away. "

But little Ruth came close to look in grandma's
    patient face,
To mark its gentle firmness, its glow of heaven's grace,
And wondered much if any before the great white
    throne
Would find a higher, nearer, better place than
    grandma's own.

                               —SYDNEY DAYRE.

Seven things that fail us,—money fails, kinsfolk
fail, strength fails, refuge fails, eyes fail, desire fails
and heart and flesh fail.

WHAT ALL CAN DO.

NO man has a right to say he can do nothing for the benefit of man-kind, who are less benefitted by ambitious projects than by the sober fulfillment of each man's proper duties. By doing the proper duty in the proper place, a man may make the world his debtor. The results of "patient continuance in well-doing" are never to be measured by the weakness of the instrument, but by the omnipotence of Him who blesseth the sincere efforts of obedient faith alike in the prince and in the cottager.

TROUBLE AND TRIALS NEVER CEASE.

MANY a young convert is surprised that, having become a Christian, he is still beset by trials and troubles. One said recently: "I thought I was over my troubles when I became a Christian, but I find they are still on hand, though there is this differ-ence—I have Jesus to help me bear them now." Old Christians and young Christians need to have this all the time in mind. "Put on the whole armour of God that ye may be able to stand against the wiles of the devil."

Keep on, weary struggling, fainting Christian, sur-rounded with troubles and trials without measure, for, "These are they which have come out of great tribula-tion and have washed their robes and made them white in the blood of the Lamb."

348

A DEAR ACQUAINTANGE.

LITTLE child, left at home alone one cold tempestuous day, was applied to by a poor wanderer for shelter.

"I can't let you in," said the little one from an upper window, "because my father don't know you;" and she would not be entreated.

Suddenly the child's voice was heard again: "Do you know Jesus?"

The poor woman burst into tears and declared that Jesus was her only friend.

Instantly the door flew open. "Oh, if you know Jesus," said the child, "it's all right, because he's our friend too."

THE SECRET OF HAPPINESS.

HAPPINESS comes most to people who seek her least and think least about her. It is not an object to be sought; it is a state to be induced. It must follow and not lead. It must overtake you, and not you overtake it." In the course of his sound philosophizing he says: "A contented mind is the first condition of happiness, but what is the first condition of a contented mind? You will be disappointed when I tell you what this all-important thing is, it is so common, so near at hand, and so many people have so much of it and yet are not happy. They have too

much of it, or else the kind that is not best suited for
them. What is the best thing for a stream? It is to
keep moving. If it stops it stagnates. So the best
thing for a man is that which keeps the current going,
the physical, moral and intellectual currents. Hence
the secret of happiness is—something to do; some con-
genial work. Take away the occupation of all men and
what a wretched world it would be. Half of it would
commit suicide in less than ten days."

—JOHN BURROUGHS.

IF YOU WOULD BE HAPPY.

KEEP your temper.
Gain a little knowledge every day.
Make few promises, and speak the truth.
Give full measure and weight with a just balance.
Consent to common custom, but not to common folly.
Be cautious of believing ill, but more cautious of re-
peating it.
Have courage to wear your old clothes until you can
pay for new ones.
Think of Heaven with hearty purpose and strong
hope to get there.
Do good to all, that thou mayest keep thy friends
and gain thine enemies.
Count your resources; find out what you are not fit
for, and give up wishing for it.

REST COMETH AFTER ALL.

BEYOND the toil, the burdens of the day,
　　Beyond the tempests and the storms of life,
　Far from the tumult of the weary way,
　　Beyond the longing and the ceaseless strife;
Out of the darkness and the gloom of night,
　Beyond the hills where shadows never·fall,
And far beyond the range of mortal sight,
　Rest cometh after all.'

" After the fever and the restless pain,
　After the waiting and the weary years,
After the conflict and the loss and gain,
　After the sorrow and the useless tears,
Far, far beyond the lofty heights of Fame,
　Beyond the hills where shadows never fall,
Beyond the fear of censure and of blame,
　Rest cometh after all."

EARTH TO AIR.

 LITTLE worm on branch of gray
Began his work one summer day.
He planned and built, he wove and spun,
Until his tiny house was done.

He laid the walls with leaf-green rails ;
He set the roof with golden nails ;
He wove a sheet of softest lace,
And in its folds himself found place.

He slept, and in the dark of night
Upon his sides grew wings of light.
The shining house became a veil,
And gone was every golden nail.

Through the thin walls of gauze I spied
The rainbow wings he had not tried.
They cradled close and folded tight
His velvet body, strong and light.

On sped the hours till sleep was done,
Wide swung the doors to life's new sun.
He woke !—he longed his wings to try,
And found himself—a butterfly !

No longer measuring slow his way,
No longer shut from light of day,
He does not toil with creeping things,
But floats with birds on happy wings !

Dear symbol of immortal years,
Thy lesson banishes our fears ;
For we, when done with earthly things,
Shall find, like thee, our angel wings.

—LYDIA AVERY COONLEY.

THE habit of strict and careful accuracy in speaking, of saying neither more or less than is felt, or thought or known, of recording facts, events, and scenes as correctly as possible, will form the best possible safeguard against the utterance of a conscious untruth, however strong may be the motive which may urge it.

LOVE OF DRESS HAS ITS LIMITS.

BEAUTY has a powerful influence over most of us. A humorously pathetic story is told of an old man whose life had been spent with a severely plain, ill-dressed wife, who secretly purchased a flaxen haired doll to gratify his latent love of the beautiful, will illustrate the principle. Actual physical beauty is a rare gift, but pleasant, cheery, clean looks and agreeable dressing go far toward answering the same purpose. The woman who studies the question of dress in order that she may find and appropriate that which is becoming, who makes a careful study of color and outlines from an artistic standpoint, and who seeks to emphasize every one of her good points and to disguise those which are less attractive, is adding materially to her influence for good at home and abroad. But when dress becomes a paramount consideration in a woman's life and simply a means of gratifying her vanity or eclipsing her neighbors, it is a lamentable perversion, and injures herself and all who come under her influence.

———————

ONE of an admiring group around a certain conscientious woman of boundless tact, recently asked her what she found truthfully to say when adoring parents exhibited unpromising infants or their pictures. The tactful woman smiled with justifiable pride at the score of anxious feminine faces turned toward her: " I always exclaim ardently, 'Well, that is a baby,' and," with dancing eyes, "it is, you know."

NOT LUCK, BUT WORK.

TWENTY clerks in a store, twenty hands in a printing office, twenty apprentices in a ship-yard, twenty young men in town all want to get on in the world, and expect to do so," says an old merchant.

"One of the clerks will become partner, and make a fortune; one of the compositors will own a newspaper, and become an influential citizen; one of the apprentices will become master builder; one of the villagers will get a handsome farm, and live like a patriarch—but which one is the lucky individual? Lucky? There is no luck about it. The thing is almost as certain as the rule of three. The young fellow who will distance his competitors is he who masters his business, preserves his integrity, who lives cleanly and purely, who devotes his leisure to the acquisition of knowledge; who gains friends by deserving them, and saves his spare money. There are some ways to fortune shorter than this dusty old highway, but the staunch men of the community, the men who have achieved something really worth having—good fortune, good name and serene old age—all go in this road."

~~~~~~~~~

The man who finds out that he has made a fool of himself has learned something valuable.

"THE GARDEN OF ROSES."

'TIS the Master's garden of beauty now,
    An orchard of pleasant fruits.
    As he walks in its shade at the cool of day,
With voice of approval we hear him say,
    "Blessed is she
    Who trains these human flowers for me."

Once it brought forth only briars and thorns—
No plant of beauty was here ;
No shade where the Master could love to rest,
No roses to fasten upon his breast ;
    He turned his face
    Away in grief from the wasted place.

Now he looks with joy on the tender vines,
And blesses the gardener's care ;
The winds of his providence send abroad,
Over desolate waste and dusty road,
    A fragrance rare
    From His purchased garden of roses fair.

As He walks among the beds of bloom,
A touch of His gentle hand
Breaks now and again from the parent stem
From among the buds the fairest of them ;
    But not to die—
    His touch giveth life eternally.

Awake ! O thou north wind ! and come thou
    south !
For lo ! the winter is past.
Awake, ye ! and over His garden blow,

355

That the spices thereof may outward flow,
  And fruit most sweet
  Be found when the Master comes to eat.

'Tis blessed to work in thy garden, Lord ;
Give even to me a share !
When comest in at the cool of day,
May the word be for me when Thou shalt say,
  " Blessed is she
  Who trains these human flowers for me."
                  —Mrs. J. H. Knowles.

THE RIGHTS OF OTHER PEOPLE,

TOO commonly the fact is ignored that a man's opinions and convictions are his personal private matter, with which no one else has the right to meddle.

In politics, the spending of money, in social life, in dress and education, each one should scrupulously avoid acting as a censor of others who may differ with himself.

No one is privileged while a guest to attack the opinions of a family whose hospitality he enjoys. When, for any reason he cannot acquiesce in the family regulations let him depart, and not try to reform the family to his standard of propriety.

A man may believe in homeopathy to the highest dilution, but that belief does not entitle him to the privileges of calling his neighbor to account because he chooses to seek relief by means of mercury and quinine in as heroic doses as he may fancy.

By calm personal argument, or by force of example, one may try to convince another that his way is the better, but a true courtesy requires that he shall not, unasked, present his opinions, where to do so will wound and not alter in the slightest degree the cause of his opponent.

Let no person flatter himself that because a man is loud of voice, and blunt in speech, ever ready with cruel judgment of others and free with advice in all matters, that he will pleasantly accept such treatment from others, for he is quite as likely to resent interference with his affairs as a man of gentler speech and greater charity.

It is so easy to form the habit of meddlesomeness, and to persuade one's self into the belief that one's mission is to be a "private investigator and public adviser," that one is apt to forget that in the regulation of one's own conduct, life presents enough perplexing problems without trespassing on the rights of others in a mistaken zeal to convert them to a better way.

THE POST OF DANGER.

A FRENCH GENERAL was once leading his regiment through a narrow and difficult pass. He begged his soldiers to endure with patience the fatigue and danger of the march.

"It is easy for you to talk," said one of the soldiers near him, "you who are mounted on a fine horse; but we—poor fellows!"

On hearing these words the general dismounted, and quickly proposed that the dismounted soldier should take his place on the horse. The soldier did so immediately; but he had scarcely mounted the horse, when a shot from the enemy on the surrounding heights struck and killed him.

"You see," said the general to his troops, "that the most elevated place is not the least dangerous." He then remounted his horse and continued the march.

GOD'S CALL.

COME out, come out, my people,
Oh ! hear the clarion call ;
It ringeth down the ages,
To you, to me, to all.
" Ye are the royal priesthood,
Your ransom is unpriced,
Bought not with gold or silver,
But the precious blood of Christ."

" Ye are the living temples,
Of God, the living God,
Oh ! follow in the footsteps
Your blessed Master trod.
Shun aught that can defile you,
He'd have you walk in white,
Heirs of His royal glory
And children of the light "

"Come out ! I will receive you,
Touch not the unclean thing,
Ye'll be the sons and daughters
Of an Almighty King."
Oh, cleanse both flesh and spirit,
His blessed promise claim,
He'll perfect what concerns you,
For Faithful is his name.

—ELIZABETH T. LARKIN.

MANNERS AT HOME.

THE foundation of courtesy is a desire to render happy those about us. Should not the members of one's own family receive the first consideration? It is the kind feeling of the inmates for each other that makes home a very heaven; and if they are indifferent, careless or unkind to each other, then the home is a dwelling place, not the "Home, Sweet Home," sung by Howard Paine. It is the little courtesies, the kind word, the loving smile, the gentle caress, that smooths the rough pathway of life. The one who is always waiting for some one else to show kindness may wait too long. The home that is ruled by love will be a happy one. Do not imagine the members of the family know you love them if you never show your feelings. Actions speak louder than words.

Children are apt to be reticent unless parents set the example. Many a girl has married very unhappily, casting herself into the arms of the first man who said, "I love you," just because she was hungry for the love of some one, and denied that which was hers by right. Many a boy has been driven to the saloon because there were companions there who wanted him and at home no one took pains to let him feel that his presence was desired. This feeling, "Nobody cares for me," is responsible for much of the evil in the world. It is quite true that spoiled children cause much unhappiness. But why are they spoiled? A wise parent will not gratify every desire of a child.

Self-denial is one of the things to be taught in child-hood; it is almost impossible to teach it afterward; and we all know how disagreeable a thoroughly selfish person is. In every house it should be the rule of the inmates to greet each other with "Good morning." "Thank you," and "If you please" should be said to the toddler as well as the gray-haired grand-parent. Little children taught from the cradle are always polite. And do not stop with words. If Amy is struggling to sew in a doll's sleeve not near so large as the arm-hole, lay down your work and help her to "make it fit." If Tom has trouble finding strings for his kite and you have forty things to do, help the boy now; by and by he will help you. If husband is cross, don't answer sharply back, but when the right time comes let him know you are sorry for his vexations and sympathize with him. And, husband, if wife is surly, very likely she has the neuralgia so bad she don't feel like talking. Suppose you take it for granted and do what you can to make her comfortable. One of the truest little poems I know of runs this way:

> "Love that asketh love again
> Finds the barter naught but pain ;
> Love that giveth in full store
> Aye receives as much and more ;
> Love exacting nothing back
> Never knoweth any lack ;
> Love compelling love to play
> Sees him bankrupt every day."

MYSTERY.

SEE how the flame doth cling to the lamp I bear
      in my hand !
   You think it a simple thing, easy to understand ?

Of what, then, is it made, and how was its substance
      wrought
When it sprang to life, and first obeyed the might of
      Eternal Thought ?

The match, this tiny wand, though no magician, I
But draw o'er the surface of sand, and lo ! the flame
      leaped high !

I gave to the wick the light, and here is the tongue of
      fire,
Wonderful, steadfast, bright, never to flag or tire.

While wick and oil are renewed ; changeless its place
      it keeps,
Sheltered from wild winds rude, it falters not nor
      sleeps.

And from its flame so small you might kindle the
      lights of the earth,
All the lamps of home, from hovel to hall, all the fires
      on every hearth :

And the flame would never be less, would lose no
      atom of power,
Though it gave to all, it would still possess the vigor
      of its first hour.

MYSTERY.

'Tis a mystery full of awe ; at the heart of creation it
    lies,
An engine vast of eternal law, a riddle of the wise.

Strike iron cold upon flint, or if stone upon stone you
    strike,
Out leaps the spark with its burning hint of the power
    in both alike.

Branches of wood that lie dead in the forest dark,
Rub them together rapidly, and lo ! the living spark !

Through the whole world everywhere latent the
    wonder lurks,
In the depths of earth, in the hights of air, for ever the
    marvelous works.

So the Spirit of God doth burn through the universe
    He hath made,
From the delicate frond of the fern to the Pleiades'
    tangled braid.

Seeing we do not see ; we hear, but who understands ?
We can but bow the knee and worship the work of
    His hands.

                —CELIA THAXTER.

MAY the records of our lives
    Which the winged hours bear above,
Be high resolves, nobly kept,
    Kindly words and deeds of love."

DEFEAT AND VICTORY.

THAT which to a christian may seem a sad repulse or defeat may be God's plan for victory. Paul was to see Rome, but when he entered that city a prisoner it looked as if the promise was mockery, yet he soon found that coming to Rome was productive of grand results, and even in Cæsar's household there were those who became "saints." Bunyan was imprisoned, and was thus prevented from preaching, but the best work he ever did for Christ was while he was in Bedford jail. He might have evangelized for awhile, but no work he could have done in preaching would have had the world-wide influence that has come from the "Pilgrim's Progress." When Judson was rebuffed in British India it seemed as if the door of usefulness might be closed, but forced as it were, to go to the Burham, he lighted a golden lamp, which has guided thousands to eternal life. Well is it if we, conscious of our own inability to judge what may be best, are willing to accept divine appointments, and believe that what we know not now will hereafter be proved best for ourselves and the cause of God.

About the most foolish thing that can **be** done **is** to try to live **a** christian life without religion.

He who sows thorns should not go barefoot.

ONE SOURCE OF EVIL.

THINKING well of a person is one of the best aids that can be given to lead him on toward well-doing. One reason why there are so many bad boys in the world is because the phrase "bad boy" has so rooted itself in the popular thought toward all boys. A child of five years not long ago shrewdly observed: "People don't know that little children are good, unless they keep them; then they find out they can be good." A child even at that early age, had seen enough of the world to know that the prevailing disposition is to take it for granted that a child can have no spontaneous promptings to right, no noble aspirations to goodness, no praiseworthy motives to action. And yet she knew that upon a fair trial, without prejudice, the world might reverse its hard judgment. The rule applies through all ages and conditions. One reason why so many ex-convicts are untrustworthy is because they know that no one trusts them; bad boys are bad because they are taught that badness is a necessary constituent of boyhood. Children and men find it easier to do evil when evil is expected of them.

About the poorest man you can find is the rich man who never gives.

No man has any trouble in pleasing God who loves his neighbor as himself.

THIS IS LIFE.

"I HAVE planned much work for my life," she said ;
  A girlish creature with golden hair,
  And bright and winsome as she was fair.

"The days are full, till he comes to wed ;
  The clothes to buy, and the home to make
  A very Eden, for his dear sake."

But cares soon come to the wedded wife ;
  She shares his duties, and hopes and fears,
  Which lessen not with the waning years.

For a very struggle at best is life ;
  If we knew the burdens along the line
  We would shrink to receive this gift divine.

Sometimes, in the hush of the evening hour
  She thinks of the leisure she meant to gain,
  And the work she would do with hand and brain.

"I am tired to-night ; I am lacking power
  To think," she says : " I must wait until
  My brain is rested, and pulse is still."

O ! Woman and Man, there is never rest.
  Dream not of a leisure that will not come
  Till age shall make you both blind and dumb.

You must live each day at your very best :
  The work of the world is done by few ;
  God asks that a part be done by you.

'Say oft' of the years as they pass from sight,
  "This, this is life, with its golden store :
  I shall have it once but it comes no more."

Have a purpose, and do with your utmost might :
  You will finish your work on the other side,
  When you wake in His likeness satisfied.
              —SARAH KNOWLES BOLTON.

BRINGING OUR SHEAVES WITH US.

THE time for toil has past, and night has come,
  The last and saddest of the harvest eves ;
Worn out with labor long and wearisome,
Drooping and faint, the reapers hasten home,
  Each laden with his sheaves.

Last of the laborers, thy feet I gain,
  Lord of the harvest! and my spirit grieves
That I am burdened not so much with grain
As with a heaviness of heart, of heart and brain—
  Master, behold my sheaves !

Few, light, and worthless—yet their trifling weight
  Through all my frame a weary aching leaves,
For long I struggled with my hapless fate,
And stayed and toiled till it was dark and late—
  Yet these are all my sheaves !

Full well I know I have more tares than wheat—
  Brambles and flowers, dry stalks and withered leaves,
Wherefore I blush and weep, as at thy feet
I kneel down reverently and repeat,
    "Master, behold my sheaves !"

I know those blossoms, clustering heavily,
    With evening dew upon their folded leaves,
Can claim no value or utility—
Therefore shall fragrance and beauty be
        The glory of my sheaves.

So do I gather strength and hope anew ;
    For well I know thy patient love perceives
Not what I did, but what I strove to do—
And though the full, ripe ears be sadly few,
        Thou wilt accept my sheaves.

                                    —Elizabeth Akers.

PUTTING OFF SALVATION.

THE steamship Central America on a voyage from New York to San Francisco, sprang a leak in mid-ocean. A vessel, noticing her signal of distress, bore down toward her. Seeing the danger to be very great, the captain of the rescue ship spoke to the Central America:

"What is amiss?"

"We are in bad repair, and going down; lie by till morning," was the answer.

"Let me take your passengers on board now."

But as it was night the commander of the Central America did not like to send his passengers, lest some might be lost; and thinking the ship could be kept afloat a while longer, replied:

"Lie by till morning."

"Once more the captain of the rescue ship cried, "You had better let me take them now."

"Lie by till morning," was sounded back through the trumpet.

About an hour and a half afterward her lights were missed; and though no sound had been heard, the CENTRAL AMERICA had gone down, and all on board perished, just because it had been thought they could be saved better at another time.

How much this reminds us of the fate that may await those who persist in putting off the claims of the Gospel! Jesus cries, "Come unto me, all ye that labor and are heavy laden, and I will give you rest." Alas! the folly of those who answer, "Not now; wait; 'when I have a convenient season I will call for thee.'"

GOD wants us to work for Him, not because He cannot do without us, but because we cannot do without Him. The busy farmer can cultivate his crop better alone, but he knows that if his boy never learns to work, he will be worthless, and so he gives him a hoe and a row beside him and instructs him and helps him over the hard places. He does not need the boy, but the boy needs him. After all, God does not ask us to work for Him, but to work with Him.

Jesus Christ is the friend of sinners. Not the friend of their sin, but of their souls, to rescue them from sin.

THE WAY OF THE TRANSGRESSOR.

EVER since the days of Cain, the way of the transgressor has been hard; but it should not be overlooked that the way has been equally hard for all those connected with the transgressor. For no one ever transgressed God's law without bringing trouble not only on themselves, but others.

Righteous Lot, because of the wickedness of the Sodomites, not only lost his property, but his wife also, to say nothing of his wicked sons-in-law.

Caleb and Joshua were right in the sight of the Lord, and not only desired to obey Him and enter the promised land, but had really been in it and seen its delights; but because the children of Israel refused to obey, they too, had to wander in the wilderness forty long years.

To-day there are many such true souls who suffer because of the rebellion of others.

Liquor and a few men are generally at the bottom of strikes, loyal men are kept from work, homes are destroyed, property ruined, lives lost; the innocent suffer with the guilty.

In a few hours our brightest hopes may be blasted, our most cherished plans destroyed by one rash act of a selfish person who blindly ignores the fact that all our lives are geared into the machinery of other lives, and that they may in a moment make the way of life hard to many others and forever destroy their brightness and usefulness.

"WHATEVER IS—IS BEST."

I KNOW as my life grows older,
  And mine eyes have clearer light,
That under each rank wrong somewhere
  There lies the root of right ;
That each sorrow has its purpose,
  By the sorrowing oft unguessed ;
But as sure as the sun begins morning,
  Whatever is—is best.

I know that each sinful action,
  As sure as night brings shade,
Is somewhere, sometime, punished,
  Though the hour is long delayed ;
I know that the soul is aided
  Sometimes by the heart's unrest,
And to grow, means often to suffer,
  But whatever is—is best.

I know there is no error
  In the great supernal plan,
And all things work together
  For the final good of man ;
I know when my soul speeds onward
  In its grand eternal quest,
I shall cry as I look back earthward,
  "Whatever is—is best."
              —ELLA WHEELER WILCOX.

The cross we pick out for ourselves is always the heaviest.

371

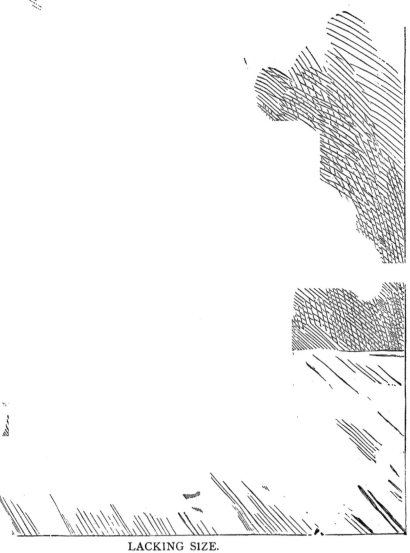

LACKING SIZE.

MISTAKES OF BOYS.

A BOY would not be worth much if he never made mistakes, or was never told of them.

There is hope for a boy just in proportion to the number of mistakes he makes and afterward corrects. One of the most common mistakes a boy makes is his ideas in regard to size. This he hankers after most of all. You will see him stretch himself trying to catch up with his big brother or playmate, measure himself and scratch the wall, count the days and almost the hours when he will be a "man."

Here we see him with his father's slippers, coat, cap and spectacles, trying to be "manly."

Ah, boys, there is something else these days that counts for manliness more than size or strength.

He is most manly who makes most of his time ; who has the best heart and brain. .It is not size that makes a man. We have seen a great six-foot specimen of humanity do a weak, cowardly act that ought to make any rightly bred seven-year-old boy blush for him.

No, it is not size you need to be manly, neither is it strength, for you can be the kindest, most truthful, patient, happy boy in the world, making the very atmosphere you live in a glorious place for yourself and all around you, with just the very size and strength you now have. Try it!

A BLESSED BANKRUPTCY.

I HEARD a man who had failed in business, and whose furniture was sold at auction, say that, when the cradle, and the piano went, tears would come, and he had to leave the house to be a man. Now, there are thousands of men who have lost their pianos, but who have found better music in the sound of their children's voices and footsteps going cheerily down to poverty, than any harmony of chorded instruments. Oh, how blessed is the bankruptcy when it saves a man's children! I see many men bringing up their children as I should bring up mine, if, when they are ten years old, I should lay them on the dissecting-table and cut the sinews of their arms and legs, so that they could neither walk or use their hands, but only sit still and be fed. Thus rich men put the knife of indolence and luxury to their children's energies, and they grow up fatty, lazy, calves, fitted for nothing at twenty-five but to squander wide; and the father must be a slave all his life, in order to make beasts of his children. How blessed then is the stroke of disaster which sets the children free and gives them over to the hard, but kind bosom of poverty, who says to them work! and working makes them men.

One trouble with the world is that so many people have more reputation than character.

374

AN OLD PROVERB.

POUTING, my darling, because it rains,
　　And flowers droop, and rain is falling,
And drops are blurring the window panes,
　　And a moaning wind through the lane is calling,
Crying, and wishing the sky was clear,
　　And roses again on the lattice twining!
Ah, well, remember, my foolish dear,
　　"'Tis easy to laugh when the sun is shining!"

When the world is bright, and fair and gay,
　　And glad birds sing in fair June weather,
And summer is gathering, night and day,
　　Her golden chalice of sweets together,
When the blue seas answer the skies above,
　　And bright stars follow the day's declining,
Why, then, 'tis no merit to smile, my love;
　　"'Tis easy to laugh when the sun is shining!"

But *this* is the time the heart to test,
　　When winter is here and storms are howling,
And the earth from under her frozen vest
　　Looks up at the sad sky, mute and scowling;
The brave little spirit should rise to meet
　　The season's gloom and the day's repining;
And *this* is the time to be glad; for, sweet,
　　"'Tis easy to laugh when the sun is shining!"

God has filled the world with things that we can see
to tell us of things we can not see.

SINCERITY NOT SUFFICIENT.

THE sentiment that it matters not what a man believes, so that he is sincere, is as unscriptural as it is absurd. Sincerity in unbelief has no more effect in warding off evil in the spiritual, than in the natural kingdom. If the teachings and persuasions of a reputed chemist should prevail on you to believe that arsenic is harmless, would it therefore be harmless? Could you mix it with your bread, and you and your children eat it without injury to health or life? Oh, no ! Neither will the sincerity of your belief save you from the consequence of error in religious faith. Right belief—truth—God's truth, brethren, is the only foundation on which you can safely rest your hope."

HE DID HIS DUTY.

THE man who has formed the habit of industry and faithfulness will not long remain unnoticed. Though he may work on for months uncommended and apparently unseen, reward will come in due time, if he keeps bravely in the path of duty.

A lad was once employed as a clerk in a large mercantile house which employed as entry clerks, shipping clerks, buyers, bookkeepers, salesmen, eighty young men, besides a small army of porters, packers and truckmen.

The boy of seventeen felt that amid such a crowd he

was lost to notice, and any efforts he might make would be unregarded.

Nevertheless, he did his duty; every morning at eight o'clock he was promptly in his place, and every power he possessed was brought to bear upon his work. After he had been there a year he had occasion to ask a week's leave of absence during the busy season. "That," was the response, "is an unusual request, and one which it is somewhat inconvenient for us to grant; but for the purpose of showing you that we appreciate the efforts you have made since you have been with us, we take pleasure in giving you the leave of absence for which you ask."

"I didn't think," said the boy, when he came home that night and related his success, "that they knew a thing about me, but it seems they have watched me ever since I have been with them."

They had, indeed, watched him, and had selected him for advancement, for shortly after he was promoted to a position of trust, with appropriate increase of salary. Conscientious devotion to duty seldom fails.

———————

PILOT was once asked if he knew all the rocks along the coast. "No," said he, "it is not necessary to know all the rocks, only the safe channel." Remember, though Christ has promised us a safe landing, he has not promised us a calm passage.

'TIS EASY TO LABOR.

'TIS easy to labor with hope as our guide,
　　To beckon us onward and brighten the way;
　To strengthen the heart till all foes are defied,
　　And strengthen the arm till all work is as play.

'Tis easy to conquer when friends us surround,
　　Ever sweet words of comfort to speak in our ear;
　To keep doubt away that else darkly had frowned,
　　And keep from our vision the phantoms of fear.

But what, when the sweet star of Hope that did guide
　　Is hidden by clouds that it may not dispart?
　And what if the comforting friends at thy side,
　　Stand silent or croak with the doubt in thy heart?

Oh! give me the heart that through silence of friend
　　May walk in the light, or with darkness may cope;
　Oh! give me the heart which, if need, to the end
　　May even fight on in the hope of a hope.

Yes, bravely strike forward, though left in the dark,
　　Still keeping the course that it held through the
　　　　light;
　Yes, strike and keep striking, lit but by the spark
　　Which its brave, ceaseless strokes bring out of the
　　　　night.

Keep up with your profession if you are going
to follow it.

378

TRUE REST.

REST is the highest condition of man. It is above work. For to work restingly, noiselessly, peacefully, lovingly, trustingly, is the perfection of work. The maturity of everything is rest. It is an approach to the Eternal One. For what is rest? The balance of the mind—the equipoise of feeling—a harmony of the inner with the outer life—the peace of desire—the response of the consciousness of truth. And where is that rest to be found? All heaven and earth answer: "In God—only in God!" Let the years that are past speak. They have given you almost everything, but one thing is wanting—rest. With many of us life has nearly been made up of going from mountain to hill, and forgetting our resting-place. A thousand things we have learned, and one after another they have thrown us off—as if they said to us indignantly, "Arise ye, and depart, for this is not your rest!" If there is anything we have learned in the pages of the past, it is this: there may be much pleasure, there may be much joy, there may be much love; but there is no REST out of God.

—Rev. Jas. Vaughan.

God never hears the prayer of a man who locks up his money before he gets down on his knees.

Until we have given ourselves to God we haven't given Him anything.

DON'T BE DISCOURAGED.

IF a man loses his property at thirty or forty years of age, it is only a sharp discipline generally, by which latter he comes to large success. It is all folly for a man to sit down in middle life discouraged. The marshals of Napoleon came to their commander and said: "We have lost the battle and we are being cut to pieces." Napoleon took his watch from his pocket and said. "It is only two o'clock in the afternoon. You have lost the battle, but we have time to win another. Charge upon the foe!" Let our readers who have been unsuccessful thus far in the battle of life not give up in despair. With energy and God's blessing, they may yet win a glorious victory.

PATIENCE.

MOTHER, why do all these years
   Sit so lightly on thy brow?
Prithee, tell us why no tears
   Ever dim thy sweet eyes now,
And the furrows, it appears,
   Father Time will not allow.

Why the single threads are few
   Mingled with thy nut-brown hair;
For of sorrow's blight, 'tis true,
   Thou hast had more than thy share,
And we know life's somber hue
   Often traces lines of care.

Ah ! 'tis patience that has wrought
   All this sweetness in thy life,
And with soothing fingers brought
   Strength to meet thy every strife ;
Patience toned thy every thought,
   Though each day with care was rife.

And thy Christian life has been
   An example wondrous rare,
An example that must win
   Admiration everywhere.
Thou hast let the sunlight in
   Thy brave heart to banish care.

Patience sweet is still thy guest,
   Though the middle line is pass'd,
On the journey to thy rest,
   Rest which thou shalt win at last.
May thy pathway yet be blest,
   And with thornless roses mass'd.

                —Ella Martin.

A KISS NOW AND THEN.

YOU may bring me the choicest of fruits and of flowers,
   The daintiest morsels that money can buy,
   To cheer me and comfort me in the dark hours,
   When under the shadows of sickness I lie ;
The couch may be soft, and the noises around me
   Subdued, so I hear not a single footfall,
And though grateful for this, yet I cannot help thinking,
   That a kiss now and then would be better than all.

A kiss now and then!   How it lightens our labors!
   It brightens our homes, and it sweetens the crust;
And when from the lips of a loved one 'tis given,
   It adds to our joy, and increases our trust.
The children demand it with innocent coaxings,
   And who will deny that our great bearded men
Are better prepared for the conflicts they're waging,
   If somebody gives them a kiss now and then?

It softens the heart of the variest miser;
   'Tis ample reward for much trouble and stress;
And none are the poorer—nay, rather the richer—
   For now and then giving a kiss or caress.
These delicate tokens of love and affection
   We may in our folly pretend to despise,
But when there's neglect of these little attentions,
   What heart-aches, and heart-breaks, and burnings arise!

Rich fruits and bright flowers may please for a moment,
   But, oh! they've no power to help or to heal
Like the lingering touch that so fondly and truly
   Express the tender emotion you feel.
Though the table may groan 'neath the weight of its viands,
   And money be plenty, the heart may not thrive;
And there's many, oh, many a lonely one sighing
   For a kiss now and then, just to keep them alive."

Bishop Whipple once remarked: "As the grave grows nearer my theology is growing strangely simple, it begins and ends with Christ as the only refuge for the lost."

THOUGHTS FOR MOTHERS.

DEAR mothers, in your zeal to reprove the children for wrong-doing, do not forget to commend them when they do well. The thought that this or that act will grieve or please mother, is a strong incentive on one hand to well-doing, or on the other a check on evil-doing. Commendation should be of such a nature as to build up a child's self-respect, and not such as to make him vain, else the good effect will be lost. The love of approbation is natural; God has planted it in the human heart, consequently it has its uses. It follows then, if a mother does not make use of this divinely implanted feeling, she wrongs the Creator of the human heart, as well as the child given her. Approbation may be expressed by approving words, smiles, or rewards. You remember the anecdote of Benjamine West, whose mother kissed him for one of his earliest efforts with the pencil. "That kiss," said he, "made me a painter." Behold the life-directing, life-lasting power of a mother's kiss!

Mothers, perhaps the fire of genius lies hidden in your children's hearts only waiting to be lighted with a word from you. Oh, do not fail to supply it.

If God were as slow to forgive sins as church members are to forgive offences, or wrong-doings repented of, there would be little chance for many of us.

—C. H. SPURGEON.

A FRIENDLY HAND.

WHEN a man 'aint got a cent, and he's feelin'
      kind o' blue,
  An' the clouds hang dark and heavy, an'
      won't let the sunshine through,
It's a great thing, oh, my brethren, for a feller just
      to lay
His hand upon your shoulder in a friendly sort o' way !

It makes a man look curious ; it makes the tear-drops
      start,
And you sort o' feel a flutter in the region of your
      heart.
You can't look up and meet his eyes ; you don't know
      what to say,
When his hand is on your shoulder in a friendly sort
      o' way !

O, the world's a curious compound, with its honey and
      its gall,
With its cares and bitter crosses ; but a good world
      after all.
And a good God must have made it—leastways that's
      what I say
When a hand rests on my shoulder in a friendly sort
      o' way !

Good thoughts are not lost though they are not prac-
ticed.

INDUSTRY.

THE way to wealth is as plain as the way to market. It depends chiefly on two words, industry and frugality; that is, waste neither time nor money, but make the best use of both. Without industry and frugality, nothing will do, and with them, everything.

Sloth makes all things difficult, but industry all easy; he that riseth late must trot all day, and shall scarce overtake his business at night, while laziness travels so slowly that poverty soon overtakes him.

Industry need not wish, and he that lives upon hopes will die fasting. There are no gains without pains; then help, hands, for I have no lands; or if I have, they are smartly taxed. He that hath a trade hath an estate, and he that hath a calling hath an office of profit and honor, but then the trade must be worked at, and the calling followed, or neither the estate nor the office will enable us to pay our taxes. If we are industrious, we shall never starve; for, at the workingman's house, hunger looks in, but dares not enter Nor will the bailiff or constable enter, for industry pays debts, while despair increaseth them.

Employ thy time well, if thou meanest to gain leisure; and since thou art not sure of a minute, throw not away an hour.

Leisure is time for doing something useful; this leisure the diligent man will obtain, but the lazy man never; for a life of leisure and a life of laziness are two things.

—FRANKLIN.

GLASS NUMBER ONE.

GLASS number one, "only in fun;"
Glass number two, "other boys do;"
Glass number three, "it won't hurt me;"
Glass number four, "only one more;"
Glass number five, "before a drive;"
Glass number six, "brain in a mix;"
Glass number seven, stars in heaven;
Glass number eight, stars in his plate;
Glass number nine, whiskey, not wine;
Glass number ten, drinking again;
Glass number twenty, not yet a plenty;

Drinking with boys, drowning his joys:
Drinking with men, just now and then;
Wasting his life, killing his wife;
Losing respect, manhood all wrecked,
Losing his friends, thus all ends.

Glass number one, taken in fun,
Ruined his life, brought on strife;
Blighted his youth, ruled his truth;
Gave only pain, stole all his gain;
Made him at last a friendless outcast.

Light-hearted boy, somebody's joy,
Do not begin early in sin;
Grow up a man brave as you can;
Taste not in fun glass number one.

INSPIRING CONFIDENCE.

HENRY Ward Beecher certainly owed a debt of gratitude to his teacher in mathematics, not only for the knowledge acquired through his tuition, but for lessons tending to strength of character. He tells this story to illustrate the teacher's method.

He was sent to the black-board, and went, uncertain, soft, full of whimpering.

"That lesson must be learned," said the teacher, in a very quiet tone, but with terrible intensity. All explanations and excuses he trod under foot with utter scornfulness. "I want that problem; I don't want any reason why you didn't get it," he would say.

"I did study it two hours."

"That's nothing to me; I want the lesson. You need not study it so long or you may study it ten hours, just suit yourself. I want the lesson."

"It was tough for a green boy," says Beecher, "but it seasoned me. In less than a month I had the most intense sense of intellectual independency and courage to defend my recitations. His cold and calm voice would fall upon me in the midst of a demonstration, 'No!'"

"I hesitated, and then went back to the beginning, and on reaching the same spot again, 'No!' uttered with the tone of conviction, barred my progress.

"'The next,' and I sat down in a red confusion.

"He, too, was stopped with 'No!' but went right on,

finished, and, as he sat down was rewarded with, 'very well.'

"Why," whimpered I, "I recited it just as he did, and you said 'No.'

" ' Why didn't you say 'Yes,' and stick to it? It is not enough to know your lesson. You must know that you know it. You have learned nothing till you are sure. If all the world says 'No!' your business is to say 'Yes!' and prove it."

TEN LITTLE FINGERS.

ONLY ten little fingers!
    Not very strong, tis true;
Yet there is work for Jesus
    Our little hands may do.
What though it be but humble,
    Winning no word of praise;
We are but little children,
    Working in little ways.

Only ten little fingers!
    But little things may grow;
And little hands now helpless
    Will not always be so.
And if we train them early,
    Unto His work alone,
They will do great service
    When they are stronger grown.

Only a band of children
    Sitting at Jesus' feet,
Fitting ourselves to enter
    Into his service sweet.

Softly his voice is calling,
  "Little ones, come unto me!
Stay not though weak and helpless;
  Child, I have need of thee."

Take us, dear Saviour, take us
  Into thy heavenly fold;
Keep our young hearts from straying
  Into the dark and cold.
Call us thy "little helpers,"
  Glad in thy work to share;
Make us thine own dear children,
  Worthy thy name to bear.

~~~~~~~~~

NEVER MIND.

IF the world don't go to suit you,
    Why repine?
  Will your caring change the matter,
    Friend of mine?
  Take life easy; it is better,
    You will find.
  Take no trouble, laugh it off, and
    Never mind.

Eat your hard crust easy-hearted,
    With a jest.
Frowns nor tears will help the matter—
    Let it rest.
Troubles will not come so thickly,
    You will find,
If unlooked for; laugh them off, and
    Never mind.

HER HEAD GOT TURNED.

BY way of telling what effect the world has upon women, let me tell what it has done for a woman whose name is known from east to west, in every home where good literature is seen. About fifteen years ago she began to write. Each bit was her best, till on the appearance of one novel, a book that stirred this country and England, it was said: "The next book she writes will be the great American novel; she is the best writer of our country." She was the worshiped woman of the finest, most learned, most cultivated society where she lived. Then she met some gayer people in this life of ovation; more showy, but less true. Her head got turned, her ideas and ideals became changed, and some portions of her last novel were expergated by the publishers as being too suggestive. The woman who of all America could have had her country at her feet, wears upon her arm as a bracelet the collar of the smallest pug dog in the world, given her by a senseless fob of Boston The duties she owes her husband if not the husband himself, are forgotten in the gay whirl of the world into which her desire for a name and reputation have led her. She is a woman of the working world. God pity her!

—PERRY PENSELL.

~~~~~~~~~

An observer says the less men think the more they talk.

STRENGTH OF CHARACTER.

WE mistake strong feeling to be strong character. A man who bears all before him—before whose frown domestics tremble, and whose bursts of fury make the children of the house quake—because he has his will obeyed, and his own way in all things, we call him a strong man. The truth is, he is a weak man; it is his passions that are strong; he, mastered by them is weak. You must measure the strength of a man by the power of the feelings he subdues, not by the power of those which subdue him. Hence, composure is very often the highest result of strength. Did we ever see a man receive a flat grand insult, and only grow pale and then reply quietly? That was a man spiritually strong. Or did we ever see a man in anguish, stand as if carved out of the solid rock, mastering himself, or one bearing a hopeless daily trial, remain silent and never tell the world what it was that cankered his home peace?

That is strength. He who, with strong passions, remains chaste—he, who, keenly sensitive, with manly power of indignation in him, can be provoked, yet can restrain himself and forgive—these are strong men, spiritual heroes.

—F. W. ROBERTSON, D. D.

~~~~~~~~~

As sure as God puts His children in the furnace, he will be in the furnace with them.

—C. H. SPURGEON.

391

THE MAN WHO ALWAYS SMILES.

THERE are those who govern nations, who can lead their
  fellow-men,
 Who gain a vast abundance by the toil of hands and
  pen ;
Who can paint a sunset glowing, who can show the world the
  right,
Who can lend the glare of noon time to the darkening hours
  of night.

They're the ones that get the notice, and the praising goes
  their way ;
For they're standing out from others in the open light of day ;
But some men who never governed, never painted, never
  wrote,
Who never preached a sermon, do our happiness promote.

It's the man who's always cheerful, with a ready laugh and
  jest,
Who's presence e'en is livening, with its bright contagious
  zest ;
The man who's friends are countless, whom no one e'er
  reviles,
Original pack of sprightliness, the man who always smiles.

His house may not a mansion be, his place inside the line
Where common people stand and note their richer neighbors
  shine ;
But yet his life's a grander one, though lacking much of
  styles,
His title is the prince of hope, the man who always smiles.

Though he never limned a landscape, he's an artist in his
    way,
He's a picture fair of joyousness in a frame that's always
    gay.
His life's a useful sermon, he's a preacher all the while,
And he's better off than governors, the man who always
    smiles.

He's one of life's physicians, without antidotes or pills,
His cures are freely given to all men's current ills ;
He's a missionary worker, leaving out the Heathen isles,
And he's aiming straight for Heaven, the man who always
    smiles.

Then worship, still, our mighty men who lead us in the
    might,
Who teaches us and who tells us how to work and act aright ;
But leave a thought for this one, too, he who our mind be-
    guiles,
Doff your hat and speak a cheery word to the man who always
    smiles.

                    —Fred. E. Smith.

ST. FRANCIS once said to a brother, "Come, let
let us go out to preach." They walked out and
St. Francis gave bread to the poor and smiles to
all, but he did not speak a word. When they came
home his brother said: "But we did not preach."
"Yes," said Francis, "for men have looked at us. We
preach by our looks and acts." Do we preach thus?
Paul did.

THE WAY OF PLEASANTNESS.

EVERY woman has an inherent longing to be attractive, and if she has not, she should have. For what would this chaos, doubt and strife of our daily warfare become, were it not that sweet woman interfuses into it her calming, cheering influences?

And the natural attribute men pay to woman's attractive qualities is admiration. If woman is incapable of appreciating the homage of man, and treats his highest gift as though it were vanity, she makes a serious mistake.

How can a girl best gain the love and respect of others? This is an all important query, and it is best answered by a concrete illustration drawn from real life. Miss A is beautiful. Her picturesque form and magnificent face are always the same, with a cold, distant aspect which even her undoubted beauty does not redeem from reproach. Miss B is neither talented nor yet so lovely, but she meets one heart to heart, and her continued pleasantness has a charm which draws around her a devoted circle of appreciative friends. She is her father's confident, her mother's joy, the recipient of her brother Jack's love trouble and sister Nellie's struggles with French.

Ah, girls! The snowiest skin will some day be sallow; the flush of youth will disappear; the bright eye grow dim and the nervy limb be uncertain and feeble. But this inward loveliness, this beauty of the spirit, is born of Heaven and knows no death. The tender ministries of Miss B will creep into any true heart, sooner than Miss A's icy beauty. Such a woman in any home is a glimpse of God's sunshine. Beauty and genius are the gifts of providence, but a good heart all can cultivate.

<hr>

JRANGIENJ JROUBLES.

MOST of us have had troubles all our lives, and each day has brought all the evil we wished to endure. But if we were asked to recount the sorrows of our lives, how many could we remember? How many that are six months old should we think worth to be remembered or mentioned? To-day's troubles look large, but a week hence they will be forgotten and buried out of sight.

If you would keep a book, and every day put down the things that worry you, and see what becomes of them, it would be a benefit to you. You allow a thing to annoy you, just as you allow a fly to settle on you and plague you; and you lose your temper (or rather get it; for when men are surcharged with temper they are said to have lost it;) and you justify yourself for being thrown off your balance by causes which you do not trace out. But if you would see what it was that threw you off your balance before breakfast, and put it down in a little book, and follow it out, and ascertain what becomes of it, you would see what a fool you were in the matter.

The art of forgetting is a blessed art, but the art of overlooking is quite as important. And if we should take time to write down the origin, the progress, and outcome of a few of our troubles, it would make us ashamed of the fuss we make over them, and we should be glad to drop such things and bury them at once in eternal forgetfulness. Life is too short to be worn out in petty worries, frettings, hatreds, and vexations. Let us think only on whatsoever things are pure, and lovely, and gentle, and of good report.

HYMN OF THANKSGIVING.

PRAISE to God, immortal praise,
For the love that crowns our days ;
Bounteous source of every joy,
Let thy praise our tongues employ !

For the blessing of the field,
For the stores the gardens yield,
For the vine's exalted juice,
For the generous olive's youth ;

Flocks that whiten all the plain,
Yellow sheaves of ripened grain,
Clouds that drop their flattering dews,
Suns that temperate warmth diffuse ;

All that spring with bounteous hand,
Scatters o'er the smiling land ;
All that liberal autumn pours
From her rich o'er-flowing stores ;

These to Thee, my God, we owe—
Source whence all our blessings flow !
And for these my soul shall raise
Greatful vows and solemn praise.

Yet should rising whirlwinds tear
From his stem the ripening ear,
Should the fig tree's blasted shoot
Drop her green, untimely fruit ;

Should the vine put forth no more,
Nor the olive yield her store,
Though the sickening flocks shall fail,
And the herds desert the stall ;

Should thine altered hand restrain
The early and the later rain,
Blast each opening bud of joy,
And the rising year destroy—

Yet to Thee my soul shall raise
Greatful vows and solemn praise,
And, when every blessing flown,
Love Thee—for Thyself alone.
—ANNA LETITIA BARBAULD.

Lose not thine own for want of asking for it; it will
bring thee no thanks.

Great things are not accomplished by idle dreams,
but by years of patient study.

CHRISTMAS GIFTS.

CHRISTMAS GIFTS.

DEAR readers, please allow a few words in regard to the preparation of Christmas gifts. I do not mean our quiet home affairs, but the public ones, those usually given in church. It has been said no church will prosper, no souls be saved, where such things are allowed in the church, on account of the envy, strife and hard feelings usually gotten up at such times.

Shall this be true of your church? If not, be careful what you do, and how you do. Avoid the spirit of striving to outdo others. Do not buy anything you are not able to get, because others will do so and so. Do not make gifts for the rich and neglect the poor. Do not knowingly wound another's feelings. Strive to make hearts glad because it is Christmas, instead of painfully reminding them of something they would like to do if they had the means.

Remember whose birthday we are celebrating and let everything be done in the spirit and harmony of such an important event.

WORDS OF WISDOM.

BE up and doing. "Life is real, life is earnest." Negligence now may place the invaluable prize of immortality beyond your reach forever, no matter how much you might desire to strive hereafter to attain it.

—ADDISON.

399

NOBILITY.

TRUE worth is in being, not seeming;
    In doing, each day that goes by
    Some little good—not in dreaming
    Of great things to do by and by.
For, what ever men say in their blindness
    And in spite of the fancies of youth,
There's nothing so kingly as kindness,
    And nothing so royal as truth.

We get back our mete as we measure—
    We cannot do wrong and feel right,
Nor can we give pain and feel pleasure,
    For justice avenges each slight.
The air for the wing of a sparrow,
    The bush for the robin or wren,
But always the path that is narrow
    And straight for the children of men.

We cannot make bargains for blisses
    Nor catch them like fishes in nets;
And sometimes the thing our life misses,
    Helps more than the thing which it gets;
For good lieth not in pursuing,
    Nor gaining of great nor of small,
But just in the doing, and doing
    As we would be done by, is all.
                   —ALICE CARY.

Society says one thing, and nature says another.

FOREIGN MISSIONARY WORK.

THERE are many christian people who are doing nothing at all in this direction simply because they do not know what to do; do not realize the claims God has upon them in this direction.

The command—"Go ye into all the world and preach the gospel to every creature," is as binding upon Christ's disciples to-day, as it was to the little band who clustered around Him and received His parting words just before He was received up into Heaven.

But you say, "I cannot go."

Perhaps God does not want you to go. But there are many who are willing and anxious to go if they only had the means to do so, and you are just as truly helping to preach if you are giving all you can to help others, as if you were there in person, unless God has especially called you.

Then, dear readers, what is your part in this great work? If you do not go, what will you give to send the gospel to those who sit in darkness?

True giving is not the throwing in of a large sum, and then sitting down and telling of it the rest of the year, but it is the daily sacrifice, the daily cross, the daily denying of self, that counts most in the eyes of Him who notices even the widow's mite.

Just how far one can deny self, must be determined between self and love for Christ. Those who seem to love most seem to find most ways to work for Him.

A few years ago when the famine was in China, and

the call came to our people for help, I knew a woman to feel so badly because she had no money to give, that she began to study how she could deny herself of even the seeming necessities of life, that she might help sustain the lives of others.

At the end of three months she had saved and sent to China seven dollars and fifty cents; but she had not eaten a piece of pie or cake, or tasted any delicacy during the time, and as often as practicable, had deprived her family of them. But so skillfully did she keep her left hand from knowing what the right hand did, that not even her husband suspected what she was doing. To-day, through a habit of self-denial and God's blessing, she is able to give much more for suffering humanity, and devote considerable of her time to the Lord's work.

Where there is a *will* to do, it will not be long before there is a way. The trouble generally is, we are not willing to work in *any* way, we want our *own* way, and as we can hardly ever have things go as we like, we hardly ever do anything.

These things ought not so to be. Time is so short, the race so quickly run, the rest so sweet, the prize so great, it pays to give up worldly pleasure and follow Him who "so loved us that He gave himself for us that he might redeem us from all iniquity and purify unto Himself a peculiar people zealous of good works."

He receives a benefit who bestows one on a worthy person.

IT NEVER PAYS.

IT never pays to fret or growl
  When fortune seems our foe ;
The better bred will push ahead
  And strike the braver blow.
    For luck is work,
    And those who shirk
Should not lament their doom :
    But yield the play
    And clear the way,
That better men have room.

It never pays to foster pride,
  And squander wealth in show ;
For friends thus won are sure to run
  In times of want or woe.
    The noble worth
    Of all the earth
Are gems of heart and brain—
    A conscience clear,
    A household dear,
And hands without a stain.

It never pays to hate a foe
  Or cater to a friend.
To fawn and whine, much less repine,
  To borrow or to lend.
    The faults of men
    Are fewer when
Each rows his own canoe,
    For friends and debts
    Are pampered pets,
Unbounded mischief brew.

It never pays to wreck the health
   In drudging after gain.
And he is sold who thinks that gold
   Is cheaply bought with pain.
     A humble lot,
     A cosy cot,
Have tempted even kings,
    For station high
    That wealth will buy,
Naught of contentment brings.

It never pays! A blunt refrain,
   Well worthy of a song ;
For age and youth must learn the truth
   That nothing pays that's wrong.
     The good and pure
     Alone are sure
To bring prolonged success !
    While what is right
    In heaven's sight
Is always sure to bless."

"Industry makes a man a purse, and carefulness gives him the strings to it. He that has it need only draw the strings as carefulness directs, and he will always find a useful penny at the bottom of it."

It is, after all, the person who stakes the least who loses the most. In the affections this is wholly true. He who risks nothing loses everything.

WORK.

"GO work to-day in my vineyard," is the divine order. God will have no idlers. Nor does he specify in all cases what we shall do. He says work.

"In my vineyard." The vineyard or the field of the Lord is the world. In the vineyard there is the setting out of new plants, pruning, tying up, grafting, gathering fruit, carrying food and drink to the workers, waiting and tending, filling gaps, mending the wall, building hedges, keeping accounts.

If we cannot do one thing let us do another—serving according to our opportunity and ability. The Lord by his providence and spirit will direct, and if we go forward in a willing and obedient spirit we shall find enough to do.

A KIND WORD.

WHO can tell the value of a kind word? It is so easily spoken, but may never be forgotten, and may have an influence for eternity.

Ah, we too often forget our Lord's example: "All wondered at the gracious words which proceeded out of his mouth." The bible enjoins us: "Be ye kind to one another. Be ye pitiful; be courteous."

Robert Lawrence had been hardened by a long course of evil, and when he found himself within the prison walls he grew desperate. A gentleman who visited him tried in vain to awaken remorse, and bring him to a sense of sin.

"My poor fellow, I would give anything to save you!" exclaimed the visitor at last, laying his hand upon the convict's shoulder.

"Why?" asked the man hoarsely.

"Because my Master loves you, and because he has put it into my heart to care for you," was the reply.

There was such earnestness and pity in the tone that the convict bowed his head in shame. Did the gentleman really care for him? Did he want to save him from the place to which the wicked go if they do not repent? And should the sinner neglect the way of escape? Was he any longer to harden his heart against the only friend who seemed to take an interest in him?

"Tell me what I am to do," he said at last.

The gentleman prayed for him, and opened to him "a door of hope," telling of one mighty to save. Before he left the dismal cell the visitor had the joy of hearing the prisoner pleading for mercy, crying in bitterness of spirit, "God be merciful to me, a sinner!"

Before you set about asking for God's blessing, make sure you have earned it.

Knowledge, like money, increases your responsibility in proportion to the amount obtained.

THE USEFUL GIRL.

HER face, though not so handsome as some,
   Is yet attractively sweet ;
Her dress, though not a costly one,
   Is tasteful, nice and neat.

She lightens her mother of many cares ;
   To her father she is kind, —
Showing in many remarkable ways,
   A well directed mind.

She can wash, sew, sweep and cook,
   And do it deftly, too,
And she can enjoy a new book
   As well as even you.

She can beautiful fancy work do,
   In the genuine Kensington stich ;
She can sing, and play the organ, too ;
   From low to highest pitch.

She can harness the team, and drive to town ;
   And, it may be shocking to you,
But she can run the reaper and gather corn
   And be a lady, too.

As our matrimonial ticket is drawn for life,
   And it's either win or lose—
Young man in search of a wife
   The useful girl will you choose ?

A FEW TABLE "DON'TS."

DON'T smack your lips.

Don't take large mouthfuls.

Don't use your knife instead of your fork.

Don't find fault and kick about your food.

Don't talk with your mouth filled with food.

Don't soil the table-cloth with bones, parings, etc.

Don't commence eating as soon as you are seated.

Don't laugh loudly, or talk boisterously at the table.

Don't retail all the slanders you can think of at the table.

Don't take bones up in your fingers to eat the meat from them.

Don't call attention to any little mistake which may have occurred.

Don't make yourself and your own affairs the chief topic of the conversation.

Don't take another mouthful, while any of the previous one remains in the mouth.

Don't blow your food in order to cool it.

Don't reach across the table for anything; but wait till it is passed to you, or ask for it.

Don't put your elbows on the table or lounge about; if not able to sit erect, ask to be excused.

Don't frown or look cross at the table; it hurts your own digestion as well as that of those eating with you.

Don't pick your teeth unless something has become edged between them, then put your napkin to your mouth while extracting it."

OVERCOMING EVIL.

IF we wish to overcome evil we must overcome it by good.

There are doubtless many ways of overcoming the evil of our own hearts, but the simplest, easiest, most universal is to overcome it by active occupation in some good word or work. The best antidote against evils of all kinds, against the evil thoughts which haunt the soul, against the heedless perplexities which distract the conscience, is to keep hold of the good we have. Impure thoughts will not stand against pure words and prayers and deeds. Little doubts will not avail against great certainties. Fix your affections on things above, and you will be less and less troubled by the cares, the temptations, the troubles and things on earth.

THOUGHTS OF MANY HEARTS.

DISREGARD or excuse your small fault, and you commit a greater one.

Talk little of your own grievances, or of others' misdoings.

Converse with those that will do you good, or to whom you may do good.

By not grasping at all within your reach, learn to bear the loss of what is out of your reach.

Do not wipe out others' blots with smeared fingers.

If someone says ill of you, do not ask who it was; so you can mend yourself and not be tempted to commit a new fault.

Who spends before he thrives, will beg before he thinks.

He is evil who is willing to make evil men his friends.

Small faults, not mended in their beginning, become great faults in the end.

Charity is the way of man to God and the way of God to man.

DON'T WHINE.

OOD people have a right to cast their burdens upon the Lord. But no one has a right to attempt to impose upon the Lord by the presentation of fictitious burdens, or to come into the Divine presence whining and finding fault with the allotments of Providence. Some people get into the habit of whining. They might have gotten into it sometime when they were really in trouble, and have forgotten to change their tone with their changed circumstances. I have known some persons to get so addicted to this thing that they would use the same whining tone in ordinary conversation, even when speaking upon the most joyous and cheerful topics. Sometimes I imagine they think it pious, a sort of holy tone. It is as far from the expression of the robust, cheerful, loving, hopeful, grateful holiness of the Bible, as the whine of the spaniel is from the songs of the happy birds of spring. So far from being holy, it is an abomination in the ear of the Giver of every good and perfect gift. Weep if you are afflicted. Groan if you are in pain. Cast your burden upon the Lord. He will sympathize with you and sustain you. He has promised it. But God has no promises for them that whine. Whatever you do, then, *do not whine.*

—J. S. SMART, D. D.

THE QUIET HOUR.

IS sweet to drop all anxious care,
 To simply rest ;
To know that for the present hour
 The soul is blest.

To cast all burdens at the feet
 Of Christ, the Lord ;
To let the soul go out and find
 Its Savior, God.

The high and holy thoughts that come
 With soothing calm,
Are like the zephyrs from the south,
 Laden with balm.

What if the future has some pain
 Hidden from view,
This quiet hour will give thee strength
 To dare and do.

Like happy bird with joyous song
 That seeks its nest,
Refreshed and soothed and filled with hope,
 The soul is blest.

Oh, quiet hour so full of peace,
    So full of love,
So full of sunlight from the throne,
    Of God above.

We greet thee like a precious friend,
    We feel thy power,
Glad refuge in a weary land,
    Oh, holy hour !

             —ELIZA H. MORTON.

PERSONAL WORK.

IT is very pleasant to have company in a good work. It is very assuring to be backed by a strong organization when one attacks a great evil. But God has generally singled out individual men to perform a great work. Moses did not wait for a vote of the Sanhedrim before he destroyed Aaron's calf. John the Baptist did not submit his sermon on repentance for the approval of a council of Pharisees before he dared to preach it. Lovejoy did not wait for the consent of conservative orthodoxy before he told his Alton neighbors it was a sin to buy and sell men. Moody is not against the church of to-day, but ahead of it. If the Church can tolerate men of crooked lives professing holiness, Moody will call saints from both hemispheres to pray them out of Northfield. Dr. Cullis may not be able to get a popular sect to sanction the healing of the sick by the prayer of faith, but hundreds of individuals will flock to him and become glad witnesses to the fact that Jesus Christ has lost none of his power over the bodies of men.

Order is good; system is good; yet God wrought mightily with Gideon, David and Samson, though they departed somewhat from common military tactics. Better far the living disorder of apostolic preaching, though it be said to turn the world upside down, than the dead forms of a worn-out ritual that leave men to perish in their sins. So in our time God has been pleased to smite giant evils by the hand of one man rather than at first by the united blow of a multitude. Not Catholic, not Episcopalian, not Independent smote the slave trade, but William Wilberforce. Not Presbyterian, not Methodist, not Baptist smote slavery, but William Lloyd Garrison. Not order, not sect, not convention smote rum, but Neal Dow. Christian men and Christian women, speak out for God! Go with your brethren as far as they follow Christ. If they halt at the cross, obey God and go forward. The Lord Jesus Christ commands individuals, not crowds. Your brethren, your church, can not answer for you at the judgment. Let God work in you both to will and to do of his good pleasure. Be of good courage, and He shall strengthen your heart, all ye that hope in the Lord. Trust in the Lord and do good; so shalt thou dwell in the land, and verily thou shalt be fed."

SOMETHING TO AVOID.

LITTLE personal pique, a bit of wounded vanity, a sudden flame of anger, often undoes the most substantial and faithful work, and nullifies the most intelligent and wise action. It is one of the painful things in experience that effort is often defeated by these small, purely personal, and often momentary feelings, which are generally unintelligent and unwise. Life would be freed from some of its most painful features if men always acted to each other on a basis of real justice and intelligence, and left their personal feelings and prejudices out of sight. A man's work ought to be judged by itself and for itself alone, and the man's position ought to rest solely upon what he is able to do. And yet most of us are constantly neutralizing the best work of others because it is not done in our way, and are constantly failing to do justice to others because of some small personal prejudice against them. The really strong, clear-sighted man is the one who is able to put himself out of the question and judge others by what they really are and do, not by their relations to him.

In this working world there is neither time nor strength to be always coddling our small vanities, and still smaller prejudices. The world does not stand in order that we may be pleased. It stands as a place for the doing of honest work in the best way, and if that work can better be done in some other way than the one we prefer, our business is to let it be done and rejoice in it.

If you wish to see things clearly, and to be just with your fellow-men, keep clear of the fumes of vanity and the thick atmosphere of mere personal feeling. Make it a rule to see what a man is and does, and to value him by these things. A person may be very distasteful to us and yet be eminently useful and successful in the world.

~~~~~~~~~~

We always find wit and merit in those who look at us with admiration.

WATCH YOUR WORDS.

KEEP watch on your words, my darling,
　For words are wonderful things ;
They are sweet like the bee's fresh honey,
　Like the bees, they have terrible stings.
They can bless like the warm, glad sunshine,
　And brighten a lonely life ;
They can cut, in the strife of anger,
　Like an open, two edged knife.

Let them pass through your lips unchallenged
　If their errand is true and kind—
If they come to support the weary,
　To comfort and help the blind ;
If a bitter, revengeful spirit
　Prompts the words, let them be unsaid,
They may flash through a brain like lightning
　Or they fall on a heart like lead.

Keep them back if they 're cold and cruel,
　Under the bar, and lock, and seal,
The wounds they make, my darlings,
　Are always slow to heal.
May peace guard your lips, and ever
　From the time of your early youth,
May the words that you daily utter
　Be the words of beautiful truth.

　　　　　　　　　　　　　—E. C.

The beam of the benevolent eye giveth value to the
bounty which the hand disburses.

FAR ABOVE BEAUTY.

IN my life I have known many women well. Among them is a fair majority of what the truly appreciative would call happy, for which fact I thank God, as it has helped me to take, on the whole, a hopeful view of life as well as human nature. Now, are these women, blest as many of them are with devoted husbands, cheerful homes, cultivated society, and leisure for the exercise of any special talent they may possess, beautiful women? With one or two exceptions, no. Indeed, more than a few of them are positively plain, if feature only is considered, while from the rest I can single out but two or three whose faces conform to any of the recognized standards of physical perfection. But they are loved, they are honored, they are deferred to. While not eliciting the admiration of every passer by, they have acquired through the force, sweetness, or originality of their character, the appreciation of those whose appreciation confers honor and happiness, and, consequently, their days pass in an atmosphere of peace and good will which is as far above the delirious admiration accorded to the simply beautiful as the placid shining of the sunbeam is to the phenomenal blaze of an evanescent flame.

Fashion is only gold front jewelry, it may appear well, but the value is not there.

SUSIE'S WISH.

"HOW I wish that dollars grew
On a bush !" said little Sue—
Pretty, blue-eyed Susie Snow—
Thinking in an idle way
Of a doll she saw one day
In a window placed for show.

" Go and seek for them awhile,"
Answered grandma, with a smile,
" Where the berry-pastures spread ;
Go with pails and baskets, quick,
Where the blueberries are thick ;
There the dollars are," she said.

Little Sue ran down the hill,
Crossed the brook beyond the mill,
Reached the pastures stretching wide,
With a shining prize in view,
Now her fingers almost flew,
Gathering fruit on every side.

When the busy day was spent,
With her berries home she went.
"Oh !" she laughed as Grandma Snow
Measured them, and every time
Counted in a silver dime—
" Now I see how dollars grow."

—M. E. N. Hatheway.

418

COME.

THE gospel is an invitation. The table is spread with the great bounties; the fountain of life and healing is open; all things are ready. The sinner has nothing to do in making the provision; Christ has provided and met the bill. All he asks of the sinner is acceptance; the surrender of himself and the taking of what Christ has to bestow. To you, fellow sinner, is this offer made—the offer of free and full salvation. . The final utterance of the New Testament is the proffer of this invitation, in which Christ and his people join: "The Spirit and the bride say, Come. And let him that is athirst come. And whosoever will, let him take of the water of life freely." No one need despair; no one need hesitate. You may be poor, halt, blind; your service may be of the poorest; no matter. You will never succeed on merit; but you may come freely, without money or price. Come just as you are to one that is mighty and able to save—to one inviting you to come. If you neglect such an offer, what excuse can you bear to the throne of judgment? What excuse can you make?

~~~~~~~~~~

Dr. Spring says: "I never knew an irreligious man to die joyous; nor a religious man to die miserable."

419

BE STEADFAST.

"BE STEADFAST"—fixed in your convictions and pronounced in their defense, even though men count you narrow, obstinate, etc—"be ye steadfast, unmovable "—not the slaves of the world, not unstable as water, not laboring to shape yourself as the world of fashion, or the like would have you to be, but " always abounding in the work of the Lord, for as much as ye know that your labor is not in vain in the Lord."

—DR. JOHN HALL.

THE LOCKED DOOR.

TWO friends once closed between them mutually,
    A door with double locks, one on each side ;
    With separate keys, fashioned with cunning art,
Sure of himself, strong in fresh-wounded pride,
Each, for his own side only, held the key.

And thus for weary weeks they dwelt apart,
Till one, at last, whose drooping tears had drowned
The fire of wrath that in his bosom burned,
Full of forgiveness, softly stole and turned
The key ; then sought to ope the door ! but found
The other lock still fast ; still locked the door !
Then the old anger leaped to sudden flame,
And, laying on his friend's hard heart the blame,
He shot again the bolt and turned once more
To nurse, in bitterness, the re-opened wound.

That night the other thought of olden days,
And melted in the memory ; they seemed
So nearer than estrangement's later hours,
That of the quarrel he thought he must have dreamed,
And so unlocked the door ; yet all his powers
Failed still to shake it.   Then he muttered, "Fool,
To think that stubborn churl would e'er repent !"
And socket-ward again the bolt he sent.
And thus before the first friend's wrath could cool,
The other's heart grew hard again and kept
The bar between them while they waked or slept.

But one calm eve they both waked from a dream
Of what has been, so clear foreshadowing, too,
The golden prophecy of what may be ;
Each rises in the moonlight's softened gleam,
Resolves to try again all he can do,
Once more before the barrier he stands ;
And as, again, slowly each iron key
Rasps in his rusted wards, an answering sound
Comes from the other side.   The great door flies
Open and leaves the old friends, newly found,
Lovingly looking in each other's eyes,
With re-united hearts and firm-clasped hands.

—C. W. BAKER.

We build barriers against the flood tide, we should place some restraint to all prosperity.

The jest that gives pain is no jest.

LET HIM PROVE IT.

THE most complete and satisfactory prosperity is that enjoyed by the individual who has earned his good fortune by his own efforts. It may appear like a herculean undertaking for a young man to go forth into the great, grasping, jostling world and fight the battle of life unassisted, but such a course is the one that leads generally to the most enduring success.

"If more fathers would take a course with their sons similar to the one my father took with me," observed one of the leading business men of Boston, "the boys might think it hard at the time, but they'd thank them in after life."

"What sort of a course?" was asked.

"Well, I was a young fellow of twenty-two, just out of college; and I felt myself of considerable importance. I knew my father was well off, and my head was full of foolish notions of having a good time and spending lots of money. Later on I expected my father to start me in business, after I'd 'swelled' round a while at the clubs and with fine horse-flesh.

"Like a wise man, father saw through my folly, and resolved to prevent my self-destruction, if possible.

"'If the boy's got the right stuff in him, let him prove it,' I heard father say to mother one day. I worked hard for my money, and I don't intend to let Ned squander it, and ruin himself besides.

"That very day father came along and handed me fifty dollars, remarking, 'Ned, take that money, spend it as you choose, but understand this much : it's the last dollar of my money you can have till you prove yourself capable of earning money and taking care of it on your own account.'

"I took the money in a sort of dazed manner, and stammered out, 'I—why—I—I—want to go into business.'

"'Business!' exclaimed father, contemptuously, 'what do you know about managing the mercantile business ? Get a clerkship and learn the alphabet before you talk to me about business.' Then he left me to ponder on his words. And that fifty dollars was the last money my father gave me, till at his death I received my part of the property.

"I felt hard and bitter at the time I received the fifty dollars ; felt my father was a stingy old fogy, and mentally resolved to prove to him that I could live without his money. He had roused my pride—just what he intended, I suppose.

"For three days I looked about for a place to make 'lots of money.' But I found no such chance, and at length, I accepted a clerkship in a large retail store at four hundred dollars a year.

"Another bit of my father's 'stinginess' at this time was demanding two dollars a week for my board through that first year.

"At the end of my first year I had laid aside two hundred dollars, and next year my salary being raised one hundred dollars, I had five hundred laid by.

"One hundred cents meant more to me in those days than one hundred dollars had, previously.

"At the end of four years' clerking I went to my father with fifteen hundred dollars of my own, and asked him if he was willing to help me enter business. Even then he would only let me hire the money, two thousand dollars, at six per cent. interest.

"To-day I am called a successful business man. And have my father to thank for it. Those lessons in self-denial, self-respect and independence which he gave me, put the manhood into me.

"Years afterwards, father told me it cost him the hardest struggle of his life to be so hard with his boy. But he felt it was the only course to make a man of me. Many a time we've laughed over that two dollar board bill."

TWO LITTLE OLD LADIES.

TWO little old ladies, one grave, one gay,
  In the self-same cottage lived day by day.
   One could not be happy, " because," she said,
"So many children were hungry for bread ; "
And she really had not the heart to smile,
When the world was so wicked all the while.

The other old lady smiled all day long
As she knitted, or sewed, or crooned a song.
She had not time to be sad, she said,
When hungry children were crying for bread.
So she baked, and knitted, and gave away,
And declared the world grew better each day.

Two little old ladies, one grave, one gay ;
Now which do you think chose the wiser way ?
                —MAUD MERRILL.

THIS LIFE IS WHAT WE MAKE IT.

ET'S oftener talk of noble deeds,
  And rarer of the bad ones,
  And sing about our happy days,
  And not about the sad ones.
We are not made to fret and sigh,
  And when grief sleeps to wake it:
Bright happiness is standing by—
  This life is what we make it.

Let's find the sunny side of men,
  Or be believers in it ;
A light there is in every soul
  That takes the pains to win it.
Oh ! there's a slumbering good in all,
  And we perchance may wake it ;
Our hands contain the magic wand—
  This life is what we make it.

Then here's to those whose loving hearts
  Shed light and joy about them !
Thanks be to them for countless gems
  We ne'er had known without them.
Oh ! this should be a happy world
  To all who may partake it :
The fault's our own if it is not—
  This life is what we make it.

ALONE WITH JESUS.

THE blue sky beams with brightness o'er me,
  The sailing clouds drift to and fro,
 The distance softly melts before me,
  The silver waves are all aglow ;
But I have fairer, brighter visions
  Than those that greet my eyes to-day,
For, twixt my soul and heaven's bright glory,
  The veil is partly torn away ;
  So happy I can only say,
    " Alone with Jesus !"

The air is filled with strains of music,
  I hardly know that I am here,
But almost fancy I'm in heaven,
  The songs of angels sound so near.
And, while I hear the happy chorus,
  It seems that I can hardly stay ;
But then, since Jesus is so near me,
  Heaven is not far away ;
  'Twere heaven itself e'en here to stay
    " Alone with Jesus."

Should storm and tempest rage around me,
  And waves of sorrow flood my soul ;
Should loved ones turn and frown upon me,
  And earthly ties be severed all,
O, Jesus, thou would'st not forsake me ;
  The brightness of thy holy face
Should chase away all gloom and darkness,
  And, sinking in thy loved embrace,
  My soul should find sweet resting place
    " Alone with Jesus."

426

Alone with Jesus, when earth's praises
   Shall turn to hate, and scoff, and scorn ;
Alone with Jesus in the sunshine,
   Alone with Jesus in the storm.
And when the lengthened shadows tell me
   It is the close of life's short day,
I'll sing one song of holy triumph
   To Him who's ever been my stay,
   Then fold my hands and pass away,
      " Alone with Jesus."
               —Mrs. Anna Crouch.

PRAYER AND WORK.

A DEVOUT WRITER has said: "Work may disturb and dissipate our communion with God ; it may weaken the very motive from which it should arise ; it may withdraw our gaze from God, and fix it on ourselves. It may puff us with conceit of our own powers; it may fret us with annoyances of resistance ; and in a hundred other ways may waste and wear away our personal religion. The more we work the more we need to pray. In this day of activity there is great danger, not of doing too much, but of praying too little for so much work. " Lord, teach us to work ; Lord, teach us to pray."

How may we preserve a due proportion between these two—work and prayer ? We are to remember that there is no well balanced living without wholeheartedness ; without a continual surrender of all to God ; with a fixed purpose to glorify Him in whatever

427

we undertake. To be fully consecrated to God and his service, according to his own word, is, therefore, the first requisite.

Next in importance to this is a proper sense of our littleness and God's greatness. No workman or work is necessary to the advancement of God's glory in the earth. Work is the privilege granted to us ; not a meritorious yielding of ourselves to God. His character is so ineffably glorious that to be linked in service with Him in any way is unspeakable condescension on his part. To know God and also ourselves enables us, therefore, so to work that holy communion with Him will be steadily maintained. And then, if we would have this connection unbroken, we should lovingly consider the example of our Lord, who, when upon earth, withdrew himself from human gaze to seek refreshment at the fountain sources of spiritual comfort. We are taught that ''for our sakes'' he thus fulfilled all righteousness. Think of his manner in the disciples' presence. Doubtless all along his toilsome way he "lifted up his eyes to Heaven" and called upon the Father.

Partaking of his spirit, no one will so work as to lose the desire to pray ; on the other hand, no one will so pray as to abridge his relish or ability for work in the Master's service.

Excessive labor is wrong, but judicious labor is the safety valve of life.

428

WORKERS AND WINNERS.

KEEP striving; the winners are those who have striven
  And fought for the prize that no idler has won;
To the hands of the steadfast alone it is given,
  And before it is gained there is work to be done.

Keep climbing: the earnest and steadfast have scaled
  The height where the path-way was rough to the feet;
But the faint-hearted faltered, and faltering failed,
  And sank down by the way-side in hopeless defeat.

Keep hoping: the clouds hide the sun for a time,
  But sooner or later they scatter and flee,
And the path glows like gold to the toilers who climb
  To the heights where men look over landscape and sea.

Keep onward—right on, till the prize is attained;
  Front the future with courage, and obstacles fall.
By those, and those only, the victory's gained
  Who keep faith in themselves and the God over all.
                                        —EBEN S. REXFORD.

BE GENEROUS WHILE ALIVE.

I HAVE felt that it is a great mistake to put off being
  generous till after you are dead. In the first place
you lose the pleasure of witnessing the good that you
may do; and, again, no one can administer your gifts
for you as well as you can do it yourself. It is a great
pleasure to be brought into personal relations of that

kind, and to make people feel that you are not a philanthropist in the abstract, but that you are interested in them personally and care for their welfare. In that way you benefit them not merely in a natural way, but you make them feel that men are really brothers, and they were made to help one another. That feeling is not only agreeable in itself, but it will be apt to prompt them to carry out the principle themselves. Put yourself into all you do, and let others feel that you are there. Do not only contribute to a charitable fund, but go yourself and help. It may seem inconvenient at first, but soon you will come to consider it worth any inconvenience.

—G. W. CHILDS.

JOHN AND JOE.

JOHN has risen before the sun,
   His cows are milked and his horses fed,
   Joe is somewhere out with his gun
      Or lying soundly asleep in his bed.
Tall weeds are waving in Joseph's field,
   Small and meager his corn appears,
Small and meager will be the yield
   When it comes to shocking the shining ears.

John pays cash when he has to buy,
   He never gambles, or drinks, or bets ;
Joe gets on tick till his score runs high,
   Then pledges his farm to pay his debts ;
And each contraction or new device
   Of springs and pulleys for catching fools,
Joe buys—no matter how steep the price—
   To rust and rot with his other tools.

John's garden gives of the best to eat,
 He's seldom bothered with doctor's bills ;
Joe lives mostly on bread and meat,
 Stomach bitters and patent pills.
John works hard with muscle and mind,
 Side by side with the world he stands ;
Joe is daily falling behind,
 Losing his grip with both his hands.

This relation is strictly true,
 Be no object to tell you a lie ;
John and Joe lives neighbors to you,
 You know 'em as well as I.
Whether you dwell where Nature fair
 Blushes with roses or pales with snow,
John and Joe are sure to be there
 Just as I tell you—'specially Joe.

BRIGHT FACES.

ONE of my friends who seems to have gained the secret of perpetual youth and good spirits said : " Do you notice I always put on my sweetest, most unruffled expression when I'm in a hurry or get caught in a crowd, a thing I detest, or whenever I want to look worried, because most other women do look so like crazy frights in the least crisis?" It is not the great men or women who look the most borne down by responsibility and anxiety. Gladstone showed less lines of care than a woman out on a shopping excursion on " bargain day."

ALABASTER BOXES OF HUMAN SYMPATHY.

DO not keep the alabaster boxes of your love and tenderness sealed up until your friends are dead. Fill their lives with sweetness. Speak approving, cheering words while their ears can hear them, and while their hearts can be thrilled and made happier by them ; the kind things you mean to say when they are gone, say before they go. The flowers you mean to send for their coffins, send to brighten and sweeten their homes before they leave them. If my friends have alabaster boxes laid away full of fragrant perfumes of sympathy and affection, which they intend to break over my body, I would rather they would bring them out in my wearied and troubled hours, and open them that I may be refreshed, and cheered by them while I need them. I would rather have a plain coffin without a flower, a funeral without an eulogy, than a life without the sweetness of love and sympathy. Let us learn to anoint our friends beforehand for their burial Post-mortem kindness does not cheer the burdened spirit. Flowers on the coffin cast no fragrance backward over the weary way.

EITHER be a possessor or do not profess. The open sinner is not condemned of the Lord as the hypocrite. Jesus says to the worldly christians: "I would thou wert cold or hot."

"JESUS LOVES ME."

I WAS sitting in my study, with my sermon almost done,
  When there slowly up the stairway came the well known
      children's song :
" Jesus loves me, Jesus loves me," and I, listening, dropped the
      pen,
For the truth so old and precious, never seemed so sweet as
      then.

Of this love I have been writing, trying hard to make it plain,
That people might believe it and find solace for their pain ;
But that I should be his loved one, and that He *my* sorrow
      bears,
Was a thought not fully pondered till that song came up the
      stairs.

Well I knew that not a lily lifts its cup to catch the showers,
But drinks in the sun's full treasures though the fields are filled
      with flowers ;
The mother to her children never gives her love in part,
But to each and every member gives an undivided heart.

But somehow I'd miss the lesson, that, while Christ loves all
      the race,
All his love is poured *on me*, through the fullness of God's
      grace.
Now I bless Him I have learned it, for it cheers me on my
      way,
And I ne'er shall cease to thank Him for the song I heard that
      day.

—REV. R. F. COYLE.

WINGS.

WINGS.

WHAT matter it though life uncertain be
    To all? What though its goal
    Be never reached? What though it fall
        and flee,
      Have we not each a soul?

A soul that quickly must arise and soar
    To regions far more pure—
Arise and dwell where pain can be no more,
    And every joy is sure.

Be like the bird that on a bough too frail
    To bear him, gayly swings;
Carols though the slender branches fail—
    He knows that he has wings.

                    —Victor Hugo.

HONEST ANYHOW.

IT is one thing to be true to principle when surrounded
by those who are upright, and quite another thing
when others are immoral. Moreover, when the
world seems to be against a man and the clouds hang
low—this is the time to test his true nobility of char-
acter. A good many years ago in one of the southern
states a bright, active colored boy was offered for sale
in one of the slave markets. A gentleman taking pity
on the lad determined to buy him and insure him kind
treatment. Before he bid for him, he said to the boy:

"If I buy you will you be honest?" Quickly came the reply, "I will be honest whether you buy me or not." This was a noble answer. The poor slave boy could not allow his surroundings to make a difference in his relations with God. Honesty with him was not a matter dependent upon others' treatment of him.

The world will be very much better when men look above erring human nature and allow divine influence to mold their thought and purpose.

GOOD MANNERS AT HOME.

THE presence of good manners is no where more needed, or more effective, than in the household, and, perhaps, no where more rare. Whenever familiarity exists, there is a chance to loosen the check upon selfish conduct which the presence of strangers involuntarily produces. Many persons who are kind and courteous in company are rude and careless with those they love best.

Emerson says, "Good manners are made up of petty sacrifices," and certainly nothing can more thoroughly secure the harmony and peace of the family circle than the habit of making small sacrifices one for another. Children thus learn good manners in the best and most natural way, and habits thus acquired will never leave them.

Courtesy and kindness will never lose their power or their charm, while all spurious imitations of them are to be despised.

THE ROYAL WAY OF THE CROSS.

WE may spread our couch with roses,
  And sleep through the summer day,
But the soul that in sloth reposes,
  Is not in the narrow way.
If we follow the chart that is given,
  We need not be at a loss ;
For the royal way to heaven
  Is the royal way of the Cross.

To one who is fond of splendor,
  The cross is a heavy load ;
And the foot that is soft and tender
  Complains of the thorny road.
But the chains of the soul must be riven,
  And gold must be as dross ;
For the royal way to heaven
  Is the royal way of the Cross.

We say we will walk to-morrow
  The path we refuse to-day ;
And still, with our luke-warm sorrow,
  We shrink from the narrow way.
What heeded the chosen eleven
  How the fortunes of life might toss,
As they followed their Master to Heaven,
  By the royal way of the Cross.

BE ABLE TO SAY "NO."

MANY a boy has entered the downward path merely because he lacked courage to refuse his companionship to those who had already taken that road. Mrs. Bottome says :

"It takes character to say 'No.' The three Hebrew children said, 'We will not serve thy God;' and there they rested. They had nothing to do with the result. If the king threw them into the fiery furnace, that was his business; and it was God's business to look after the fire when they were thrown into it. They simply said and acted, 'No, we will not.' Dare to say 'No!'"

A BLIGHTED HOME.

TO the weak and the strong a word I would say,
It is for all that my words are to-day;
A demon there is that lurks in the dark,
Of good will and friendship he has not a spark.

He despises the light, your lives he will blight,
If you list to his voice in the darkness of night.
He gloats in sight of the homes he has broken,
By the absence of loved ones and other sad tokens.

From the heads of kings he has torn off the crown,
From the heights of glory he has cast men down ;
He has taken the bread from the mouths of babes,
And the love of home from the man he degrades.

438

As I look o'er the past a home I can see,
A father, a mother, and a child there in glee ;
The father is tall, honest, handsome and brave,
Not a cloud does he see, not a joy does he crave.

His home is so bright with gladness and song,
He cares not to mingle with the death-dealing throng.
His child is his idol, his wife is his pride,
Through paths that are pleasant their footsteps he'll guide.

Now, look again at the home of the drunkard :
The wife's white brow with sadness is furrowed ;
With husband she's pleading, with tears in her eyes,
To stay with her dear one that near to death lies.

But no ! from their side, with a blow and an oath,
He leaves them in darkness.   God pity them both !
He starts for the tavern, and with him he takes
The shoes of the little one that he forsakes.

He steps to the bar with the shoes in his hand,
To pay for his rum this way he has planned ;
He passes them over, the rumseller recoils.
Oh, think of the many happy homes that he spoils !

" I cannot take these," the rumseller says,
"O, take them back home, she will need them," he says,
But the poor drunken wretch, says, " No !" to him now,
" You have caused me to fall, and before you to bow.

You have ruined my home, and prospects in life,
You've taken my child, you've taken my life ;
So give me the rum or by me you will be cursed,
O, do take the shoes, and then do your worst ! "

439

The rum is refused the poor drunkard at last,
By the very same man that gave the first glass ;
He reels to the door.   Ah ! list to the sound—
A report of a pistol, and a dull, heavy sound.

The drunkard at last from temptation is free,
No more to the demon will he bow the knee ;
He is missed by no one ; his life was a spark
That did not light home that now is so dark.

Such scenes as this, my friends, you may see,
In the homes where all should be gladness and glee ;
But the rum-selling curse o'ershadows our land,
And crushes our hopes like houses of sand.

Let us go to the home of the poor drunkard's wife,
And by our kind deeds let us brighten her life ;
And fight the dread demon of rum from our door,
Until all such sights shall be seen nevermore.

                                    —Herbert J. Leighton.

No man or woman, however humble, can really be
strong, gentle, pure and good, without the world being
helped and comforted by the very existence of good-
ness.

Be the kind of a man that you would like to have
your boys become.

A KIND WORD.

A KIND WORD costs but little, but it may bless the one to whom it is spoken all day. Nay, have not kind words been spoken to you which have lived in your heart through years, and borne fruit of joy and hope? Let us speak kindly to one another. We have burdens and worries, but let us not, therefore, rasp and irritate those near us, those we love, those Christ would have us save. Some one has given us these impressive words: ''Speak kindly in the morning; it lightens the cares of the day, and makes the household and all its affairs move along smoothly. Speak kindly at night, for it may be that before dawn some loved one may finish his or her space of life for this world, and it will be too late to ask forgiveness.''

CHRISTIAN SYMPATHY.

THERE was once a man who had fallen over-board, and someone held out to him a plank lying on the pier, one end of which was covered with ice. He reached out the plank to the man with the icy end to him. The man seized the end of the plank, and again and again his hands slipped off. At last he cried out in despair: "For God's sake give me the warm end of the plank!" This illustrates the truth that there must be the warmth of sympathy if we expect to move the intellect and will. Cold demonstrations do not reform men; icy sermons and lectures, however grammatically written or properly delivered, will fall as useless as icicles on a stony pavement. Very proper, precise, and learned teachers are seldom useful. They shine, but the light that comes from them is like the sunshine reflected from an iceburg. There must be heat.

BE TRUE.

BE true to every impulse
   Within the upright soul,
That pointeth toward duty—
   Like magnet to the pole.

Be true to the affections,
   Wherever thou dost go.
Free from the heart's deep fountains
   These glad'ning streams should flow.

True to the soul's monitions;
   True to the heart's best love,
To friendships and to charities,
   To sordid self above.

True to the land that bore thee,
   Loving its very sod;
Loyal unto thy country,
   Upright before thy God.

—MACK STERLING.

TO-DAY IF YOU WILL HEAR HIS VOICE.

IS there some noble deed that you may do ?
  Some point to gain on high ?
Act now, and thus to thyself be true,
  To-morrow ye may die.

Is there some cheering word that you may speak
  While day is passing by ?
Go, let that precious word the silence break,
  To-morrow ye may die.

Is there some grievous wrong that you may right,
  Or hush some deep drawn sigh ?
Remember while so swiftly comes the night,
  To-morrow ye may die.

Go, pour sweet balm into some wounded heart ;
  Go, wipe some tearful eye ;
Let not the act undone with day depart,
  To-morrow ye may die.

Yea, go, and make your peace with God and man
  Ere on your couch you lie ;
Secure a crown of life, 'tis wisdom's plan,
  To-morrow ye may die.

The right kind of a Christian character is something
that the devil's mud won't stick to.

DON'T SNEER.

WE pray you not to get in the habit of sneering. You may indulge this tendency until it utterly destroys the spirit of christian gentleness and kindness in your hearts. Your neighbors are full of faults, to be sure ; your fellow-christians fail to come up to the standard of their professions, it is true. But are these good reasons why you should become sour, censorious and malignant ? What about yourself ? Are you perfect ? Suppose God should judge you as rigorously as you judge other people ? In that event where would you stand ? Be forbearing; be magnanimous ; be Christ-like. Remember it is not easy to reach the highest levels of conduct. and do not expect of others what you fail to do in your own life.

THE SECRET OF A HAPPY HOME.

I HAVE passed into quiet parlors where the carpet is clean and not old, and the furniture polished and bright, into rooms where the chairs are neat and the floors carpetless, into the kitchen where the family live and the meals are cooked and eaten, and the boys and girls are as blithe as the sparrows overhead; and I see that it is not so much wealth and learning nor clothes nor servants nor toil nor idleness nor town nor country nor station, as tone and temper that renders home happy or wretched. And I see, too, in the town or country, good sense and God's grace makes life what no teacher or accomplishments, or means or society can make it—the fair beginning of an endless existence, the goodly, modest, well proportioned vestibule to a temple of God's building that shall never decay, wax old or vanish away.

—REV. JOHN HALL.

HOME SONG.

STAY, stay at home, my heart, and rest;
Home-keeping hearts are happiest,
For those that wander they know not where
Are full of trouble and full of care ;
To stay at home is best.

Weary, and home-sick, and distressed,
They wander east, they wander west,
And are baffled, and beaten, and blown about
By the winds of the wilderness of doubt ;
To stay at home is best.

Then stay at home, my heart, and rest ;
The bird is safest in its nest;
O 'er all that flutter their wings and fly
A hawk is hovering in the sky ;
To stay at home is best.

—LONGFELLOW.

Success is on the hill top, you cannot get there without climbing.

IN GOD'S GOOD TIME.

LOW hang the clouds, a leaden pall
   That shows no gleam of azure rift.
But hark ! soft as a spirit's call
   "In God's good time the clouds shall lift."

Fierce break the billows at my feet,
   No hint of help my eyes discern ;
But hark ! again a whisper sweet :
   "In God's good time the tide shall turn."

Oh, heart, in this glad word abide,
   Repeated like a silver chime :
Unharmed is he by storm or tide
   Who waits in faith for God's good time.
               —MARY B. SLEIGHT.

EXILED.

IT comes to me often in silence,
   When the firelight sputters low—
When the black uncertain shadows
   Seem wraiths of the long ago ;
Always with a throb of heart-ache
   That thrills each pulsive vein,
Comes the old unquiet longing,
   For the peace of home again.

I am sick of the roar of cities,
   And of faces cold and strange ;
I know where there's warmth of welcome,
   And my yearning fancies range

446

Back to the dear old homestead,
  With an aching sense of pain.
But there 'll be joy in the coming,
  When I go home again.

When I go home ! There's music
  That never may die away,
And it seems the hands of angels,
  On a mystic harp at play,
Have touched with a yearning sadness
  On a beautiful broken strain,
To which is my fond heart wording—
  When I go home again.

Outside of my darkening window
  Is the great world's crash and din,
And slowly the autumn shadows
  Come drifting, drifting in.
Sobbing, the night wind murmurs
  To the splash of the autumn rain ;
But I dream of the glorious greeting
  When I go home again.

             —EUGENE FIELD.

A MAN who is unable to discover any errors or mistakes in the opinions he formerly held, is not likely to advance very fast in the acquirement of knowledge.

Romance is one thing, but making an honest living and paying your debts is another.

447

THE TRUE PEACEMAKER.

DON'T be a grumbler. Some people contrive to get hold of the prickly side of everything, to run against all the sharp corners and disagreeable things. Half the strength spent in growling would often set things right. You may as well make up your mind to begin with that no one ever found the world quite as he would like it ; but you are to take your part of the trouble and bear it bravely. You will be sure to have burdens laid upon you that belong to other people, unless you are a shirker yourself; but don't grumble. If the work needs doing, and you can do it, never mind about that other fellow who ought to have done it and didn't. Those workers who fill up the gaps and smooth away the rough spots and finish up the jobs that others leave undone—they are the true peacemakers and worth a whole regiment of growlers.

"BUSINESS IS BUSINESS."

THERE is a man who lives in the city of New York who has accumulated quite a fortune by simply advising people what to do. There always will be a large number of persons who are unable to rely on their own judgment. Others come to a conclusion with ease and certainty.

A young man had accumulated $1,000, and was debating whether he should buy a small candy store with it or whether he should lend it on a mortgage. This latter he knew was the secure way. The other promised great profits. In this perplexity he saw an advertisement: "Advice given to those going into business."

After stating his case the counsellor said: "My fee will be $5 in advance."

When this was paid, he asked:

"Do you understand the candy business?"

"No; I did not think it was necessary. I expect to supervise it merely."

"Then you will lose all your money in three months."

"You think I had better lend the money on the mortgage?"

"I do not say that. What is your business; that is, what do you perfectly understand?"

"I know the pickle business through and through. I can make pickles of all kinds but do not like it."

"Never mind what you like. Go and get a small place and make pickles. Go from hotel to hotel, restaurant to restaurant, and sell them. In ten years come back and see me. You will have $10,000 at least."

As the young man was going away he was called back.

"Here is a card. I want you to put it where you can see it a hundred times a day."

These were the words on the card: "Business is Business. Men don't do what they like; they do what they can."

The card had a strange fascination for him. He read

it with care as he walked along the street. As he studied it new light seemed to enter his mind.

He found a dingy basement, and began to arrange for his operations. Of course, vinegar must be got, several barrels of it. Some was offered him at ten cents a gallon, some more was shown at five cents. "Which shall I take?" He thought of the words on his card. He seemed to see people testing his pickles, and not liking them depart without buying.

"They will know good vinegar," thought he; and so he bought the honest stuff.

In a few days several tubs of the materials were ready, and he knew he must market them. Now he greatly hated to face strange people, and push his goods upon their notice. He never had courage when a boy, and now as a man he felt more timid, it seemed, but he thought of the words of the card, and entered a restaurant. The evident manager was a blooming young woman; and the pickle-dealer was more afraid of women than men. But "business is business" repeated itself over and over in his mind.

The answer to his statement was that his pickles should be tried, and if found all right, would be purchased.

"Glad I got that good vinegar," thought the young man; and he began to feel that there was a certain power in the maxim his advisor had given. He began to feel a courage he had never expected in meeting people and trying to sell his goods to them.

Calling at a store to get, if possible, an order for pickles in bottles, he was quickly and rudely met with,

"Don't want to see any such stuff." Noticing the utter dismay on the young man's face, the merchant said, short and sharp, "Don't you know enough of business to put up your goods attractively?"

As he retreated, ruffled and disheartened, the maxim repeated itself over and over, with this additional sentence, "It is business to put up goods attractively." He sought out a lithographer, and had some handsomely colored labels printed.

"They will buy the bottles," said a friend, just for the picture you have on them."

When he had gained sufficient courage, he sought out again the merchant who had rebuffed him. "I wish to make you a present of a bottle of fine pickles."

"Why do you make me a present of them?"

"Because you gave me advice that is worth a good deal."

The morning of one Fourth of July came, and he pondered whether to go to his store or not. All at once he thought, "People going on picnics will want pickles." It was the magic words on the little card that ran through his mind. He found as he thought, a large number of buyers waiting for him.

The little card was consulted in all sorts of weather. If a man made a proposition to him of any kind, and he was in doubt, he would go and look at the words, and study them intently, trying to think their application to the case in hand. "Men do what they can," he reflected. "I would like to sell something else; but I know I can sell pickles." Then he returned. Now he was resolute and firm, although by nature easily swayed by the words of others.

"Business is business," he said. "I am in the pickle business. If I cannot make money this way I shall quit, and go into something else; but I will not have two kinds on my hands."

It was a turning-point. After this he could refuse all influence to go into something at the time more lucrative.

He was not only industrious; it is plain he had a fixed principle of action. Of course he was successful. All men who put industry and mind to their work are bound to be successful. When the ten years were up, of course he had the $10,000 and more too.

HARD KNOTS.

MY little three-year-old came to me stamping with rage, because in trying to untie her bonnet-strings she had drawn them into a hard knot. She was pulling with all her might, but the more she pulled the tighter they became.

At last she consented to let me untie them for her, but just as I began to get them loose, she would grow impatient and give them another jerk that would tighten them and cause another long delay.

And I thought, it is just so with the hard knots of our lives. By our impatience we make them harder. We should patiently wait until the hard things can be straightened, the rough places made smooth.

The little tangles in our daily life will not last long if we will only stand still and let God straighten them for us.

SOME MOTHER'S CHILD.

AT home or away, in the alley or street,
  Whenever I chance in this wide world to meet
  A girl that is thoughtless, a boy that is wild,
My heart echoes softly: " 'Tis some mother's child."

And when I see those o'er whom long years have rolled,
Whose hearts have grown hardened, whose spirits are cold,
Be it woman all fallen, or man all defiled,
A voice whispers sadly: " Ah! some mother's child."

No matter how far from the right she has strayed,
No matter what inroads dishonor hath made;
No matter what elements have cankered the pearl—
Though tarnished or sullied, she is some mother's girl.

No matter how wayward his footsteps have been,
No matter how deep he is sunken in sin;
No matter how low is his standard of joy—
Though guilty and loathsome, he is some mother's boy.

That head has been pillowed on the tenderest breast;
That form has been wept o'er, those lips have been pressed;
That soul has been prayed for in tones sweet and mild;
For her sake deal gently with some mother's child.

—FRANCIS L. KELLER.

Help somebody worse off than yourself, and you will
find that you are better off than you fancied.

453

WATCHING OUR CONVERSATION.

NOTWITHSTANDING the Divine word says that for every idle word men shall speak they shall give account thereof in the day of judgment, many really good people are constantly saying something that kills their influence in the church, and hinders the growth of grace in their own heart.

Recently during a severe storm, a dear brother who claims to enjoy the blessing of holiness, on coming out out of church, remarked:

"I think it is time it stopped raining, we have had enough of it."

Instantly a man whom the brother had often exhorted to lead a better life, replied:

"You seem to know more about it than the Almighty, perhaps you can change affairs if you should take the lines in your own hands."

Of course the brother felt hurt, as well as rebuked, but he was really at fault, as he had forgotten to set a watch upon his lips that the door of his mouth might be kept.

When the time comes, (if it ever does) when christians learn to have their conversation without covetousness, and such as "becometh the gospel of Christ," the world will have more confidence in Christianity, and God will be able to use them more fully to His glory.

~~~~~~~~~

It is better to know when to say yes, and no, than to know the meaning of every word in the dictionary.

MAKING THE BENCH.

GOOD STORY is told of a United States sena-
tor who began life as a carpenter.

"I will not always be a carpenter," he used to
declare, for it seemed he had set his heart upon some-
time entering the legal profession. He did not slight
his carpenter's work for his day dreams of what he
should do and become, but was noted for his honest,
conscientious labor.

One day the young man was planing a board that was
to become a part of a "judge's bench," when a friend
observing his painstaking, inquired :

"Why do you take such pains to smooth that board?"

Instantly the young carpenter replied : "Because I
want a smooth seat when I come to sit on it."

His friend laughed, and thought the joke so good
that he reported it in the shop, and the young man was
bantered not a little about the "judge's bench." He
always replied, good-naturedly :

"Wait and see. He laughs who wins, and I may sit
there yet."

And he did ; but the distance between the carpenter's
and judge's bench was paved with heroic struggles and
self-sacrifice.

~~~~~~~~~~

The success of our friends pleases us until it sur-
passes our own, and then we resent it.

WANTED—A CAREER.

 TO do something," my heart kept repeating—
"Something so beautiful, noble or fine,
That bright it should bloom like a flower in the
    desert ;
    That clear like a star in the night it should
    shine ! "

Then I looked in the sky ; 'twas a-quiver already
    With star upon star, through the glittering night ;
I looked o'er the land, 'twas a-flutter with flowers ;
    What need of my wee one to make it more bright ?

Then I looked in my heart, and I saw 'mid its motives
    What from my own vision I gladly would hide ;
Commingled with longings for art and for beauty,
    Ah! much of ambition, of envy, of pride !

Then I looked where no star-beam e'er comes pene-
    trating,
    Where the flow'rs are crushed out in the unceas-
    ing strife,
The pitiful struggle for merest existence
    That mockery makes of the thing we call life !

And I gave to a child that was wailing with hunger,
    The comfort, the beauty of every-day bread ;
To a soul that was starving for sympathy's music
    A commonplace word of encouragement said.

O, rich this new field for my thought and my labor,
    And soothed was my longing for beauty and art,
For a flower sweetly bloomed on my own barren path-
    way,
    A star softly rose in my own shadowed heart!
                                —MARGARITE C. MOORE.

456

AS WE HAVE OPPORTUNITY.

"AS we have therefore opportunity, let us do good unto all men." Oh, how these words have cheered my heart.

What a comfort it is to know the dear Master requires no more of us than we are able to do. Sometimes when I look around and see so much to be done, such a harvest of souls to be gathered in, and the laborers so few, and they spending their time inventing machinery, seemingly indifferent as to the storm that is gathering over the fields, my heart cries out, Oh, that I could go forth, Oh, that I could snatch souls from destruction; for I can say like Jeremiah of old, " His words are in mine heart like fire shut up in the bones, and I am weary with forbearing."

But God knows best, perhaps it is a needed discipline that means are withheld, and time so limited. God will have a tried people, and they who are not faithful in the little, will never have the honor of much.

How glad I am for that word "opportunity." Had it not been for that I should many times have been so discouraged as to believe it impossible for me to do God's will. But all His plans are perfect, His demands right. In the great reckoning day the question will not be asked how much have we done for the Master, but if we have improved our opportunities. What shall we answer?

457

WANTED.

WANTED : Men.
 Not systems fit and wise,
 Not faiths with rigid eyes,
Not wealth in mountains piles,
Not power with gracious smiles,
Not even the potent pen :
 Wanted : Men.

 Wanted : Deeds.
Not words of winning note,
Not thoughts from life remote,
Not fond religious airs,
Not sweetly languid prayers,
Not love of scent and creeds ;
 Wanted : Deeds.

 Men and deeds.
Men that can dare and do,
Not longings for the new,
Not partings of the old ;
Good life and action bold—
These the occasion needs ;
 Men and deeds.

~~~~~~~~~~

How much easier it is to sit by the fire and resolve to do
than it is to go out in the cold and do it.

WAIT.

I SAW the proprietor of a garden standing at his fence and call to his poor neighbor:

"Would you like some grapes?"

"Yes, and very thankful," was the ready answer.

"Then bring your basket."

The basket was quickly handed over the fence. The owner took it and disappeared among the vines; and I marked that he deposited into it rich clusters from the fruitful labyrinth in which he hid himself. The woman stood at the fence quiet and hopeful. At length he re-appeared with a well-filled basket, saying, "I have made you wait a good while, but there is all the more grapes."

It is so, thought I, with the proprietor of all things. He says: "What shall I give thee? Ask and thou shalt receive." So I bring my empty vessel—my needy but capacious soul. He disappears; but I am not always so patient and trustful as the poor woman. Sometimes I cry out, "How long! how long!"

At last He comes to me richly laden, and kindly chides my impatience, saying: "Have I made thee wait long? See what I have treasured up for thee all the while."

Then I look and see fruits richer than I had asked for, and I pour out my heart's thanks to my generous Benefactor, and grieve that I distrusted Him. Surely the longer He makes me wait, the more He gives.

GOOD NIGHT.

GOOD-NIGHT.

THERE is a tender sweetness about some of our common phrases of affectionate greeting, simple and unobtrusive as they are, which falls like dew upon the heart. Good-night! The little one lisps it as, gowned in white, with shining face and hands, and prayers said, she toddles off to bed. Sisters and brothers exchange the wish; parents and children; friends and friends.

Familiar use has robbed it of its significance to some of us; we repeat it automatically without much thought. But consider. We are as voyagers, putting off from time to time upon an unexplored sea. Our barques of life set sail and go onward into darkness, and we asleep on our pillows, take no such care as we do when awake and journeying by daylight. Of the perils of the night, whatever they may be, we take no heed. An unsleeping vigilance watches over us, but it is the vigilance of one stronger and wiser than we, who is the Eternal Good. Good and God spring from the same root, and are the same in meaning. "Good-bye" is only "God be with you." "Good-night" is really "God-night," or "God guard the night." It would be a churlish household in which these gentle forms of speech were ignored or did not exist. Alike the happy and the sorrowful, day by day, may say "Good-night."

461

REST IN HEAVEN.

THERE are no weary hearts in Heaven,
    No tired, aching feet,
  But joys and smiles innumerable,
    As saints each other greet.

When in the new Jerusalem,
  We'll walk the golden street,
And sing the praises of our Lord,
  Or sit at Jesus' feet.

The storms of life which o'er us rise,
  And darken all our way,
Will not be felt beyond the skies,
  For there 'tis always day.

There in our Father's home above,
  The dwelling of the blest,
We'll meet with loved ones 'round the throne,
  And there forever rest,

A rest from sin, a rest from toil,
  From suffering and pain ;
No earthly cares our bliss can mar,
  We'll not return again.

Toil on, toil on, ye weary ones,
  With grief and sorrow pressed,
'Tis but a little while below,
  Then joy and endless rest.

           —MRS. EMMA V. SWEETEN.

LIST OF AUTHORS.

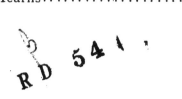